OVID

— Selections from —

Ars Amatoria

Remedia Amoris

OVID

— Selections from —

Ars Amatoria
Remedia Amoris

Text, Commentary, Vocabulary

Graves Haydon Thompson

Bolchazy-Carducci Publishers, Inc.

Mundelein, Illinois USA

Cover Illustration: from a fragment of an Attic kylix, late 6th century BCE,
Metropolitan Museum of Art, New York

1997 Reprint of the 1958/1995 privately published edition.

Bolchazy-Carducci Publishers, Inc.
1570 Baskin Road
Mundelein, Illinois 60060
www.bolchazy.com

Printed in the United States of America
2014
by United Graphics

ISBN 978-0-86516-395-9

Library of Congress Cataloging-in-Publication Data

Ovid, 43 B.C.-17 or 18 A.D.
     [Ars amatoria. Selections]
     Selections from Ars amatoria, Remedia amoris : text, commentary, vocabulary /
Graves Hayden Thompson
          p.   cm.
     Originally published: Farmville, Va. : Farmville Printing, 1952.
     Introduction and commentary in English, text in Latin.
     ISBN 0-86516-395-2 (pbk. : alk paper)
     1. Latin language--Readers. 2. Ovid, 43 B.C.-17 or 18 A.D.--Problems, exercises,
etc. 3. Love poetry, Latin--Problems, exercises, etc. 4. Rome--Poetry--Problems,
exercises, etc.
I. Ovid, 43 B.C.-17 or 18 A.D. Remedia amoris. Selections.
II. Thompson, Graves H., 1907-   . III Title. IV. Title: Remedia amoris.
PA2099.09T48 1997
871.01--dc21

                                                                    97-22080
                                                                         CIP

DEDICATION AND EXPLANATION

Since every work of any pretension or pretense must have
a dedication, this modest production is accordingly ded-
icated to that Forgotten and too often Forgetting Man, the
ordinary student who would like to get something, even a
little enjoyment, out of the study of Latin, but who
decides that either he is hopeless or Latin is hopeless.
He must feel that there is something worth-while in this
ancient and honorable language. For a couple of millennia
it has provided profit and pleasure to millions of people
(no exaggeration: even one thousand times two thousand
would give two million). In this number have been included
not only the best minds of the human race, but countless
others of just average ability. And it is exactly because
of this eternal interest that the language has continued
to survive. But interest, like fire, does not exist on
nothing. There must be something solid and stimulating
beneath it all.

The problem, then, is in some way to bridge the diffi-
cult gap between the great storehouse of Latin and the
ordinary student, who may be regarded as at least pas-
sively receptive, just wanting to be shown. It is hoped
that this work may help point the way. It is frankly aimed
at making Latin as painless and enjoyable as possible,
without failing to recognize that one of the language's
great virtues has always been and must continue to be the
demand it makes upon the individual's faculty of inde-
pendent reasoning.

In this attempt to render Latin more enjoyable, there
were two steps. The first was the selection of a work
which would be eminently readable. Ovid's *Ars Amatoria,*
with its companion work the *Remedia Amoris,* is just that.
Yet as a textbook it has always been shunned as though it
had the leprosy, largely because in places Ovid expressed

himself a little more frankly and unreservedly than is our custom today, at least in print. A modicum of judicious pruning remedies that. We have left a work that can hardly fail to be universally interesting, since it deals with a subject of universal interest - the way of a man with a maid, or what happens when boy meets girl. Hollywood and journalistic advisers of the lovelorn have built fortunes on this theme. What we read in this *Art of Love* is nothing politely remote, but good advice for some everyday situations. For seasoning Ovid has added well-told stories and a wit sparkling and modern. Perhaps modernity is the quality that will project above everything else, and Ovid may help his readers to realize the timelessness of human nature.

The second step was somehow to eliminate as much as possible the student's mechanical and constant thumbing of a vocabulary or dictionary in unending pursuit of elusive meanings. This has been the source of much useless weariness and boredom. The problem has already been recognized and met in various ways. Among the most successful solutions has been that of Professor Clyde Pharr's edition of Vergil's *Aeneid*. With his gracious permission, I have borrowed the idea of the extensible vocabulary sheet inside the back cover. Here will be found the approximately two hundred Latin words which occur ten times or more in the 1594 lines of the *Ars Amatoria* and *Remedia Amoris* that are printed in this book.

All the other words will be found in the notes at the bottom of each page. Here, in what I believe is a new scheme, vocabulary and explanatory notes for each line of text have been combined. Accordingly, except for the most common words, which are on the extensible sheet and are therefore readily visible, *all the information needed (it is hoped) to translate a given line will be found together in one place.*

This means that there is considerable repetition of vocabulary and information in the footnotes. For many this will be helpful. Those who find it unnecessary may readily and happily skip the repetitive matter.

No description of Ovid's meter is given in this book,
simply because experience has shown that no written expla-
nation of scansion can be half so effective as verbal
explanation and demonstration by a competent instructor.
Suffice it to say that Ovid used the elegiac couplet, an
alternation of the dactylic hexameter line and the dac-
tylic pentameter line. There is considerable pleasure to
be had from reading Ovid's smooth Latin metrically, and
the scansion will often help to determine the length of
doubtful vowels and hence the forms of words.

The Latin text used in this book is based more or less
on the Teubner edition of R. Ehwald (Leipzig, 1916), but
a good many changes have been made in readings, spellings,
and punctuation.

This book is dedicated to L.B.T., with all thanks for countless
acts of help, encouragement, and inspiration.

SUPPLEMENTARY NOTE

Ovid is open to the charge of being a male chauvinist. But he
was writing two millenia ago, and that concept would have
meant nothing to him. He liked women, but he did satirize
them sometimes, as he did the stratagems of lovers of both
sexes. Ovid is long dead now, and there is nothing that we can
do about that. We have to take him for what he is, and enjoy
his keen and witty perception of human nature.

GRAVES HAYDON THOMPSON
Hampden-Sydney, Virginia
May, 1997

The author places a bouquet of wildflowers at the monument dedicated to Ovid in the city of his exile and death, Tomis (the modern city of Constantsa, Romania).

TABLE OF CONTENTS

Modern sculpture of head of Publius Ovidius Naso in the Museum
of Constantsa, Romania (the ancient city of Tomis, where Ovid
was exiled in AD 8 and died in AD 17).

INTRODUCTION

The Story of Ovid's Life

Ovid's life may well be described as a story, embodying as it does one of the basic patterns of fiction - and of life. It is the dramatic story of the small-town boy who comes to the big city and makes good; then, at the height of his fame and success, like Oscar Wilde, he meets a stunning reversal of fortune and plunges into the depths.

Publius Ovidius Naso, born on March 20, 43 B.C., came into the world during a period of great doubt and turmoil. Scarcely a year before, the great Julius Caesar had been assassinated. A long period of tension and strife ensued. When Ovid was eleven, Octavian Caesar finally achieved his victory over Mark Antony and Cleopatra; the Mediterranean world began to settle down into a long period of stability, and Roman society into a gay whirl of dissolute pleasure.

Ovid's father, a well-to-do gentleman of Sulmo, ninety miles east of Rome, wanted his son to have a good education in preparation for a life of public service. So it was that Ovid, just entering his teens, came to Rome, and the threads of life began to be woven into that pattern which was to bring him the brightest happiness and the blackest tragedy.

The legal and political career Ovid's father had planned for him did not work out too well. Despite a few minor offices, Ovid's facile mind and light-hearted disposition led him into the pleasant life of the literary and social circles of the Roman capital. He was a born poet - he tells us that whatever he tried to write automatically turned into verse - and his poetry helped him enter the ranks of the highest society, which included the Emperor's daughter Julia. His love poems, the *Amores*, mainly celebrating the charms and whimsicalities of a lovely wench

ix

named Corinna, quickly became the rage of Rome. Everyone was inquiring, 'Who is Corinna?' - a secret Ovid gaily refused to divulge, possibly because she was not one girl but an amalgam of several.

Ovid followed up this success with a series of letters written (in verse, of course) supposedly by various anguished heroines of mythology to their absent sweethearts, lovers, or husbands. These letters, the *Heroides,* showed a tremendous understanding of female psychology which was to be manifested in Ovid's next major work, the *Ars Amatoria.* This poem, published at the turn of the century, must dispute with the later *Metamorphoses* the title of Ovid's greatest work. It is bright, witty, satiric, carried forward with great verve. The *Remedia Amoris* followed, ostensibly to reduce the suicide rate among disappointed lovers, but undoubtedly to capitalize on the success of the *Ars Amatoria.* Like most sequels, it is not quite up to the standard of the earlier work.

In passing, it is interesting to note that Ovid must have made good use of the knowledge contained in both these poems. He had three marriages, two separations.

With his next publication, the *Metamorphoses,* Ovid regained the literary heights. The stories of mythology, which had been popping out here and there in his earlier poems, were now woven into one continuous whole, running from the creation of the world down through the death of Julius Caesar and his metamorphosis into a star. In the course of this engaging work, Jupiter and the other majestic gods of Ólympus lose much of their dignity under Ovid's irreverent handling, from which, to this day, they have never fully recovered.

Ovid was halfway through the *Fasti,* a poem on the Roman calendar and festivals, when a thunderbolt from a more potent (or at least a more vindictive) Jupiter struck. In 8 A.D. the Emperor Augustus ordered him into exile at Tomi, a desolate town on the Black Sea near the mouth of the Danube.

The cause of Ovid's banishment is one of the great mysteries in literary history - a mystery which apparently

will never be solved for certain. Two reasons are cited by
Ovid - *carmen et error* - a poem and an error. The poem is
the *Ars Amatoria*, but that had been published some eight
years earlier. Granted that it was a poem the tone of
which ran counter to the moral reforms Augustus was trying
to institute; yet eight years is a long time for even
governmental bureaucracy to react. The 'error' must have
been the true cause for the banishment, but at its nature
Ovid barely hints, saying that he had seen more than he
should have seen.

Mysteries and the solution of mysteries have always
fascinated the human mind. Scholars have offered many
suggestions as to the nature of Ovid's error: he had seen
the Empress Livia in her bath (!) or the Emperor Augustus
in some embarrassing situation; he was involved in some
political intrigue against the ruling dynasty, or was
caught up in a plot of Livia against the two Julias,
daughter and granddaughter of Augustus; or (most probably)
he was suspected of conniving at the adultery of the
younger Julia with a Roman named Silanus. Julia and
Silanus were exiled. Ovid's banishment at almost the same
time is a suspicious coincidence.

At Tomi, far removed from the friends, Romans, country-
men, from the city and social life he loved so well, Ovid
passed the last years of his life in alternating hope and
despair. His hope and despair were translated into poetic
epistles which were sent to his friends, to his faithful
wife, or to the Emperor as Ovid strove for an end to
his sentence of exile. These letters compose his last
major works, the *Tristia* and the *Epistulae ex Ponto*.
Except as a release for his troubled thoughts, they did
him no good. Augustus died in 14 A.D., unrelenting. His
successor, Tiberius, was an even more implacable soul. In
17 A.D. Ovid obtained the only liberation open to him -
death.

On Reading the *Ars Amatoria*

A person who translates this *Art of Love* needs more than
a moderate knowledge of Latin. A sense of humor is quite

important, for instance. One of Ovid's patron goddesses whom he invokes is Thalia, the Muse of comedy. Let no one be deceived by the serious pose Ovid adopts at the beginning of his poem. He is Professor Ovid, M.A. - Magister Amoris, Master of the Art of Love. His is a didactic or teaching poem, like Lucretius' *De Rerum Natura* or Vergil's *Georgics*, but a burlesque one. He dons the horn-rimmed spectacles of the classroom, sets them well down on the end of his nose, and gazes in mock solemnity upon his pupils. The reader must join in the fun in the same spirit.

It helps to have a feeling for satire, too. Love is Ovid's subject, but what is love? The most serious and far-reaching of emotions, or a fleeting, fickle phenomenon? For Ovid, both. Love is king, and Ovid is his prophet; yet in the final analysis, his glorification of Love only reveals its many absurdities. So it is with girls. The feminine sex has no more ardent admirer than the kind and gentlemanly Ovid, yet when one has done with the poem, there may well be the feeling that this has been a scintillating satire on the ways, wiles, and whims of womankind, plus a few accurate shots at the males.

An alert mind is needed to read the *Ars Amatoria*. One must keep his eyes open and his wits keen, for Ovid is a clever writer. He is seldom obvious. After the Latin has been translated, the subtleties of his ideas must sometimes be searched out. That is part of the pleasure of reading Ovid.

The *Ars Amatoria* and the *Remedia Amoris* are especially easy to translate because of their verse form, the elegiac couplet. It will be observed that long lines (dactylic hexameter) and short lines (dactylic pentameter) alternate in these poems, and that every two such lines almost invariably contain a complete thought and often a complete sentence. It is not necessary to hunt over half a page to round up stray and roving parts of a sentence, as in some Latin writers. Ovid's thoughts come generally in neat and logical packets, yet seldom slip into monotony.

Ovid is a modern writer. He thinks like a modern. It is necessary, then, that he be translated in modern idiom. A student should not feel restricted to the definitions of words and the translations of phrases suggested in the vocabulary and footnotes. Once the meaning is clear, his own sense of English idiom may suggest a better or more natural rendition. Thus he may in a measure partake anew of the creative act that once was Ovid's, two thousand years ago.

Inscription on the monument dedicated to Ovid in Constantsa, Romania (ancient Tomis). The inscription, written by Ovid himself, reads:

Hic ego qui iaceo tenerorum lusor amorum
      ingenio perii Naso poeta meo
at tibi qui transis ne sit grave quisquis amasti
      dicere Nasonis molliter ossa cubent
                      Tristia III.3.73–76

I who lie here was a writer
Of tales of tender love
Naso the poet, done in by my
Own ingenuity.
You who pass by, should you be
A lover, may you
Trouble yourself to say that
Naso's bones
May rest softly.

(Translated by Paul Shore in *Rest Lightly: An Anthology of Latin and Greek Tomb Inscriptions.* Wauconda, IL: Bolchazy-Carducci Publishers, 1997.)

P. OVIDI NASONIS

A R S   A M A T O R I A

Liber Primus

In a manner burlesquing other more serious didactic works, Ovid proclaims himself the outstanding expert on the subject of love and urges those who wish information thereon to read his poem.

Siquis in hoc artem populo non novit amandi,
  hoc legat et lecto carmine doctus amet!
Arte citae veloque rates remoque moventur,
  arte leves currus: arte regendus Amor.
Curribus Automedon lentisque erat aptus habenis,   5
  Tiphys in Haemonia puppe magister erat:
me Venus artificem tenero praefecit Amori:
  Tiphys et Automedon dicar Amoris ego.

After assuring his readers that he is master of his subject and is writing from experience (*'Usus opus movet hoc'*), Ovid proceeds to outline the three great divisions of the first two books of the *Ars Amatoria*; namely, how to find the girl, how to win her, and how to keep her.

---

1   **populus, -i**, m., *people*. **nosco, -ere, novi, notus**, *become acquainted with;* (perf.) *know.*

2   **lego, -ere, legi, lectus**, *collect, choose, read*. **carmen, -inis**, n., *song, poem*.

3   **citus, -a, -um**, *quick, swift, rapid*. **velum, -i**, n., *cloth, sail*. **ratis, -is**, f., *raft, boat, ship*. **remus, -i**, m., *oar*.

4   **currus, -us**, m., *chariot*. **rego, -ere, rexi, rectus**, *guide, control, govern*.

5   **currus, -us**, m., *chariot*. **Automedon, -ontis**, m., *Automedon, the charioteer of Achilles*. **lentus, -a, -um**, *pliant, flexible, tough, slow, calm*. **habena, -ae**, f., *rein*.

6   **Tiphys, -yos**, m., *Tiphys*, the pilot of the Argo. **Haemonius, -a, -um**, *Haemonian, Thessalian*. **puppis, -is**, f., *stern of a ship, ship*. **Haemonia puppis**: the Argo, which sailed from Thessaly under command of Jason in search of the Golden Fleece. **magister, -tri**, m., *master, pilot*.

7   **artifex, -ficis**, m., *master, artist, expert*. Here in apposition with **me**. **praeficio, -ere, -feci, -fectus**, *place in authority over, place in charge of, set over*.

8   **Tiphys, Automedon**: see lines 6 and 5. --It will be observed that Ovid was hardly a shrinking violet.

1

35   Principio, quod amare velis, reperire labora,
            qui nova nunc primum miles in arma venis!
        Proximus huic labor est placitam exorare puellam;
            tertius, ut longo tempore duret amor.
        Hic modus; haec nostro signabitur area curru,
40   haec erit admissa meta premenda rota.

Ovid now takes up his first topic, how to find the girl. It is important, he says, to know just what places will offer you an opportunity for meeting girls. It is not necessary to go abroad. There are all kinds right in Rome.

        Dum licet, et loris passim potes ire solutis,
            elige cui dicas 'Tu mihi sola places.'
        Haec tibi non tenues veniet delapsa per auras:
            quaerenda est oculis apta puella tuis.

---

35   **principio,** *first, in the first place.* **velis:** pres. subj. of
        volo. **quod amare velis:** either regard this whole clause as
the object of **reperire,** or supply **id** as the antecedent of **quod** and
the object of **reperire.** **reperio, -ire, repperi, repertus,** *find,*
meet with. **laboro, -are, -avi, -atus,** *labor, take pains, exert*
oneself, strive.

36   **qui** with a verb in the 2nd person is to be translated 'you
        who.' **primum,** *first, for the first time.* **miles, -itis,** m.,
soldier. --Ovid regards love as a kind of warfare, as indeed it
is. Cf. James Thurber's cartoon series dealing with the war be-
tween the sexes; also, 'All's fair in love and war.'

37   **proximus, -a, -um,** *next, second.* **labor, -oris,** m., *labor,*
        task. **placitus, -a, -um,** *pleasing, agreeable, acceptable.*
exoro, -are, -avi, -atus, *prevail upon, win* (by entreaty).

38   **tertius, -a, -um,** *third.* **duro, -are, -avi, -atus,** *endure,*
        continue, last, remain.

39   **hic modus:** supply **erit.** **modus:** 'the ground I intend to
        cover.' **signo, -are, -avi, -atus,** *mark.* **area, -ae,** f.,
space, ground, field. **currus, -us,** m., *chariot.*

40   **admissa . . . rota** (abl.): 'wheel driven at full speed.'
        meta, -ae, f., *goal, turning post.* **premo, -ere, pressi,**
pressus, *press, touch, graze.* --Ovid is figuratively comparing the
writing of his book to the driving of a chariot in a race. In each
case a prescribed course is laid out and there is a goal or turn-
ing post to aim at.

41   **loris . . . solutis:** 'with loosened reins'; i.e., 'fancy-
        free.' **passim,** *hither and thither, everywhere.*

42   **eligo, -ere, elegi, electus,** *pick out, choose.* **cui:** supply
        puellam as antecedent.

43   **delabor, -i, delapsus,** *fall, slip down, glide down, descend.*

Scit bene venator, cervis ubi retia tendat,   45
   scit bene, qua frendens valle moretur aper;
aucupibus noti frutices; qui sustinet hamos,
   novit, quae'multo pisce natentur aquae:
tu quoque, materiam longo qui quaeris amori,
   ante frequens quo sit disce puella loco.   50
Non ego quaerentem vento dare vela iubebo,
   nec tibi, ut invenias, longa terenda via est.
Andromedan Perseus nigris portarit ab Indis,
   raptaque sit Phrygio Graia puella viro:

---

45   **scio, -ire, -ivi, -itus,** *know.* **venator, -oris,** m., *hunter.* **cervus, -i,** m., *stag, deer.* **rete, -is,** n., *net.* **tendo, ere, tetendi, tentus,** *stretch, extend.*

46   **scit:** see 45. **qua . . . valle:** as often in poetry, **in** is omitted. **frendo, -ere, -ui, fres(s)us,** *gnash the teeth.* **valles, -is,** f., *valley.* **moror, -ari, -atus,** *delay, tarry, stay, wait.* **aper, -pri,** m., *wild boar.*

47   **auceps, -cupis,** m., f., *birdcatcher, fowler.* **notus, -a, -um,** *(well) known.* **frutex, -icis,** m., *bush.* **sustineo, -ere, -tinui, -tentus,** *hold up, support.* **hamus, -i,** m., *fishhook.*

48   **nosco, -ere, novi, notus,** *become acquainted with;* (perf.) *know.* **piscis, -is,** m., *fish.* **nato, -are, -avi, -atus,** *swim.*

49   **materia, -ae,** f., *stuff, matter, material* (a not too flattering way of speaking about a young lady!).

50   **frequens, -entis** (adj.), *frequent(ly), numerous, (assembled) in great numbers.* **quo . . . loco** introduce an indirect question after **disce. puella:** singular used for plural.

51   This and the following lines mean simply that a fellow does not have to take a long trip by sea or land to find a girl. There are plenty in Rome (or Farmville). **quaerentem:** remember that all participles *must* modify some noun or pronoun either expressed or implied; if implied, it must usually be expressed in English. Here supply **te.** Translate 'in your search.' **vento dare vela:** 'to give sails to the wind' obviously means 'to sail' or 'to take a sea voyage.' **velum, -i,** n., *cloth, sail.*

52   **invenio, -ire, -veni, -ventus,** *find, discover.* **tero, -ere, trivi, tritus,** *rub, wear out, tread.*

53   **Andromeda, -ae** (acc. **-an**), f.: a beautiful princess of Ethiopia rescued from a sea monster by **Perseus,** who completed the job by marrying her and begetting three children. **niger, -gra, -grum,** *black, dark, dusky.* **porto, -are, -avi, -atus,** *bear, carry, bring.* **portarit** is a syncopated form standing for **portaverit** (perf. subj.). The subjunctive is probably concessive ('granted that . . .', 'though . . .'), as is **rapta sit** (54). **Indi, -orum,** m., *the inhabitants of India, Indians* (here seemingly used for the Ethiopians).

54   **Phrygius, -a, -um,** *Phrygian, Trojan.* **Graius, -a, -um,** *Greek.* --There should be no question as to the names of the Greek girl (Helen) and the Trojan man (Paris), who was also a kind of

55   tot tibi tamque dabit formosas Roma puellas,
    'Haec habet' ut dicas 'quidquid in orbe fuit.'
    Gargara quot segetes, quot habet Methymna racemos,
      aequore quot pisces, fronde teguntur aves,
    quot caelum stellas, tot habet tua Roma puellas;
60   mater in Aeneae constitit urbe sui.
    Seu caperis primis et adhuc crescentibus annis,
      ante oculos veniet vera puella tuos;
    sive cupis iuvenem, iuvenes tibi mille placebunt,
      cogeris et voti nescius esse tui;
65   seu te forte iuvat sera et sapientior aetas,

Trojan horse, operating as he did in the guise of a family friend.
Ovid's point in these last two lines is that Perseus and Paris had
to go far afield to find their lady loves, but that this is quite
unnecessary for the gentle reader.

55   **tot** (indecl. adj.), *so many.* **Roma, -ae,** f., *Rome.* --**Tot** and
    tam lead up to the result clause **ut dicas**, which governs the
direct quotation in 56.

56   **haec:** i.e., Rome. **orbis, -is,** m., *circle, earth, world.*

57   **Gargara, -orum,** n.: the upper part of Mt. Ida, in Troas; also
    a city at its foot. **seges, -etis,** f., *field of grain, crop.*
Methymna, -ae, f.; a city on the island of Lesbos, famous for its
excellent wine. **racemus, -i,** m., *cluster of grapes.*

58   **aequor, -oris,** n., *level surface, sea.* **piscis, -is,** m.,
    fish. **frons, -dis,** f., *leafy branch, foliage, leaves.* **tego,**
-ere, -xi, -ctus, *cover, hide, conceal, protect.* **avis, -is,** f.,
bird.

59   **caelum, -i,** n., *sky, heaven, the heavens.* **stella, -ae,** f.,
    star. **tot** (indecl. adj.), *so many, as many.* **Roma, -ae,** f.,
Rome.

60   **mater, -tris,** f., *mother.* **Aeneas, -ae,** m.: son of Venus and
    Anchises, and ancestor of the Romans. **consisto, -ere,**
-stiti, *stand, halt, stop, take up one's abode.* **urbs, urbis,** f.,
city. **sui** here = 'of her son.' --In other words, Rome is now the
headquarters of Venus.

61   **seu . . . sive** (63) . . . **seu** (65): 'if . . . or if . . . or
    if.' **primis:** 'first' here = 'youthful.' **adhuc,** *still, yet.*
cresco, -ere, crevi, cretus, *grow, increase.*

62   **verus, -a, -um,** *true, real, actual, genuine.* **puella** here =
    'young girl.'

63   **sive:** see 61. **cupio, -ere, -ivi (-ii), -itus,** *long for, de-*
    sire, wish. **mille** (indecl. adj.), *a thousand.*

64   **cogo, -ere, coegi, coactus,** *collect, force, compel.* **et:** a
    case of anastrophe; should be translated before **cogeris.** **vo-**
tum, -i, n., *vow, wish, desire.* **nescius, -a, -um,** *ignorant.*

65   **seu:** see 61. **forte,** *by chance, perchance, perhaps.* **serus,**
    -a, -um, *late, mature.* **sapiens, -entis,** *wise, sensible.*
aetas, -atis, f., *period of life, time of life, life, age.*

hoc quoque, crede mihi, plenius agmen erit.

Ovid mentions a few of the places to frequent, such as the por-
ticoes of Pompey, Octavia, or Livia, or various temples; even the
law courts, where many a lawyer has been smitten by Love and,
though eloquent, has stumbled for words to speak for himself (67-
88). But especially fruitful are the theaters. Here flock all the
most attractive women. Ever since the first Romans obtained their
wives by force in a theater, such places have afforded opportuni-
ties for flirtation.

Sed tu praecipue curvis venare theatris:

    haec loca sunt voto fertiliora tuo.   90

Illic invenies quod ames, quod ludere possis,

    quodque semel tangas, quodque tenere velis.

Ut redit itque frequens longum formica per agmen,

    granifero solitum cum vehit ore cibum,

aut ut apes saltusque suos et olentia nactae   95

    pascua per flores et thyma summa volant,

sic ruit in celebres cultissima femina ludos:

---

66   **plenus, -a, -um,** *full, abundant, plentiful.* **agmen, -inis,**
       n., *army* (on the march), *crowd, throng, band.*

89   **praecipue,** *chiefly, especially, particularly.* **curvus, -a,**
       -um, *curved.* **venor, -ari, -atus,** *hunt, chase.* **theatrum, -i,**
   n., *theater.* Here ablative of place where; cf. 46.

90   **votum, -i,** n., *vow, wish, desire.* **fertilis, -e,** *fruitful,*
       fertile, productive.

91   **illic,** *in that place, there.* **invenio, -ire, -veni, -ventus,**
       come upon, find, discover. **ames:** this and the following sub-
   junctives are potential. **ludo, -ere, -si, -sus,** *play, play with,*
   have fun with.

92   **semel,** *once, a single time.* **tango, -ere, tetigi, tactus,**
       touch. **velis:** pres. subj., 2nd pers. sing., of **volo.**

93   **redeo, redire, redii, reditus,** *go back, come back, return.*
       Logically, this should here be translated after it. **fre-**
   quens, -entis, *in great numbers, numerous.* **formica, -ae,** f., *ant.*
   Here singular for plural. **agmen, -inis,** n., *line of march, pro-*
   cession, army, multitude.

94   **granifer, -era, -erum,** *grain-bearing.* Ovid may have made up
       this word, as we know of no other author who used it. How did
   Ovid form it? **solitus, -a, -um,** *accustomed, usual.* **veho, -ere,**
   -xi, -ctus, *bear, carry, convey.* **cibus, -i,** m., *food.*

95   **apis, -is,** f., *bee.* **saltus, -us,** m., *forest pasture, wood-*
       land. **-que . . . et,** *(both)* . . . *and.* **olens, -entis,** *sweet-*
   smelling, fragrant. **nanciscor, -i, nactus,** *happen on, find.*

96   **pascuum, -i,** n., *pasture.* **flos, -oris,** m., *blossom, flower.*
       thymum, -i, n., *thyme.* **volo, -are, -avi, -atus,** *fly.*

97   **sic** introduces the concluding clause of the comparison, thus
       balancing the two subordinate clauses beginning with **ut** - a
   very common device in Latin. **ruo, -ere, rui, rutus,** *fall down,*
   hasten, hurry, rush. **celeber,-ebris, -ebre,** *crowded.* **cultus, -a,**
   -um, *cultivated, polished, elegant, well-dressed.* **femina:** singu-

copia iudicium saepe morata meum est.
Spectatum veniunt; veniunt spectentur ut ipsae:
100   ille locus casti damna pudoris habet.
Primos sollicitos fecisti, Romule, ludos,
    cum iuvit viduos rapta Sabina viros.
Tunc neque marmoreo pendebant vela theatro,
    nec fuerant liquido pulpita rubra croco;
105   illic, quas tulerant nemorosa Palatia, frondes
    simpliciter positae, scaena sine arte fuit;
in gradibus sedit populus de caespite factis,
    qualibet hirsutas fronde tegente comas.

---

lar for plural. **ludus, -i,** m., *play;* (plur.) *public games, shows.*

98   **copia, -ae,** f., *abundance, ample supply, large number.* **iudi-cium, -ii,** n., *judgment, decision.* **moror, -ari, -atus,** *delay, retard, hinder.*

99   **spectatum:** supine expressing purpose. --An often quoted line expressing an eternal truth.

100   **castus, -a, -um,** *pure, chaste, virtuous, modest.* **damnum, -i,** n., *harm, damage, injury, loss.* **pudor, -oris,** m., *shame, modesty, decency, good manners, propriety.*

101   **sollicitus, -a, -um,** *full of anxiety, full of excitement, disturbed, exciting.* **Romulus, -i,** m.: founder and first king of Rome. **ludus, -i,** m., *play;* (plur.) *public games, show(s).*

102   **viduus, -a, -um,** *mateless, widowed, wifeless.* **Sabina, -ae,** f., *Sabine woman* or *women* (the Sabines being an ancient Italian people adjoining the Latins). --Ovid here begins a brief recounting of the famous story ('The Rape of the Sabines') how the first Romans, men without women, obtained wives by an elementary sort of blitzkrieg.

103   **tunc,** *then, at that time.* **marmoreus, -a, -um,** *(made) of marble, marble.* **pendeo, -ere, pependi,** *hang* (intr.), *be suspended.* **velum, -i,** n., *cloth, awning, curtain, sail.* **theatrum, -i,** n., *theater.*

104   **liquidus, -a, -um,** *flowing, clear, bright.* **pulpitum, -i,** n. (sing. and plur.), *platform, stage.* **ruber, -bra, -brum,** *red, ruddy.* **crocus, -i,** m., *saffron.*

105   **illic,** *in that place, there.* **quas:** the antecedent is **frondes. nemorosus, -a, -um,** *woody, leafy, shady.* **Palatium, -ii,** n. (sing. and plur.), *the Palatine hill* (first of the seven hills of Rome to be built on). **frons, frondis,** f., *leafy branch, green bough, foliage.*

106   **simpliciter,** *simply, naturally.* **positae:** supply **sunt. scaena, -ae,** f., *stage, scene.*

107   **gradus, -us,** m., *step, tier of seats.* **populus, -i,** m., *people.* **caespes, -itis,** m., *turf, sod.*

108   **quilibet, quaelibet, quodlibet,** *any . . . at all, any . . . whatsoever.* **hirsutus, -a, -um,** *rough, shaggy, bristly.* **fronde:** see 105. **tego, -ere, texi, tectus,** *cover.*

Respiciunt oculisque notant sibi quisque puellam
    quam velit, et tacito pectore multa movent.   110
Dumque, rudem praebente modum tibicine Tusco,
    ludius aequatam ter pede pulsat humum,
in medio plausu (plausus tunc arte carebant)
    rex populo praedae signa petita dedit.
Protinus exsiliunt, animum clamore fatentes,   115
    virginibus cupidas iniciuntque manus.
Ut fugiunt aquilas, timidissima turba, columbae,
    utque fugit visos agna novella lupos,
sic illae timuere viros sine more ruentes;

---

109 **respicio, -ere, respexi, respectus,** *look back, look about.*
    noto, -are, -avi, -atus, *mark, note, observe.* **quisque**: Note
this not unusual use with a plural verb to make the action more
particular. It shows clearly that all the men are engaged in the
action, but each one is picking out a different girl for himself.

110 **velit**: a potential subj.: 'he would like.' **tacitus, -a, -um,**
    silent.

111 **rudis, -e,** *rude, rough, unpolished.* **praebeo, -ere, -ui,**
    offer, furnish, supply. **tibicen, -inis,** m., *piper, flute*
player. **Tuscus, -a, -um,** *Tuscan, Etruscan.* The Etruscans were a
people settled in Italy who had great influence on the development
of Roman civilization in the early days. Music at public perform-
ances was one of their contributions.

112 **ludius, -ii,** m., *stage player, actor, dancer.* **aequo, -are,**
    -avi, -atus, *make equal, level, smooth.* **ter,** *three times,*
thrice. **pulso, -are, -avi, -atus,** *beat, strike.* **humus, -i,** f.,
earth, ground. --This is a classic and rather picturesque way of
describing a dance (solo, not the modern gliding embrace).

113 **plausus, -us,** m., *clapping, applause.* **tunc,** *then, at that*
    time. **careo, -ere, -ui, -itus,** *be without, lack* (with abl.).

114 **rex, regis,** m., *king.* **populus, -i,** m., *people.* **praeda, -ae,**
    f., *booty, plunder, prey.* **signum, -i,** n., *sign, signal.*

115 **protinus,** *straightway, immediately.* **exsilio, -ire, exsilui,**
    spring forth, leap up, jump up. **clamor, -oris,** m., *shout,*
cry. **fateor, -eri, fessus,** *confess, acknowledge, reveal.*

116 **virgo, -inis,** f., *maiden, young woman, girl.* **cupidus, -a,**
    -um, *desirous, eager.* **iniciunt manus**: 'lay hands on,' 'take
hold of,' 'seize.' **Inicio** takes both a direct and indirect object.
-que: to be translated at the beginning of the line.

117 **aquila, -ae,** f., *eagle.* **timidus, -a, -um,** *timid.* **turba,**
    -ae, f., *crowd, throng.* Here in apposition with **columbae.**
columba, -ae, f., *dove, pigeon.*

118 **agna, -ae,** f., *ewe lamb.* **novellus, -a, -um,** *young, new.*
    lupus, -i, m., *wolf.*

119 **timuere**: note the use (very frequent in Ovid) of the ending
    -ere for **-erunt. sine more**: 'without custom' = 'in an un-
precedented manner.' **ruo, -ere, rui, rutus,** *fall, hasten, rush.*

120   constitit in nulla, qui fuit ante, color.
          Nam timor unus erat, facies non una timoris:
            pars laniat crines, pars sine mente sedet;
          altera maesta silet, frustra vocat altera matrem;
            haec queritur, stupet haec; haec manet, illa fugit
125   Ducuntur raptae, genialis praeda, puellae,
            et potuit multas ipse decere timor.
          Siqua repugnarat nimium comitemque negabat,
            sublatam cupido vir tulit ipse sinu
          atque ita 'Quid teneros lacrimis corrumpis ocellos?
130   Quod matri pater est, hoc tibi' dixit 'ero.'
          Romule, militibus scisti dare commoda solus!
          Haec mihi si dederis commoda, miles ero.

---

120   A poetic way of saying 'They all changed color.' **consisto,**
      -ere, -stiti, *stand, remain unchanged, continue.*

121   **nam** (conj.), *for.* **timor, -oris,** m., *fear.*

122   **lanio, -are, -avi, -atus,** *tear.* **crinis, -is,** m., *hair.*

123   **maestus, -a, -um,** *sad, dejected, melancholy.* **sileo, -ere,**
      -ui, *be still, be silent.* **frustra,** *uselessly, in vain.*
      voco, -are, -avi, -atus, *call.* **mater. -tris,** f., *mother.*

124   **queror, queri, questus,** *complain, lament.* **stupeo, -ere, -ui,**
      be stunned, be astounded, be stupefied. **maneo, -ere, mansi,**
      mansus, *stay, remain.*

125   **duco, -ere, duxi, ductus,** *lead (away).* **genialis, -e,** *pleas-*
      ant, delightful. **praeda, -ae,** f., *booty, plunder, prey.* Here
      in apposition with **puellae.**

126   **timor, -oris,** m., *fear.*

127   **repugno, -are, -avi, -atus,** *fight back, resist.* **repugnarat =**
      repugnaverat. nimium, *too much.* (A *little* coyness, it seems,
      makes things more interesting.) **comes, -itis,** m., f., *companion,*
      comrade. **nego, -are, -avi, -atus,** *say no (to), deny, refuse.*

128   **tollo, -ere, sustuli, sublatus,** *lift up, raise.* **cupidus, -a,**
      -um, *desirous, eager.*

129   **ita,** *thus, so, in this way.* **corrumpo, -ere, -rupi, -ruptus,**
      ruin, mar; make red (?). **ocellus, -i,** m.: diminutive of **ocu-**
      lus; a Latin way of saying 'dear little eye' in one word.

130   The antecedent of **quod** is **hoc. mater, -tris,** f., *mother.*
      --A very good psychological approach to a difficult situation
      complicated by the fact that the girl is crying, always a mascu-
      line hazard.

131   **Romulus, -i,** m.: founder and first king of Rome. **miles,**
      -itis, m., *soldier.* **scio, -ire, -ivi, -itus,** *know (how).*
      scisti = scivisti. commodum, -i, n., *advantage, reward, pay.*

132   **commoda:** see 131. **miles:** see 131.

Scilicet, ex illo sollemni more, theatra
nunc quoque formosis insidiosa manent.

The horse races at the Circus and the gladiatorial shows are
also recommended. There are various devices by which you can make
a favorable impression on young ladies who attend.

Nec te nobilium fugiat certamen equorum;   135
    multa capax populi commoda Circus habet.
Nil opus est digitis, per quos arcana loquaris,
    nec tibi per nutus accipienda nota est:
proximus a domina, nullo prohibente, sedeto,
    iunge tuum lateri qua potes usque latus;   140
et bene, quod cogit, si nolit, linea iungi,

---

133 **scilicet,** *evidently, undoubtedly.* **sollemnis,** -e, *estab-*
        lished, sacred; hallowed by time (?). **theatrum,** -i, n., *the-*
ater. --In the expression **ex illo sollemni more** Ovid seems to im-
ply that the passage of time and the halo surrounding the name of
Romulus have given an almost religious sanction to an act of vio-
lence. In his more modern and civilized age Ovid regards this as a
precedent for flirtation at the theater. Undoubtedly the more
strict people of Rome frowned on the theater just as many good
people have in recent centuries.

134 Note that **quoque** always emphasizes the word it follows; this
        should be brought out in translation. **insidiosus,** -a, -um,
deceitful, dangerous. **maneo,** -ere, -nsi, -nsus, *remain, continue.*

135 **nobilis,** -e, *famous, renowned, highborn, noble, thoroughbred.*
        certamen, -inis, n., *contest, struggle.* --This line simply
means, don't miss the horse races (as a place to meet girls).

136 **capax,** -acis (with gen.), *spacious, large, holding a lot.*
        populus, -i, m., *people.* **commodum,** -i, n., *advantage, re-*
ward. **Circus,** -i, m: probably the *Circus Maximus.* Chariot races,
games, and public shows were held in the circuses.

137 **nil opus est** (with abl.): 'there is no need of.' **arcanum,**
        -i, n., *secret, private matter.*

138 **nutus,** -us, m., *nod.* **nota,** -ae, f., *mark, sign, signal.*

139 **proximus,** -a, -um, *next.* **proximus a:** Latin is just as logi-
        cal in saying 'next from' as English is in saying 'next to.'
prohibeo, -ere, -ui, -itus, *hinder, prevent, forbid, prohibit.*
sedeto: future imperative.

140 **iungo,** -ere, -nxi, -nctus, *join, (press).* **latus,** -eris, n.,
        side. **usque,** *all the way, continuously.*

141 **bene,** *well, successfully, easily.* Here to be taken closely in
        conjunction with the preceding clause: 'and you can do this
easily . . . .' **quod,** *because.* **cogo,** -ere, coegi, coactus, *col-*
lect, force, compel. **nolo, nolle, nolui,** *not wish, be unwilling.*
The subject here is *she.* **linea,** -ae, f., *line* (here the line used
to mark off one seat from another, as in our stadia or bleachers).
iungi: 140. As subject supply **latera** (from 140).

quod tibi tangenda est lege puella loci!
Hic tibi quaeratur socii sermonis origo,
   et moveant primos publica verba sonos.
145 Cuius equi veniant, facito studiose requiras,
   nec mora, quisquis erit, cui favet illa, fave.
At cum pompa frequens certantibus ibit ephebis,
   tu Veneri dominae plaude favente manu;
utque fit, in gremium pulvis si forte puellae
150   deciderit, digitis excutiendus erit;
   et si nullus erit pulvis, tamen excute nullum:
   quaelibet officio causa sit apta tuo.

---

142 **quod**: 141. **tango, -ere, tetigi, tactus,** *touch.* **lex, legis,**
   f., *law, regulation, rule.*

143 **socius, -a, -um,** *united, mutual, sociable, friendly.* **sermo,**
   -onis, m., *talk, conversation.* **origo, -inis,** f., *beginning,*
commencement, source, origin.

144 **publicus, -a, -um,** *public, usual, ordinary, general.* **sonus,**
   -i, m., *sound, word.* --In the following lines Ovid gives ex-
amples of *publica verba,* ordinary, impersonal topics of conversa-
tion (personal topics would not be, or certainly should not be,
publica). Oddly, he neglects to suggest the weather as a possible
subject. Perhaps Roman weather was not so variable as our own, and
hence less subject to comment; or else the Romans were conversa-
tionally more resourceful.

145 **studiose,** *eagerly, anxiously, with an air of concern.* **re-**
   quiro, -ere, -sivi (-sii), -situs, *ask, inquire.*

146 **nec mora (sit** may be understood) = 'without delay.' **faveo,**
   -ere, favi, fautus (with dat.), *favor, be favorable to, be*
inclined toward, applaud.

147 **pompa, -ae,** f., *procession, parade.* The *Circensis pompa* was
   headed by the presiding magistrate with his civil and mili-
tary escort. The charioteers and other performers followed, then
the ceremonial group (priests and bearers of sacred objects), in-
cluding the images of the gods. It is such an image of Venus that
in the next line is to be applauded (why Venus?). **frequens, fre-**
quentis, *crowded.* **certo, -are, -avi, -atus,** *contend, compete.*
ephebus, -i, m., *youth* (strictly, a Greek, from 18 to 20).

148 **plaudo, -ere, -si, -sus,** *clap, applaud.* **favente**: 146. --It
   is an amusing picture Ovid presents of the young man, anxious
to impress the attractive girl in the adjoining seat and making a
point of shouting 'Yea-a-a Venus,' as it were, to show in what
direction his interests lie.

149 **fit**: supply **saepe. gremium, -ii,** n., *lap, bosom.* **pulvis,**
   -eris, m., *dust.* **forte,** *by chance, perhaps, perchance.*

150 **decido, -ere, -cidi,** *fall (down), drop.* **excutio, -ere,**
   -cussi, -cussus, *shake off, knock off, brush off.*

151 **pulvis**: 149. **excute**: 150. **nullum**: 'that no dust.' --This
   is one of Ovid's neatest lines.

152 **quilibet, quaelibet, quodlibet,** *any . . . at all, any . . .*
   whatsoever. **officium, -ii,** n., *service, kindness, courtesy,*
duty.

Pallia si terra nimium demissa iacebunt,
  collige et immunda sedulus effer humo;
protinus, officii pretium, patiente puella   155
  contingent oculis crura videnda tuis.
Respice praeterea, post vos quicumque sedebit,
  ne premat opposito mollia terga genu.
Parva leves capiunt animos: fuit utile multis
  pulvinum facili composuisse manu;   160
profuit et tenui ventos movisse tabella

---

153 **pallium, -ii, n.**, *cloak, mantle* (a Greek garment for males,
     worn also by the more emancipated women of Greece and Rome).
Here plural for singular. **terra, -ae, f.**, *earth, ground.* **nimium,**
too much, too, very much. **demissus, -a, -um,** *low, drooping,
falling, hanging down, downcast.*

154 **colligo, -ere, -legi, -lectus,** *collect, gather up, pick up.*
     immundus, -a, -um, *unclean, dirty, filthy.* **sedulus, -a, -um,**
diligent, zealous, careful, solicitous. **effero, efferre, extuli,
elatus,** *bring out, lift up, raise.* **humus, -i, f.**, *earth, ground.*

155 **protinus,** *immediately.* **officii:** 152. **pretium, -ii, n.**,
     price, pay, reward. Here in apposition with the rest of the
sentence. **patior, pati, passus,** *suffer, endure, allow, permit.*
patiente puella: the ablative absolute properly should be regarded
as conditional!

156 **contingo, -ere, -tigi, -tactus** (with dat.), *touch, happen,
     befall, fall to one's lot, attain.* **crus, -uris, n.**, *leg,
shin, ankle.* **contingent oculis . . . videnda:** 'eyes will have an
opportunity to glimpse' - but work out literally.

157 **respicio, -ere, -spexi, -spectus,** *look back at, look around
     at, glare back at.* **praeterea,** *besides this, besides, more-
over.* **post** (with acc.), *behind, after.* **post . . . sedebit:** the
whole clause is the object of **respice.**

158 **premo, -ere, pressi, pressus,** *press.* **oppono, -ere, -posui,
     -positus,** *place against.* **tergum, -i, n.**, *back.* Here plural
for singular. Whose back is meant? **genu, -us, n.**, *knee.* --The
implication is that such an occasion will almost inevitably arise
(it still does, frequently). But Ovid would not have been above
feigning the situation if it would permit him to show solicitude
for a pretty girl in the next seat.

159 **parva** (from **parvus, -a, -um,** *little, small*): 'little things,'
     'trifles.' --The first four words of this line are a clever
if unchivalric stigmatization of the female sex. There is at least
part truth in what Ovid says. It is notorious that women like
frills: bright ribbons around packages, the right labels on their
dresses, maraschino cherries on their desserts, countless little
attentions. Whether this tendency also indicates frilly minds is a
question. Regardless of that, Ovid's advice is certainly sound.
utilis, -e, *useful.*

160 **pulvinus, -i, m.**, *cushion, pillow.* **facilis, -e,** *easy, ready,
     courteous.* **compono, -ere, -posui, -positus,** *put together,
arrange, adjust.*

161 **prosum, prodesse, profui,** *be useful, be of use, be advanta-
     geous.* **tabella, -ae, f.**, *tablet, fan.*

12 P. OVIDI NASONIS

Hos aditus Circusque novo praebebit amori
sparsaque sollicito tristis harena foro.
165 Illa saepe puer Veneris pugnavit harena,
et qui spectavit vulnera, vulnus habet:
dum loquitur tangitque manum poscitque libellum
et quaerit posito pignore, vincat uter,
saucius ingemuit telumque volatile sensit
170 et pars spectati muneris ipse fuit.

Mention of a mock naval battle staged by Augustus Caesar (2 B.C.) leads Ovid into a long but diplomatic digression in praise of the young Gaius Caesar, grandson of Augustus, who was about to lead a campaign against the Parthians. This in turn leads to the subject of the triumphal procession which will eventually take place. The up-to-the-minute young man will be ready to give any girl who asks, the names of the kings, places, mountains, or rivers represented in the parade. Even if she does not ask, he will give the names all the same; and if he does not know the names, he will make up some that sound just as good (171-228). Dinner parties also enable a person to meet girls. But be careful: wine and artificial light often impair the judgment.

---

162 **cavus, -a, -um,** *hollow.* **scamnum, -i,** n., *stool.*

163 **aditus, -us,** m., *approach.* **Circus, -i,** m., *the Circus, the Circus Maximus* (scene of chariot races, etc.). **praebeo, -ere, -ui, -itus,** *offer, give, furnish, supply.*

164 **spargo, -ere, sparsi, sparsus,** *scatter, sprinkle.* **sollicitus, -a, -um,** *troubled, disturbed, exciting.* **tristis, -e,** *sad, melancholy.* **harena, -ae,** f., *sand.* Sand was strewn in arenas where fights were held. **forum, -i,** n., *market place, forum.* Gladiatorial contests were sometimes held in the Forum.

165 In the next six lines Ovid plays with the idea that a person fallen in love is as much wounded (by the weapons of Cupid) as the defeated gladiator in the arena. Cf. the double meaning of our word 'smitten.' **pugno, -are, -avi, -atus,** *fight.* **harena:** see 164.

166 **habet:** the traditional cry of the people when a gladiator was wounded.

167 **tango, -ere, tetigi, tactus,** *touch, take hold of.* **manum:** whose? **posco, -ere, poposci,** *ask for, request.* **libellus, -i,** m., *booklet, program.*

168 **pignus, -oris,** n., *pledge, wager, stake, bet.* **uter, utra, utrum** (interr.), *which* (of two).

169 **saucius, -a, -um,** *wounded, smitten.* **ingemo, -ere, -ui,** *groan.* **telum, -i,** n., *dart, javelin, spear, arrow.* Here, Cupid's arrow. **volatilis, -e,** *flying, winged, swift.* **sentio, -ire, -si, -sus,** *feel, perceive.*

170 In this last sentence Ovid has referred to one and perhaps two old Roman customs which do not seem peculiarly Roman: betting on athletic contests and holding hands.

Dant etiam positis aditum convivia mensis:
  est aliquid praeter vina, quod inde petas.   230

*   *   *   *   *   *   *

Illic saepe animos iuvenum rapuere puellae,
  et Venus in vinis ignis in igne fuit.
Hic tu fallaci nimium ne crede lucernae: 245
  iudicio formae noxque merumque nocent.
Luce deas caeloque Paris spectavit aperto,
  cum dixit Veneri 'vincis utramque, Venus.'
Nocte latent mendae, vitioque ignoscitur omni,
  horaque formosam quamlibet illa facit.   250
Consule de gemmis, de tincta murice lana,
  consule de facie corporibusque diem.

---

229 **aditus**, **-us**, m., *approach.* **convivium**, **-ii**, n., *banquet, din-*
ner party. **mensa**, **-ae**, f., *table.*

230 **praeter** (acc.), *past, besides.* **vinum**, **-i** (also plur.), n.,
wine. **inde**, *from that place, from there.*

243 **illic**, *in that place, there.*

244 If for nothing else, this line is notable for its double play
  on words, a thing dear to Ovid's heart. His idea is, com-
bining love and wine is like combining fire and fire.

245 **tu**: with an imperative, best omitted in translation. **fallax**,
  -acis, *deceitful, deceptive.* **nimium**, *too much.* **lucerna**,
-ae, f., *lamp.* --A very sensible line. Moonlight, which is noto-
rious for the effect it has, should be included in the same cate-
gory as lamplight.

246 **iudicium**, **-ii**, n., *(power of) judgment.* **merum**, **-i**, n., *(un-*
mixed) wine. **noceo**, **-ere**, **-cui**, **-citus** (with dat.), *hurt,*
harm, injure, impair.

247 **lux, lucis**, m., *light, light of the sun, daylight.* **dea**, **-ae**,
  f., *goddess.* The reference here, of course, is to Juno, Mi-
nerva, and Venus. **caelum**, **-i**, n., *sky, air.* **Paris**, **-idis**, m.,
Paris, who caused the Trojan War by carrying off Helen. He decided
a famous beauty contest ('Miss Heaven') in favor of Venus. **aper-
tus**, **-a**, **-um**, *open, clear.*

248 **uterque, utraque, utrumque**, *each, both.*

249 **lateo**, **-ere**, **-ui**, *lie hid, be concealed.* **menda**, **-ae**, f.,
  fault, defect, blemish. **ignosco**, **-ere**, **-novi**, **-notus**, *par-*
don, forgive, overlook. When **ignosco** is used in the impersonal
passive, the English subject will be found in the dative in Latin;
or for the literal 'it is pardoned' etc. we may substitute some
such phrase as 'pardon is granted' etc.

250 **hora**, **-ae**, f., *hour.* **quilibet, quaelibet, quodlibet**, *any-*
(one) at all, any(one) whatsoever.

251 **consulo**, **-ere**, **-ui**, **-tus**, *consult.* **gemma**, **-ae**, f., *bud, gem,*
  jewel. **tingo**, **-ere**, **-nxi**, **-nctus**, *wet, dye, color.* **murex**,
-icis, m., *purple dye, purple.* **lana**, **-ae**, f., *wool.*

252 Anyone who, buying a suit, has been told to take it to the

Having concluded the first portion of his discussion, how to
find the girl, Ovid now proceeds to his second topic, how to win
the girl. The first requisite is confidence that no woman is be-
yond your reach.

> Hactenus, unde legas quod ames, ubi retia ponas,
>   praecipit imparibus vecta Thalia rotis.
> 265 Nunc tibi, quae placuit, quas sit capienda per artes,
>   dicere praecipuae molior artis opus.
> Quisquis ubique, viri, dociles advertite mentes,
>   pollicitisque favens vulgus adeste meis!
> Prima tuae menti veniat fiducia, cunctas
> 270   posse capi; capies, tu modo tende plagas.
> Vere prius volucres taceant, aestate cicadae,
>   Maenalius lepori det sua terga canis,

door and examine it by natural light will appreciate the
soundness of this advice.

263 **hactenus**, *so far, thus far*. **unde**, *from which (what) place,
whence*. **rete**, **-is**, n., *net*.

264 **praecipio**, **-ere**, **-cepi**, **-ceptus**, *advise, teach*. **impar**,
-aris, *unequal*. **veho**, **-ere**, **vexi**, **vectus**, *bear, carry, con-
vey*. **Thalia**, **-ae**, f.: the Muse of Comedy, claimed by Ovid as the
source of his inspiration. **rota**, **-ae**, f., *wheel*. The 'unequal'
wheels refer to the alternating long (hexameter) and short (pen-
tameter) lines used in the *Ars Amatoria*, as if they were the
wheels of the Muse's chariot.

265 The antecedent of **quae** is the subject of **sit capienda**, which
is a subjunctive in an indirect question depending on **dicere**.

266 **praecipuus**, **-a**, **-um**, *particular, special*. **molior**, **-iri**,
-itus, *undertake, attempt*. **opus** is either in apposition with
dicere, the object of **molior**; or is itself the object of **molior**,
and **dicere** is in apposition with **opus**.

267 With each of the first two words of the line supply 'you
are.' **ubique**, *wherever*. **docilis**, **-e**, *teachable, docile, at-
tentive*. **adverto**, **-ere**, **-ti**, **-sus**, *turn*.

268 **pollicitum**, **-i**, n., *promise*. **faveo**, **-ere**, **favi**, **fautus**, *be
well disposed, be favorable, favor*. **vulgus**, **-i**, n., *(common)
people, crowd*. Here vocative.

269 **fiducia**, **-ae**, f., *confidence, assurance*. **cunctus**, **-a**, **-um**,
all. Note the gender here.

270 **tendo**, **-ere**, **tetendi**, **tentus** (**-sus**), *stretch, spread*. **plaga**,
-ae, f., *hunting net, snare*.

271 **ver**, **veris**, n., *springtime, spring*. **prius . . . quam**, *sooner
. . . than; before* (not to be translated 'before' until the
clause headed by **quam** is reached). **volucris**, **-is**, f., *bird*. **ta-
ceo**, **-ere**, **-cui**, **-citus**, *be silent*. **aestas**, **-atis**, f., *summer*.
cicada, **-ae**, f., *cicada, tree cricket, grasshopper, locust*.

272 **Maenalius**, **-a**, **-um**, *Maenalian, Arcadian* (here referring to a
hound bred in that region). **lepus**, **-oris**, m., *hare*. **tergum**,
-i, n., *back*. Here plur. for sing. Obviously 'give the back to'
means 'run away from.' **canis**, **-is**, m., f., *dog*.

femina quam iuveni blande temptata repugnet;
  haec quoque, quam poteris credere nolle, volet.
Utque viro furtiva Venus, sic grata puellae;   275
  vir male dissimulat, tectius illa cupit.
Conveniat maribus, ne quam nos ante rogemus,
  femina iam partes victa rogantis agat!
Mollibus in pratis admugit femina tauro,
  femina cornipedi semper adhinnit equo;   280
parcior in nobis nec tam furiosa libido:
  legitimum finem flamma virilis habet.

  *   *   *   *   *   *   *

Ergo age, ne dubita cunctas sperare puellas!   343

---

273 **quam**: see 271. **blande**, *flatteringly, courteously, pleasant-
     ly, charmingly*. **tempto**, -are, -avi, -atus, *handle, assail,
court, woo, make love to*. **repugno**, -are, -avi, -atus, *fight
against, fight back, resist*.

274 **quam**: subject of **nolle**, which depends on **credere**, which de-
     pends on **poteris**. **nolo, nolle, nolui**, *not wish, be unwill-
ing, be reluctant; be unfriendly (?)*.

275 Both clauses of this line have **Venus** for subject, **est** (under-
     stood) for verb, and **grata** for predicate adjective. **furti-
vus**, -a, -um, *stolen, secret, hidden*. **gratus**, -a, -um, *pleasing,
agreeable*. --This line may be taken as meaning that girls are as
susceptible to the secret fires of love as are men.

276 **dissimulo**, -are, -avi, -atus, *disguise, hide, conceal, keep
     secret*. Supply 'his love' as the object. **tecto**, *secretly,
hiddenly, cautiously*. **cupio**, -ere, -ivi (-ii), -itus, *desire, be
in love*.

277 **convenio**, -ire, -veni, -ventus, *come together, suit, be
     agreed (on) among*. Here we have the protasis of a condition
with **si** omitted; English sometimes does the same thing ('should it
be agreed'). **mas, maris**, m., *a male*. **qui, quae, quod** (after **si,
nisi, ne, num**), *anyone, any*.

278 **rogantis**: With such participles used alone always supply some
     substantive in the same case: 'of the one making love,' 'of
the one who makes love,' etc.

279 **pratum**, -i, n., *meadow*. **admugio**, -ire, -ii, *low to, bellow
     to*. **femina** does not mean *woman* here! **taurus**, -i, m., *bull*.

280 **cornipes**, -pedis, *horn-footed, hoofed*. **adhinnio**, -ire, -ivi
     (-ii), -itus, *neigh to, whinny to*.

281 **parcus**, -a, -um, *sparing, moderate*. **furiosus**, -a, -um, *mad,
     raging, frantic*. **libido**, -inis, f., *desire, eagerness, long-
ing, passion*.

282 **legitimus**, -a, -um, *lawful, just, proper*. **finis**, -is, m.,
     limit, bound, end. **flamma**, -ae, f., *flame, flame of love,
love, passion*. **virilis**, -e, *of a man, manly, masculine*.

343 **ergo**, *therefore, then, accordingly*. **dubito**, -are, -avi,
     -atus, *doubt, hesitate*. **cunctus**, -a, -um, *all*. **spero**, -are,
-avi, -atus, *hope (for)*. --This line is reminiscent of the com-
mencement speaker who created a sensation some years ago by urging

Vix erit e multis, quae neget, una tibi.
345   Quae dant quaeque negant, gaudent tamen esse rogatae;
        ut iam fallaris, tuta repulsa tua est.
      Sed cur fallaris, cum sit nova grata voluptas,
        et capiant animos plus aliena suis?
      Fertilior seges est alienis semper in agris,
350   vicinumque pecus grandius uber habet.

It is well to be on good terms with the lady's maid. She can
tell you the best times to press your suit. But do not fall for
the maid (351-398). Certain days must be avoided; especially those
on which presents are given, such as the day of the Matronalia
(= St. Valentine's) (399-416). Worst of all is your girl friend's
birthday. But one way or another she will get presents out of you.

417   Magna superstitio tibi sit natalis amicae,
        quaque aliquid dandum est, illa sit atra dies.
      Cum bene vitaris, tamen auferet; invenit artem

---

the graduating class to aspire to marrying the boss's daughter.

344   **vix**, *hardly, scarcely*.   **erit**: cultivate the trick of supply-
        ing the English expletive 'there' when needed, as here:
'there will be.'   **nego, -are, -avi, -atus,** *say no, deny, refuse*.
tibi: more easily read with **neget**.

345   A statement of the general truth that all women, whether they
        accept or decline, are flattered by a proposal of marriage.
quae dant: 'girls who consent.'   **negant**: 344.   **gaudeo, -ere, gavi-
sus sum,** *rejoice, be glad*.

346   **tutus, -a, -um,** *safe, without danger, harmless, without loss*.
      repulsa, -ae, f., *rejection, refusal, repulse*.

347   **cur,** *why*.   **gratus, -a, -um,** *pleasing, agreeable*.   **voluptas,**
        -atis, f., *enjoyment, pleasure, delight*.   --The advantage of
being a new face would, of course, be only temporary, but would
afford at least a beginning.

348   **alienus, -a, -um,** *belonging to another person, not one's own,*
        another's. Here used substantively; supply 'things' or the
like.   **suis**: 'than one's own.'

349   Another of Ovid's pat illustrations which he slips in so
        smoothly.   **fertilis, -e,** *fertile, productive*.   **seges, -etis,**
f., *grainfield, crop*.   **alienis**: 348.   **ager, agri,** m., *field*.

350   **vicinus, -a, -um,** *neighboring*.   **pecus, pecoris,** n., *cattle,*
        herd, flock.   **grandis, -e,** *large, full, abundant*.   **uber,**
uberis, n., *udder*.

417   **superstitio, -onis,** f., *superstition; a thing of dread*.   **na-
talis, -is,** m., *birthday*.

418   **qua**: the antecedent is **dies**.   **ater, atra, atrum,** *black, dark,*
        dismal, unlucky, sad.

419   **vito, -are, -avi, -atus,** *shun, seek to escape, avoid*.   **vitaris**
        = **vitaveris**.   **aufero, auferre, abstuli, ablatus,** *carry off,*
obtain. As often, an object must be supplied here; e.g., 'the
loot.'   **invenio, -ire, -veni, -ventus,** *come upon, find, discover*.
invenit, the scansion shows, is present tense.

femina, qua cupidi carpat amantis opes.   420
Institor ad dominam veniet discinctus emacem,
    expediet merces teque sedente suas,
quas illa inspicias, sapere ut videare, rogabit,
    oscula deinde dabit; deinde rogabit, emas.
Hoc fore contentam multos iurabit in annos,   425
    nunc opus esse sibi, nunc bene dicet emi.
Si non esse domi, quos des, causabere nummos,
    littera poscetur - ne didicisse iuvet.
Quid, quasi natali cum poscit munera libo

---

420 **cupidus, -a, -um,** *desirous, eager, fond, passionate.* **carpo,**
    -ere, -psi, -ptus, *pluck, gather, snatch, fleece.* **amans,**
amantis, m., *lover.*

421 An example of how a woman may go about getting presents out
    of a man follows. Presumably Ovid is speaking from experi-
ence; his words seem to come from the heart. **institor, -oris,** m.,
peddler. **discinctus, -a, -um,** *ungirt, slovenly, carelessly
dressed, dissolute.* **emax, -acis,** *eager to buy, fond of buying.*

422 **expedio, -ire, -ivi (-ii), -itus,** *set free, bring out, set
    forth.* **merx, -cis,** f., *goods, wares, merchandise.* **-que**
should be translated at the beginning of the line.

423 **inspicio, -ere, -spexi, -spectus,** *look at, inspect, examine.*
    inspicias depends on **rogabit, ut** being omitted. **sapio, -ere,**
-ivi (-ii), *taste, have good taste, have discernment, be wise.*
--Another instance of Ovid's keen insight into human psychology,
male and especially female. The man is more or less indifferent to
the goods on display, while the woman is anxious that in front of
outsiders, at least, he make a show of having good taste and ap-
preciating nice things.

424 **osculum, -i,** n., *little mouth, kiss.* **deinde,** *then, next.*
    emo, -ere, emi, emptus, *buy, purchase.* --This procedure
speaks for itself. Eve undoubtedly used it on Adam.

425 **hoc:** abl. **fore** is fut. inf. of **sum; se** is understood as the
    subject. **contentus, -a, -um,** *satisfied, content.* **iuro,**
-are, -avi, -atus, *swear.*

426 **nunc . . . nunc:** the emphatic word in this line. *Now* is the
    time; no putting off! **opus esse sibi:** 'that there is need to
herself' = 'that she needs (it).' **bene,** with **emo,** means 'cheaply'
or 'at a bargain.' **emo:** 424.

427 **domus, -us** & **-i,** f., *house, home.* **causor, -ari, -atus,**
    plead, give as a reason, pretend, make excuse. **nummus, -i,**
m., *coin, money, cash.*

428 **littera, -ae,** f., *letter, document, promissory note, check.*
    posco, -ere, poposci, *ask for (urgently), beg, demand, re-*
quest. **ne didicisse iuvet** is Ovid's own parenthetical and sardon-
ic comment, and means roughly 'So that you will be sorry you ever
learned to write.'

429 **quid:** 'what's to be said?' or 'what's to be done?' **quasi,** *as
    if.* Here to be read only with **natali . . . libo:** 'as if for

430   et, quotiens opus est, nascitur illa sibi?
       Quid, cum mendaci damno maestissima plorat,
       elapsusque cava fingitur aure lapis?
       Multa rogant utenda dari, data reddere nolunt;
          perdis, et in damno gratia nulla tuo.

Letters may be used to pave the way. Use flatteries and prom-
ises. Anyone can be rich in promises (437-458). But to write ef-
fective letters, you must have eloquence based on a good educa-
tion. If she does not answer at first, persevere.

       Disce bonas artes, moneo, Romana iuventus,
460   non tantum trepidos ut tueare reos:
       quam populus iudexque gravis lectusque senatus,
          tam dabit eloquio victa puella manus.

(i.e., to buy) a birthday cake.' **natalis, -e,** natal, birthday.
libum, -i, n., cake.

430 **quotiens,** how often, as often as. **nascor, nasci, natus,** be
     born. **sibi:** read either with **opus est** ('she has need') or
with **nascitur,** showing that it is to her own interest to have such
frequent birthdays ('she has a birthday for herself').

431 **quid:** 429. **mendax, -acis,** lying, false, feigned, fictitious.
     damnum, -i, n., harm, loss. What sort of loss, is suggested
in the next line. **maestus, -a, -um,** sad, sorrowful, dejected,
melancholy. **ploro, -are, -avi, -atus,** cry, wail, lament, weep.

432 **elabor, elabi, elapsus,** slip off, fall off. Here supply **esse.**
     cavus, -a, -um, hollow, (shell-like, pierced). **fingo, -ere,**
finxi, fictus, form, imagine, feign, pretend. **auris, -is,** f.,
ear. **lapis, -idis,** m., stone, jewel.

433 **utenda dari:** literally, 'to be given to be used,' hence 'to
     be lent.' **nolo, nolle, nolui,** not wish, be unwilling.

434 **perdo, -ere, -didi, -ditus,** destroy, waste, lose. **damno:** see
     431. **gratia, -ae,** f., favor, thanks, gratitude.

459 Ovid's discussion of carrying on one's courtship by mail is
     useful for students separated from the objects of their af-
fection by the exigencies of education. **bonas artes:** perhaps
equivalent to our terms 'liberal arts' or 'belles-lettres.' More
specifically, the phrase here seems to refer to eloquence and the
ability to express oneself well, regarded as highly important by
Romans, politicians, and would-be leaders of men (and women). **mo-
neo, -ere, -ui, -itus,** warn, advise. **Romanus, -a, -um,** Roman, of
Rome. **iuventus, -utis,** f., age of youth, young people, youth (in
a collective sense).

460 **tantum,** only, merely. **trepidus, -a, -um,** anxious, disturbed,
     alarmed. **tueor, -eri, tuitus,** gaze upon, defend, protect.
reus, -i, m., defendant.

461 **populus, -i,** m., people. **iudex, -icis,** m., f., judge. **gra-
     vis, -e,** heavy, grave, eminent, venerable. **lectus, -a, -um,**
chosen, selected, excellent. **senatus, -us,** m., senate.

462 **do . . . manus** = yield, surrender. **eloquium, -ii,** n., elo-
     quence. **puella** is contrasted with the three nominatives in

Sed lateant vires, nec sis in fronte disertus;
  effugiant voces verba molesta tuae.
Quis, nisi mentis inops, tenerae declamat amicae?   465
  Saepe valens odii littera causa fuit.
Sit tibi credibilis sermo consuetaque verba,
  blanda tamen, praesens ut videare loqui.
Si non accipiet scriptum inlectumque remittet,
  lecturam spera propositumque tene.   470
Tempore difficiles veniunt ad aratra iuvenci,
  tempore lenta pati frena docentur equi;
ferreus adsiduo consumitur anulus usu,

---

the preceding line through the use of **quam . . . tam; dabit** serves
as verb for all four of these nouns.

463 Good advice: not to make a display of your powers or learn-
    ing. **lateo, -ere, -ui,** *lie hid, be concealed.* **sis:** subjunc-
tive used as imperative. **frons, frontis,** f., *brow, front, appear-
ance.* **in fronte =** 'too obviously' or the like. **disertus, -a, -um,**
fluent, eloquent.

464 **effugio, -ere, -fugi,** *flee from, avoid, shun.* **molestus, -a,**
    -um, *troublesome, annoying, labored, affected.*

465 **inops, -opis** (with gen.), *destitute of, without.* **declamo,**
    -are, -avi, -atus, *speak oratorically, declaim.*

466 **valens, -entis,** *strong, powerful.* Probably modifies **causa**
    here. **odium, -ii,** n., *hatred, ill-will, offense, annoyance.*
littera, -ae, f., *letter.*

467 **tibi:** a dative of personal interest, most easily, if not ex-
    actly, translated by the English possessive. **credibilis, -e,**
believable, credible, plausible. **sermo, -onis,** m., *conversation,*
speech, mode of expression, language, style, diction. Here used of
letter writing. **consuetus, -a, -um,** *usual, ordinary, customary.*

468 **blandus, -a, -um,** *flattering, pleasant, agreeable, charming,*
    smooth. **praesens, -entis,** *present, in person.*

469 **scriptum, -i,** n., *writing, letter.* **inlectus, -a, -um,** *un-*
    read. **remitto, -ere, -misi, -missus,** *send back, return.*

470 **lecturam:** supply **esse,** a subject, and an object, all quite
    obvious. **spero, -are, -avi, -atus,** *hope.* **propositum, -i,**
n., *plan, intention, design, purpose.*

471 Again Ovid launches into a series of illustrations of his
    meaning, this time on the value of perseverance. **difficilis,**
-e, *difficult, hard to manage, troublesome, obstinate.* **aratrum,**
-i, n., *plow.* **iuvencus, i,** m., *young bullock, young ox.*

472 **lentus, -a, -um,** *pliant, flexible, tough.* **patior, pati, pas-**
    sus, *bear, suffer, endure, submit to.* **frena, -orum,** n., *bri-*
dle, *bit, reins.*

473 **ferreus, -a, -um,** *made of iron, iron.* **adsiduus, -a, -um,**
    continual, constant. **consumo, -ere, -sumpsi, -sumptus,** *con-*
sume, *wear away.* **anulus, -i,** m., *ring.* **usus, -us,** m., *use, wear.*

interit adsidua vomer aduncus humo.
475 Quid magis est saxo durum, quid mollius unda?
Dura tamen molli saxa cavantur aqua.
Penelopen ipsam, persta modo, tempore vinces;
capta vides sero Pergama, capta tamen.
Legerit et nolit rescribere, cogere noli:
480 tu modo blanditias fac legat usque tuas.
Quae voluit legisse, volet rescribere lectis;
per numeros venient ista gradusque suos.
Forsitan et primo veniet tibi littera tristis,
quaeque roget, ne se sollicitare velis:
485 quod rogat illa,timet;quod non rogat,optat,ut instes;

474 **intereo, -ire, -ii, -itus,** *perish, wear away.* **vomer, -eris,**
m., *plowshare.* **aduncus, -a, -um,** *hooked, curved.* **humus, -i,**
f., *earth, ground, soil.* **adsidua . . . humo** in this context
clearly means 'by continual plowing in the ground.'

475 **magis,** *more.* **saxum, -i,** n., *stone, rock.*

476 **saxa:** 475. **cavo, -are, -avi, -atus,** *make hollow, hollow out.*

477 **Penelope, -es** (acc. **-en**), f.: faithful wife of Ulysses. **per-
sto, -are, -stiti, -status,** *stand fast, persevere, persist.*

478 **sero,** *late, after a long time.* **Pergama, -orum,** n., *(the cit-
adel of) Troy.*

479 **legerit et nolit:** either conditional subjunctives (supply **si**)
or concessive: 'suppose that she has read (your letter) and
does not want . . . .' **nolo, nolle, nolui,** *not wish, not want, be
unwilling.* **rescribo, -ere, -psi, -ptus,** *write back, reply (in
writing).* **cogo, -ere, coegi, coactus,** *collect, force, compel.*
noli (with inf.) = 'do not.'

480 **blanditia, -ae,** f., *flattery.* **usque,** *all the way, all the
while, continually.*

481 **quae:** its antecedent is either the subject of **volet** ('she')
or else may be found in **lectis. rescribere:** 479. **lectis**
(dat.): 'things read,' i.e., 'what she had read'; or 'when she has
read them.'

482 **per numeros . . . gradusque suos:** 'by their own steps and
stages,' 'in their own good time' (lit. 'through their own
numbers and steps'). **iste, ista, istud,** *that, that of yours.* As
often with neuter plural pronouns, here supply 'things.'

483 **forsitan,** *perhaps.* **primo** (adv.), *at first.* **littera, -ae,**
f., *letter.* **tristis, -e,** *sad, ill-humored, stern, harsh.*

484 **quae:** 'one which.' **sollicito, -are, -avi, -atus,** *disturb,
vex, bother.*

485 **opto, -are, -avi, -atus,** *wish, desire.* **ut instes** explains
quod non rogat. insto, -are, -stiti, -status, *press on, in-
sist, persist.*

insequere, et voti postmodo compos eris.

Appear wherever she appears (487-504). Next some advice about
personal grooming.

Sed tibi nec ferro placeat torquere capillos,   505
    nec tua mordaci pumice crura teras.

*   *   *   *   *   *   *

Forma viros neglecta decet: Minoida Theseus
    abstulit a nulla tempora comptus acu;   510
Hippolytum Phaedra, nec erat bene cultus, amavit;
    cura deae silvis aptus Adonis erat.
Munditie placeant, fuscentur corpora Campo;
    sit bene conveniens et sine labe toga;

---

486 **insequor, -qui, -cutus,** *follow on, pursue, proceed, press on.*
     votum, -i, n., *vow, wish, desire.* **postmodo,** *afterwards,*
presently, shortly. **compos, -potis** (with gen.), *master of, pos-*
sessing, possessed of, in possession of.

505 **ferrum, -i,** n., *iron, implement of iron, curling irons.* **tor-**
     queo, -ere, torsi, tortus, *turn, twist, curl.*

506 **mordax, -acis,** *biting.* **pumex, -icis,** m.,*pumice stone.* **crus,**
     -uris, n., *leg.* **tero, -ere, trivi, tritus,** *rub, smooth.*
--These were practices of the up-to-date women of Ovid's time (and
more recent times, too) and of some men.

509 **neglectus, -a, -um,** *neglected, careless.* **Minois, -idis** (acc.
     -ida), f., *daughter of Minos; Ariadne* (who fell in love and
ran off with Theseus). **Theseus, -ei,** m.: Greek hero who conquered
the Minotaur.

510 **aufero, auferre, abstuli, ablatus,** *carry off.* **comptus, -a,**
     -um, *adorned, ornamented.* **tempora** (acc. of respect) **comptus:**
translate freely 'though his temples were adorned'; how literally?
acus, -us, f., *pin, hairpin, ornamental pin.*

511 These next two lines refer to two more famous love affairs of
     mythology, in each of which cases, says Ovid, the man was not
noted for the elegance of his dress. **Hippolytus** was very much in-
terested in hunting and very little interested in women, least of
all **Phaedra,** his young step-mother. The outcome, incidentally, was
catastrophic. **Adonis,** an extraordinarily handsome lad madly loved
by Venus, also enjoyed hunting (which explains **silvis aptus**) and
eventually lost his life because of it. He would have done better
to listen to Venus. **cultus, -a, -um,** *cultivated, ornamented,*
adorned, polished, dressed, elegantly dressed.

512 **dea, -ae,** f., *goddess.* **silva, -ae,** f., *wood, forest.*

513 **mundities, -ei,** f., *cleanliness, neatness.* **placeant:** the
     subject is **corpora,** or possibly **viri. fusco, -are, -avi,**
-atus, *darken, bronze, tan.* **Campus, -i,** m., *the Campus Martius,* a
field in Rome used for assemblies, drills, games, exercise, and
recreation. As the Romans took their exercise naked or nearly so,
again anticipating more recent times, they could acquire a good
sun tan at the same time.

514 **conveniens, -entis,** *fitting.* **bene conveniens** = 'a good fit.'

515   lingula ne ruget; careant rubigine dentes.
    Nec vagus in laxa pes tibi pelle natet,
    nec male deformet rigidos tonsura capillos:
    sit coma, sit scita barba resecta manu.
    Et nihil emineant et sint sine sordibus ungues,
520   inque cava nullus stet tibi nare pilus.
    Nec male odorati sit tristis anhelitus oris,
    nec laedat nares virque paterque gregis.
    Cetera lascivae faciant, concede, puellae . . .

---

    labes, -is, f., *spot, stain, blemish.* **toga, -ae,** f., *toga* (a flowing outer garment worn by Roman citizens).

515 **lingula ne ruget:** a conjecture (i.e., guess based on certain evidence) by Palmer. No one is sure what Ovid wrote here, as the manuscript readings are confused. **lingula, -ae,** f., *(little) tongue, tongue of a shoe, shoe strap.* **rugo, -are, -avi, -atus,** *become wrinkled, become coated* (?). **careo, -ere, -ui, -itus** (with abl.), *be without, be free from, lack.* **rubigo, -inis,** f., *rust, stain, yellowness.* **dens, dentis,** m., *tooth.*

516 **vagus, -a, -um,** *rambling, wandering.* **laxus, -a, -um,** *wide, loose, roomy; too large.* **pellis, -is,** f., *skin, leather, shoe.* **nato, -are, -avi, -atus,** *swim, float.* --All this is merely Ovid's way of saying not to wear shoes that are too large.

517 **deformo, -are, -avi, -atus,** *disfigure, spoil, mar.* **rigidus, -a, -um,** *stiff, stubborn.* **tonsura, -ae,** f., *clipping, trimming, cutting.*

518 **scitus, -a, -um,** *knowing, experienced, skillful.* **barba, -ae,** f., *beard.* **reseco, -are, -avi, -atus,** *cut off, cut.*

519 **nihil,** *nothing, not at all, not.* **emineo, -ere, -ui,** *stand out, project.* **sordes, -is,** f., *dirt, filth.* **unguis, -is,** m., *fingernail.*

520 **cavus, -a, -um,** *hollow.* **sto, -are, steti, status,** *stand, remain.* **naris, -is,** f., *nostril.* **pilus, -i,** m., *hair.*

521 **odoratus, -a, -um,** *odorous, fragrant, smelling.* **tristis, -e,** *sad, offensive, foul, unpleasant.* **anhelitus, -us,** m., *breathing, breath.* --This is the passage that brought Ovid to national attention when advertisements of an antiseptic manufacturer featured it in 1950.

522 **nares:** 520. **grex, gregis,** m., *flock, herd.* --The preceding line refers to halitosis, this one to B.O. (body odor). 'The husband and father of the herd' means 'the he-goat,' an animal not noted for a too pleasant smell. The Romans used these goatish expressions, just as we do B.O., to refer euphemistically to underarm odor.

523 The sense of the line is that it is proper for men to go this far in attention to their personal appearance and grooming. Anything further should be left to the women. **ceterus, -a, -um,** *the other, the rest.* **lascivus, -a, -um,** *playful, frolicsome,*

The story of Ariadne and Bacchus is related to show that the
latter is not incompatible with love.

Gnosis in ignotis amens errabat harenis,
    qua brevis aequoreis Dia feritur aquis;
utque erat e somno tunica velata recincta,
    nuda pedem, croceas inreligata comas,   530
Thesea crudelem surdas clamabat ad undas,
    indigno teneras imbre rigante genas.
Clamabat flebatque simul, sed utrumque decebat;
    non facta est lacrimis turpior illa suis.
Iamque iterum tundens mollissima pectora palmis, 535

---

frisky, roguish, wanton. **faciant** depends on **concede**, with **ut**
omitted; its subject is **puellae.** **concedo, -ere, -cessi, -cessus,**
depart, grant, concede, allow.

527 However we may feel about the use of wine (it was taken as a
    matter of course by the Romans, as it is by Europeans), Ovid
is certainly to be praised in that he warns against drunkenness.
Besides, it gives him an excuse for relating the conclusion of Ar-
iadne's adventure (cf. 509-510), after she had been deserted in
her sleep on the island of Dia by Theseus, just subsequent to
their elopement from Crete. It is a masterpiece of verbal paint-
ing. The processional scene Ovid describes has been reproduced by
several of the great masters of visual painting, including Titian
and Poussin. **Gnosis, -idis,** f., *the Cnossian girl, the Cretan
girl;* i.e., *Ariadne* (daughter of Minos, king of Crete). **ignotus,
-a, -um,** *unknown, strange.* **amens, amentis,** *out of one's senses,
frantic, distracted.* **erro, -are, -avi, -atus,** *wander (up and
down), rove.* **harena, -ae,** f., *sand, shore, beach.*

528 **brevis, -e,** *little, small.* **aequoreus, -a, -um,** *of the sea.*
    Dia, -ae, f.: either of two islands (Standia or Naxos) north
of Crete. **ferio, -ire,** *strike, beat.*

529 **ut erat:** 'just as she was (on awaking).' **somnus, -i,** m.,
    sleep. **tunica, -ae,** f., *undergarment, tunic.* **velo, -are,
-avi, -atus,** *cover, clothe.* **recingo, -ere, -xi, -ctus,** *ungird,
loose.*

530 **nudus, -a, -um,** *naked, bare.* **pedem, comas:** accusatives of
    specification. **croceus, -a, -um,** *saffron-colored, golden,
yellow.* **inreligatus, -a, -um,** *unbound.*

531 **Theseus, -ei** (acc. **-ea**), m.: Greek hero who conquered the
    Minotaur with Ariadne's help. **crudelis, -e,** *hard-hearted,
cruel.* **surdus, -a, -um,** *deaf.*

532 **indignus, -a, -um,** *unworthy, undeserved.* **imber, -bris,** m.,
    rain, shower (of tears). **rigo, -are, -avi, -atus,** *wet, mois-
ten, bedew.* **gena, -ae,** f., *cheek.*

533 **simul,** *at the same time.* **uterque, utraque, utrumque,** *each,
    both.*

534 **non . . . turpior** is a roundabout way of saying 'prettier.'
    This device is called *litotes.*

535 **iterum,** *again, a second time.* **tundo, -ere, tutudi, tunsus**

'Perfidus ille abiit! Quid mihi fiet?' ait.
'Quid mihi fiet?' ait: sonuerunt cymbala toto
litore et attonita tympana pulsa manu.
Excidit illa metu rupitque novissima verba;
540   nullus in exanimi corpore sanguis erat.
Ecce Mimallonides sparsis in terga capillis,
ecce leves satyri, praevia turba dei,
ebrius ecce senex: pando Silenus asello
vix sedet et pressas continet arte iubas.

(tussus, tusus), *beat, strike (repeatedly)*. **palma, -ae,** f.,
palm, hand. --This classic way of expressing grief is not so much
in fashion as it used to be.

536 **perfidus, -a, -um,** *faithless, false, treacherous, perfidious.*
abeo, -ire, -ivi (-ii), -itus, *go away, depart, disappear.*
aio, *say.*

537 A very dramatic line. Its power is based on the repetition of
Ariadne's words, then the sudden sound of the cymbals break-
ing in on her lonely lament. This startling succession of soft and
loud effects has often been strikingly used by the great compos-
ers, such as Tschaikowsky and Wagner. **ait:** 536. **sono, -are, -ui,**
-itus, *sound, resound.* **cymbalum, -i,** n., *cymbal* (especially asso-
ciated with Bacchus). **totus, -a, -um,** *all, whole, entire.*

538 **litus, -oris,** n., *seashore, beach.* **attonitus, -a, -um,** *thun-
der-struck, frantic, frenzied.* Ablative case here. **tympanum,**
-i, n., *drum, tambourine.* **pello, -ere, pepuli, pulsus,** *beat,*
strike, drive.

539 **excido, -ere, -cidi,** *fall down, faint, swoon, collapse.* It is
doubtful if Ariadne actually faints, since a few lines later
she is quite conscious and tries to run away. **metus, -us,** m.,
fear, dread. **rumpo, -ere, rupi, ruptus,** *break (off), interrupt.*
--As Ariadne has already begun to repeat herself, it may be just
as well that she breaks off talking.

540 **exanimis, -e,** *lifeless, breathless, terrified.* **sanguis,**
-inis, m., *blood.*

541 **ecce,** *lo! see! behold! here are (is).* **Mimallonis, -idis,** f.,
a Bacchante, a female follower of Bacchus. **spargo, -ere,**
-si, -sus, *scatter, strew, spread.* **tergum, -i,** n., *back.*

542 **ecce:** 541. **satyrus, -i,** m., *satyr* (a goat-footed forest dei-
ty). **praevius, -a, -um,** *going before, leading the way, pre-
ceding.* **turba, -ae,** f., *crowd, throng, band, troop.* **dei:** the god
here is Bacchus, god of wine.

543 **ebrius, -a, -um,** *drunken, intoxicated.* **ecce:** 541. **senex,**
senis, m., *old man* (i.e., Silenus). **pandus, -a, -um,** *bent,*
crooked, curved, sway-backed. **Silenus, -i,** m.: the tutor and con-
stant attendant of Bacchus; bald, flat-nosed, perpetually drunk;
excessively fond of young women; one of the clowns of mythology.
asellus, -i, m., *(little) ass, donkey.*

544 **vix,** *with difficulty, scarcely, barely.* **premo, -ere, -essi,**
-essus, *press, hold fast, firmly grasp.* **contineo, -ere,**

Dum sequitur Bacchas,Bacchae fugiuntque petuntque, 545
    quadrupedem ferula dum malus urget eques,
in caput aurito cecidit delapsus asello;
    clamarunt satyri 'surge age, surge, pater!'
Iam deus in curru, quem summum texerat uvis,
    tigribus adiunctis aurea lora dabat: 550
et color et Theseus et vox abiere puellae
    terque fugam petiit terque retenta metu est;
horruit, ut steriles agitat quas ventus aristas,
    ut levis in madida canna palude tremit.

-tinui, -tentus, *hold together, hold fast, cling to.* **arte,** *close-ly, fast, firmly.* **iuba, -ae,** f., *mane.*

545 **sequor, -qui, secutus,** *follow, chase, pursue.* **Baccha, -ae,** f., *a Bacchante, a female follower of Bacchus.* --The girls are having some fun, in an immemorial female way, by tantalizing the old fellow.

546 **quadrupes, -pedis,** m., f., n., *quadruped.* **ferula, -ae,** f., *staff, (walking) stick, whip.* **malus, -a, -um,** *bad, unlucky, awkward, unskillful.* **urgeo, -ere, ursi,** *press, drive, urge on.* **eques, -itis,** m., *horseman, rider.*

547 **caput, -itis,** n., *head.* **auritus, -a, -um,** *long-eared.* **cado, -ere, cecidi, casus,** *fall.* **delabor, -bi, -lapsus,** *fall, slip down, slide off.* **asellus, -i,** m., *(little) ass, donkey.*

548 **clamarunt = clamaverunt. satyri:** 542. **surgo, -ere, surrexi, surrectus,** *rise, get up, stand up.*

549 **currus, -us,** m., *chariot.* **summum:** must be translated before **quem. tego, -ere, -xi, -ctus,** *cover.* **uva, -ae,** f., *grape, bunch of grapes.*

550 **tigris, -is (-idis),** m., f., *tiger, tigress.* Bacchus used ti-gers for drawing his chariot. Everyone to his own taste. **ad-iungo, -ere, -nxi, -nctus,** *join, yoke, harness.* **aureus, -a, -um,** *of gold, golden.* **lora, -orum,** n., *reins.* To give reins is to slacken reins, or to let go unrestrained.

551 **Theseus:** 531. Here could mean either Theseus himself or the thought of Theseus. **abeo, -ire, -ii (-ivi), -itus,** *go away, depart, leave, disappear, vanish.* The ending **-ere = -erunt.**

552 **ter,** *three times, thrice.* **fuga, -ae,** f., *flight, escape.* **retineo, -ere, -ui, -tentus,** *hold back, keep back, restrain.* **metus, -us,** m., *fear, dread.*

553 **horreo, -ere, -ui,** *bristle, tremble, shake, shudder.* **steri-les . . . aristas** have been incorporated into the relative clause and have taken the case of the relative pronoun. Properly they should be in the nominative case and the line written thus: 'horruit, ut steriles aristae quas ventus agitat.' **sterilis, -e,** *barren, dry.* **agito, -are, -avi, -atus,** *drive, shake, toss about, move to and fro.* **arista, -ae,** f., *ear of grain, (stalk).*

554 **madidus, -a, -um,** *moist, wet.* **canna, -ae,** f., *reed, cane.* **palus, -udis,** f., *swamp, marsh.* **tremo, -ere, -ui,** *shake,*

555 Cui deus 'en, adsum tibi cura fidelior,' inquit;
        'pone metum: Bacchi, Gnosias, uxor eris!
     Munus habe caelum: caelo spectabere sidus;
        saepe reget dubiam Cressa Corona ratem.'
     Dixit, et e curru, ne tigres illa timeret,
560   desilit (imposito cessit harena pede),
     implicitamque sinu (neque enim pugnare valebat)
        abstulit: in facili est omnia posse deo.
     Pars 'Hymenaee' canunt,pars clamant Euhion,'euhoe!'
        Sic coeunt sacro nupta deusque toro.

---

quiver, tremble.

555 **en**, *lo! behold! see!* **fidelis**, -**e**, *trusty, faithful, true.*
     inquam, *say.*

556 **metus**, -**us**, m., *fear, dread.* **Bacchus**, -**i**, m.: god of wine.
     Gnosias, -**adis**, f., *Cnossian girl, Cretan girl.* **uxor**, -**oris**,
     f., *wife.*

557 **munus**: in apposition with **caelum**. **caelum**, -**i**, n., *sky, heav-
     en, the heavens.* **sidus**, -**eris**, n., *constellation, star.* Here
     in apposition with the subject 'you.' --This is the mythical ori-
     gin of that circular group of stars still known as 'Corona' (see
     next line) or 'Ariadne's Crown.'

558 **rego**, -**ere**, -**xi**, -**ctus**, *guide, direct, rule.* **dubius**, -**a**,
     -**um**, *doubting, doubtful, uncertain.* **Cressa**, -**ae** (adj.), *Cre-*
     tan. **corona**, -**ae**, f., *wreath, crown.* **ratis**, -**is**, f., *boat, ship.*

559 **currus**, -**us**, m., *chariot.* **tigres**: 550.

560 **desilio**, -**ire**, -**silui**, -**sultus**, *leap down.* **impono**, -**ere**, -**po-**
     sui, -**positus**, *place on.* **cedo**, -**ere**, **cessi**, **cessus**, *go,*
     withdraw, yield. **harena**, -**ae**, f., *sand.* --This parenthetical
     statement is perhaps thrown in to show the eagerness with which
     Bacchus jumped from his chariot and hence to indicate that he was
     not merely interested in allaying Ariadne's fear of the tigers.

561 **implico**, -**are**, -**ui** (-**avi**), -**itus** (-**atus**), *enfold, embrace,*
     clasp. With **implicitam** supply **eam**. **neque enim**, *for . . .*
     not. **pugno**, -**are**, -**avi**, -**atus**, *fight, struggle.* **valeo**, -**ere**,
     -**ui**, -**itus**, *have strength, have the power, be in condition, be*
     able.

562 **aufero**, **auferre**, **abstuli**, **ablatus**, *carry off.* **in facili est:**
     'it is easy.' **omnia posse**: 'to be able (to do) all things.'
     --Ovid's wistful envy of the gods, especially in affairs of the
     heart, is evident.

563 **Hymenaeus**, -**i**, m., *Hymen* (god of marriage, who was invoked
     when a wedding was taking place). **cano**, -**ere**, **cecini**, **can-**
     tus, *sing.* **Euhius**, -**ii** (acc. **Euhion**), m.: a surname of Bacchus.
     euhoe: a shout of joy at the festivals of Bacchus.

564 **coeo**, -**ire**, -**ivi** (-**ii**), -**itus**, *come together, meet, be unit-
     ed, unite.* **sacer**, -**cra**, -**crum**, *holy, sacred.* **nupta**, -**ae**,
     f., *bride, wife.* **torus**, -**i**, m., *couch, bed, marriage, wedlock.*

Ergo ubi contigerint positi tibi munera Bacchi,   565
    atque erit in socii femina parte tori,
Nycteliumque patrem nocturnaque sacra precare,
    ne iubeant capiti vina nocere tuo.
Hic tibi multa licet sermone latentia tecto
    dicere, quae dici sentiat illa sibi,   570
blanditiasque leves tenui perscribere vino,
    ut dominam in mensa se legat illa tuam,
atque oculos oculis spectare fatentibus ignem:
    saepe tacens vocem verbaque vultus habet.
Fac primus rapias illius tacta labellis   575
    pocula, quaque bibit parte puella, bibas;

---

565 Ovid's story is ended and he returns to his subject. **ergo,**
therefore, accordingly. **contingo, -ere, -tigi, -tactus** (with
dat.), *touch, befall, fall to the lot of.* **Bacchus, -i,** m., *Bac-
chus* (god of wine), *the vine, wine.* --It would seem more logical
for **positi** to agree with **munera** than with **Bacchi.**

566 **socius, -a, -um,** *sharing, shared, social.* **tori:** 564. **socii**
    . . . **tori** refers, of course, to the Roman custom of reclin-
ing on long couches at meals, several to a couch.

567 **Nyctelius, -a, -um,** *Nyctelian,* an epithet of Bàcchus (because
    his mysteries were celebrated at night, the word being de-
rived from the Greek for 'night'). **nocturnus, -a, -um,** *of the
night, nocturnal.* **sacrum, -i,** n., *sacred thing, sacred rite.*
precor, -ari, -atus, *entreat, pray (to), call upon, beseech.* **pre-
care** is imperative.

568 **caput, -itis,** n., *head.* **vinum, -i,** n. (also in plur.), *wine.*
    noceo, -ere, -ui, -itus (with dat.), *do harm to, injure, (go
to).*

569 **sermo, -onis,** m., *talk, conversation.* **latens, -entis,** *lying
    hid, hidden, concealed, secret.* **tectus, -a, -um,** *hidden, se-
cret, concealed, disguised, cautious.*

570 **sentio, -ire, -si, -sus,** *feel, perceive.* Note the mood here.

571 **blanditia, -ae,** f., *flattery;* (plur.) *flatteries, loving
    words.* **perscribo, -ere, -psi, -ptus,** *write (trace) out.* **vi-
no:** 568. --It should be understood here that the wine has been
spilled on the table and the finger is used as a writing instru-
ment.

572 **mensa, -ae,** f., *table.* **se:** subject of **esse** understood.

573 **fateor, -eri, fassus,** *confess, show, declare.*

574 **tacens, -entis,** *silent.* **vultus, -us,** m., *expression, fea-
tures, face, countenance.*

575 **tango, -ere, tetigi, tactus,** *touch.* **labellum, -i,** n.,*(lit-
tle, dear, sweet) lip.*

576 **poculum, -i,** n., *cup, goblet.* --A more obvious order of
    words for the rest of the line would be: 'bibasque parte (po-

       et quemcumque cibum digitis libaverit illa,
578   tu pete dumque petes, sit tibi tacta manus.
   Do not drink to excess; but be entertaining.
       Certa tibi a nobis dabitur mensura bibendi:
590   officium praestent mensque pedesque suum.
       Iurgia praecipue vino stimulata caveto
         et nimium faciles ad fera bella manus:
       occidit Eurytion stulte data vina bibendo;
         aptior est dulci mensa merumque ioco.
595   Si vox est, canta; si mollia bracchia, salta;
         et quacumque potes dote placere, place.

   As the guests leave the table, seize the opportunity for a few
private words with the girl. Pour on the compliments. Everybody
loves flattery.

-----

culi) qua bibit puella.' As often happens, the antecedent has been
incorporated into the relative clause. --The little act of devo-
tion referred to here is surely no more repulsive or unsanitary
than the modern traditional gesture of gulping champagne from a
lady's slipper.

577   **cibus, -i**, m., *food*. **libo, -are, -avi, -atus**, *taste, touch*.

578   **tibi:** dat. of agent. That this is basically a dative of per-
      sonal interest must be quite apparent here. **tacta:** 575.

589   **certus, -a, -um**, *fixed, sure, reliable, certain, definite.*
      mensura, -ae, f., *measure, quantity, extent, limit.*

590   **officium, -ii**, n., *service, duty, function, office.* **praesto,
      -are, -avi, -atus**, *stand before, fulfil, perform, show.*

591   **iurgium, -ii**, n., *quarrel, dispute, strife.* **praecipue,** *espe-
      cially, particularly.* **vinum, -i**, n., *wine.* **stimulo, -are,
      -avi, -atus**, *arouse, incite, stimulate.* **caveo, -ere, cavi, cau-
      tus,** *beware of, guard against, avoid.* **caveto:** fut. imperative.

592   **nimium,** *too much, too.* **facilis, -e**, *easy, ready, quick.* **fe-
      rus, -a, -um**, *wild, savage, fierce.* **bellum, -i**, n., *war,
      battle, fight.* **manus:** accusative plural.

593   **occido, -ere, -cidi, -casus**, *fall down, perish, die.* **Euryti-
      on, -onis,** m.: a centaur who became drunk at a wedding and
      tried to make off with the bride, Hippodamia. The bridegroom, Pi-
      rithous, and his friends resented this and there was quite a
      fight, with results disastrous to Eurytion. **stulte,** *foolishly.*
      Could modify either **data** or **bibendo. vina:** 591.

594   **dulcis, -e**, *sweet, delightful, pleasant.* **mensa, -ae**, f., *ta-
      ble, dining.* **merum, -i**, n., *(unmixed) wine.* **iocus, -i**, m.,
      jest(ing), joke, joking, mirth. --In these last lines, a pretty
      good temperance lesson.

595   In both **si** clauses, **tibi** should be understood, as well as
      sunt in the second one. **canto, -are, -avi, -atus**, *sing.*
      bracchium, -ii, n., *arm.* **salto, -are, -avi, -atus**, *dance.*

596   **dos, dotis**, f., *dowry, gift, talent.*

At cum discedet mensa conviva remota,
  ipsa tibi accessus turba locumque dabit.
Insere te turbae, leviterque admotus eunti   605
  velle latus digitis et pede tange pedem.
Colloquii iam tempus adest; fuge rustice longe
  hinc Pudor! audentem Forsque Venusque iuvat.
Non tua sub nostras veniat facundia leges;
  fac·tantum cupias: sponte disertus eris.   610
Est tibi agendus amans imiᵗ ndaque vulnera verbis;
  haec tibi quaeratur qual⸗pet arte fides.

---

603 **discedo, -ere, -cessi, -cessus,** *separate, depart, go away,*
    leave. **mensa:** 594. **conviva, -ae,** m., f., *table companion,*
guest. Here may refer in a collective sense to all the guests
rather than to the one girl in question. **removeo, -ere, -movi,**
-motus, *move back, take away, remove.*

604 **accessus, -us,** m., *approach, access, chance to approach.*
    turba, -ae, f., *crowd, throng.*

605 **insero, -ere, -serui, -sertus,** *insert, mix with.* **insere te**
    (with dat.): 'mingle with.' **turbae:** 604. **leviter,** *lightly,*
easily, gently. **admoveo, -ere, -movi, -motus,** *move towards.* **ad-**
motus eunti: 'drawing near to her as she goes.'

606 **vello, -ere, vulsi, vulsus,** *pluck, tweak, pinch.* **latus,**
    -eris, n., *side.* **tango, -ere, tetigi, tactus,** *touch.*

607 **colloquium, -ii,** n., *conversation.* **rusticus, -a, -um,** *rus-*
    tic, provincial, prudish. This is Ovid's favorite word for
describing anyone or anything too strait-laced to suit his tastes.
'Mid-Victorian' sometimes conveys the same idea. **longe,** *far, far*
off, far away.

608 **hinc,** *from this place, from here, hence.* **pudor, -oris,** m.,
    shame, shyness, modesty. Here personified and in the vocative
case. **audens, -entis,** *daring, bold, brave.* **fors, fortis,** f.,
chance, luck, fortune. Also personified as the goddess of chance.

609 These next two lines mean that Ovid can give you no specific
    rules as to what you should say in such a situation; if you
are sufficiently interested (or can just get started), words
should come of themselves. **facundia, -ae,** f., *eloquence, fluency.*
lex, legis, f., *law, precept, rule.*

610 **tantum** (adv.), *only.* **cupio, -ere, -ivi (-ii), -itus,** *desire,*
    wish, be eager. Some editors here substitute **incipias,** 'that
you make a beginning,' which they think makes better sense. It
certainly makes good sense. Whether it is what Ovid wrote in the
first place is another question. **sponte,** *of one's own accord,*
spontaneously. **disertus, -a, -um,** *fluent, eloquent.*

611 **Est tibi agendus amans:** 'you must act the part of a lover.'
    imitor, -ari, -atus, *imitate, feign, pretend.* Here supply
sunt. **vulnera** = 'wounds of love.' --At the start, at least, Ovid
visualizes a mere flirtation rather than a serious case of love.

612 **quilibet, quaelibet, quodlibet,** *any . . . at all, any . . . .*
    whatsoever. **fides, -ei,** f., *trust, faith, belief.* --Ovid

Nec credi labor est: sibi quaeque videtur amanda;
  pessima sit, nulli non sua forma placet.
615 Saepe tamen vere coepit simulator amare,
  saepe, quod incipiens finxerat esse, fuit.
Quo magis o, faciles imitantibus este, puellae:
  fiet amor verus, qui modo falsus erat.
Blanditiis animum furtim deprendere nunc sit,
620   ut pendens liquida ripa subitur aqua:
nec faciem nec te pigeat laudare capillos
  et teretes digitos exiguumque pedem.

---

means you must put on a convincing performance.

613 **labor, -oris,** m., *work, trouble; a hard thing.* **amanda:** 'to
be loved' = 'worthy of love' or 'lovable.'

614 **pessimus, -a, -um** (superlative of **malus**), *very bad, very ugly.*
sit: concessive subjunctive ('though . . . .'). **nulli non
sua forma placet:** lit., 'to no (woman) is her own appearance not
pleasing.' This should be rephrased in more idiomatic English.

615 **vere,** *truly, really, in fact.* **coepi, coepisse, coeptus**
(perf. tenses only), *have begun, began.* **simulator, -oris,**
m., *feigner, pretender.*

616 **incipio, -ere, -cepi, -ceptus,** *begin.* **fingo, -ere, finxi,
fictus,** *form, imagine, feign, pretend.* --The sense of the
line: 'often he has become what in the beginning he had (only)
pretended to be.'

617 **quo,** *wherefore, for which (this) reason.* **magis** (adv.), *more,
rather.* **o,** *O! oh!* Goes with **puellae** here, but very effective
in this particular position. **facilis, -e,** *easy, pleasant, not
harsh, kind.* **imitor, -ari, -atus,** *imitate, pretend.* The partici-
ple is used here as a substantive: 'to those who . . . .' **este:**
imperative of **sum.** --The implication may be that women are not
fooled by men; they just pretend to be fooled.

618 **verus, -a, -um,** *true, real, genuine.* **falsus, -a, -um,**
feigned, pretended, false.

619 **blanditia, -ae,** f., *flattery; (plur.) flatteries, smooth
words.* **furtim,** *stealthily, secretly.* **deprendo, -ere, -di,
-sus,** *take away, seize, capture, take possession of.* **sit:** in Eng-
lish some predicate must be supplied, such as 'your purpose' or
'the time.'

620 **pendeo, -ere, pependi,** *hang.* **liquidus, -a, -um,** *flowing,
liquid, clear, bright, limpid.* **ripa, -ae,** f., *bank.* **subeo,
-ire, -ii, -itus,** *go under, undermine, approach.*

621 **piget, -ēre, piguit (pigitum est),** *it irks, annoys, dis-
pleases, disgusts.* It is an impersonal verb which in English
is best turned around and translated with the personal object as
the subject; so that **te pigeat** ('let it displease you') = 'be dis-
pleased,' or with a negative, 'be sure to.' **laudo, -are, -avi,
-atus,** *praise.*

622 **teres, -etis** (adj.), *round, smooth, slender.* **exiguus, -a,
-um,** *small, little, tiny.*

Delectant etiam castas praeconia formae;
  virginibus curae grataque forma sua est.
Nam cur in Phrygiis Iunonem et Pallada silvis   625
  nunc quoque iudicium non tenuisse pudet?
Laudatas ostendit avis Iunonia pinnas:
  si tacitus spectes, illa recondit opes;
quadrupedes inter rapidi certamina cursus
  depexaeque iubae plausaque colla iuvant.   630

Since girls are mostly a deceptive race, it is fair and proper
to practice a little deception in dealing with them (631-658).
Tears may be useful.

---

623 **delecto, -are, -avi, -atus,** *delight, please.* **castus, -a,**
     -um, *pure, chaste, virtuous, modest.* Used here as a feminine
substantive. **praeconium, -ii,** n., *a proclaiming, laudation, com-*
mendation, praise.

624 **virgo, -inis,** f., *maiden, young woman, girl.* **curae:** 'for a
     care,' i.e., 'a concern,' 'a source of interest,' or the
like. **gratus, -a, -um,** *pleasing.*

625 **nam** (conj.), *for.* **cur,** *why.* **Phrygius, -a, -um,** *Phrygian,*
     Trojan. **Iuno, -onis,** f., *Juno,* queen of the gods, wife of
Jupiter. **Pallas, -adis** or **-ados** (acc. **-ada**), f., *Pallas,* sur-
name of *Minerva (Athene),* goddess of wisdom, etc. As both she and
(to a lesser degree) Juno were of a very strict moral character,
Ovid is trying to show that even such women are inclined to be
vain about their looks. **silva, -ae,** f., *wood, forest.*

626 **iudicium, -ii,** n., *judgment, decision.* **tenuisse** here = 'to
     have won.' **pudet, -ere, -uit** or **puditum est,** *it makes*
ashamed, one is ashamed. Like **piget** (621), this is an impersonal
verb whose object should be translated as the subject, replacing
the word *one* in the meaning given above.

627 **laudo, -are, -avi, -atus,** *praise.* **ostendo, -ere, -di, -sus**
     and **-tus,** *spread out, show, exhibit, display.* **avis, -is,** f.,
bird. **Iunonius, -a, -um,** *of* or *belonging to Juno* (whose bird was
the peacock). --Unfortunately some peacocks, not having read
Ovid, do not react in the prescribed manner.

628 **tacitus, -a, -um,** *silent, in silence.* **recondo, -ere, -didi,**
     -ditus, *shut up, hide, conceal.*

629 **quadrupes, -pedis,** m., f., n., *quadruped, horse.* **inter** (with
     acc.), *between, among, amid.* **rapidus, -a, -um,** *swift, rapid.*
certamen, -inis, n., *contest, struggle.* **cursus, -us,** m., *running,*
race. Here genitive case.

630 **depecto, -ere, --, -xus,** *comb.* **iuba, -ae,** f., *mane.* **plaudo,**
     -ere, -si, -sus, *clap, pat.* **collum, -i,** n., *neck.* --A typ-
ical Latin usage appears in this line. The logical subjects are
implied in the two participles, which should be translated by Eng-
lish gerunds; the two nouns, the grammatical subjects, should then
be translated as though in the genitive case. The famous example
of this construction is **ab urbe condita,** which means literally

Et lacrimae prosunt: lacrimis adamanta movebis!
660 Fac madidas videat, si potes, illa genas.
Si lacrimae (neque enim veniunt in tempore semper)
  deficient, uda lumina tange manu.
Quis sapiens blandis non misceat oscula verbis?
Illa licet non det, non data sume tamen!
665 Pugnabit primo fortassis et 'improbe!' dicet:
  pugnando vinci se tamen illa volet.
Tantum ne noceant teneris male rapta labellis,
  neve queri possit dura fuisse, cave.

Most women like to be swept off their feet. Some, however, are just the opposite and are attracted by that which seems to avoid them (669-722). Paleness and thinness are appropriate to a lover, so that everyone may see that he is in love.

723 Candidus in nauta turpis color: aequoris unda
  debet et a radiis sideris esse niger;

'from the city having been founded,' i.e., 'from the founding of the city.'

659 **prosum, prodesse, profui,** *be useful, be of use, help.* **adamas, -antis** (acc. **-anta**), m., *adamant, the hardest iron.*

660 **madidus, -a, -um,** *moist, wet.* **gena, -ae,** f., *cheek.*

661 **neque enim,** *for . . . not.*

662 **deficio, -ere, -feci, -fectus,** *fail, be lacking.* **udus, -a, -um,** *wet, moist, damp.* Here abl. **lumen, -inis,** n., *light, eye.* **tango, -ere, tetigi, tactus,** *touch.*

663 **sapiens, -entis,** *wise, knowing, sensible.* **blandus, -a, -um,** *smooth, flattering, caressing, coaxing.* **misceo, -ere, miscui, mixtus,** *mix, mingle.* **osculum, -i,** n., *little mouth, kiss.*

664 **data** modifies **oscula** understood. **sumo, -ere, sumpsi, sumptus,** *take.*

665 **pugno, -are, -avi, -atus,** *fight, resist.* **primo** (adv.), *at first.* **fortassis,** *perhaps, probably, possibly.* **improbus, -a, -um,** *bad, wicked, shameless, impudent.* **improbe** corresponds remarkably to our expression, now burlesqued, 'You naughty man!'

666 **pugnando:** 665.

667 **tantum** (adv.), *only.* **noceo, -ere, -cui, -citus** (with dat.), *harm, injure, hurt.* **rapta** modifies **oscula,** understood as the subject of **noceant.** **labellum, -i,** n., *(little) lip.*

668 **neve,** *and (that) not, and lest.* **queror, queri, questus,** *complain.* **dura:** pred. acc. agreeing with **oscula,** understood as subject of **fuisse.** **caveo, -ere, cavi, cautus,** *take care, beware.* The two preceding **ne** clauses depend on **cave.**

723 **candidus, -a, -um,** *white, clear, bright.* **nauta, -ae,** m., *sailor.* **aequor, -oris,** n., *level surface, sea.*

724 **debeo, -ere, -ui, -itus,** *owe, ought, must, should.* **radius, -ii,** m., *rod, ray, beam.* **sidus, -eris,** n., *constellation,*

turpis et agricolae, qui vomere semper adunco   725
    et gravibus rastris sub Iove versat humum;
et tua, Palladiae petitur cui palma coronae,
    candida si fuerint corpora, turpis eris.
Palleat omnis amans! Hic est color aptus amanti;
    hoc decet; hoc stulti non valuisse putent.   730

*   *   *   *   *   *   *

Arguat et macies animum, nec turpe putaris
    palliolum nitidis imposuisse comis.
Attenuant iuvenum vigilatae corpora noctes   735
    curaque et, in magno qui fit amore, dolor.
Ut voto potiare tuo, miserabilis esto,
    ut qui te videat, dicere possit 'amas!'

---

star, sun, sky. **niger, -gra, -grum**, *black, dark, tan.*

725 Both subject (from 723) and verb must be supplied in this
    first clause. **agricola, -ae**, m., *farmer.* **vomer, -eris**, m.,
plowshare. **aduncus, -a, -um**, *bent, hooked, curved.*

726 **gravis, -e**, *heavy.* **rastri, -orum**, m., *toothed hoe, rake,
    mattock.* **Iuppiter, Iovis**, m., *Jupiter, heaven, sky.* **verso,
-are, -avi, -atus**, *turn (up).* **humus, -i**, f., *earth, ground, soil.*

727 **tua** modifies **corpora**. By its advanced position it affords a
    quasi antecedent for **cui**, which refers to the person directly
addressed here: 'you by whom.' **Palladius, -a, -um**, *of Pallas
(Athene, Minerva).* **palma, -ae**, f., *palm, prize.* **corona, -ae**,
f., *garland, wreath, crown.* --This crown of Pallas (to whom the
olive tree was sacred) was the olive wreath, given as a prize in
athletic contests.

728 **candida:** 723. **corpora:** plural for singular.

729 **palleo, -ere, -ui**, *be pale, look pale.* **amans, -antis**, m.,
lover.

730 **stultus, -i**, m., *fool, the foolish.* **valeo, -ere, -ui, -itus**,
be strong, be healthy, have influence, be effective, avail.

733 **arguo, -ere, -ui, -utus**, *make clear, make known, show, ac-
    cuse.* **macies, -ei**, f., *leanness, thinness.* **puta(ve)ris:**
with **nec**, a prohibitive subjunctive: 'do not think (it).'

734 **palliolum, -i**, n., *hood.* **nitidus, -a, -um**, *shining, bright,
    neat, trim.* **impono, -ere, -posui, -positus**, *place on, put
on.* --The present-day equivalent might be to pull the hat down
over the eyes.

735 **attenuo, -are, -avi, -atus**, *make thin, thin, weaken.* **vigilo,
-are, -avi, -atus**, *watch, be awake, spend in wakefulness,
pass without sleeping.*

736 **dolor, -oris**, m., *pain, ache, anguish.*

737 **votum, -i**, n., *vow, wish, desire.* **potior, -iri, potitus**
    (with abl.), *become master of, get, obtain.* **miserabilis, -e**,
pitiable, miserable, wretched, sad. **esto:** fut. imperative of **sum.**

738 **qui:** 'he who,' 'whoever.' **amas:** 'you are in love!'

Beware of your closest friend. He may steal your sweetheart
(739-754). There are all sorts of girls, and each must be ap-
proached in a different way.

755   Finiturus eram; sed sunt diversa puellis
           pectora: mille animos excipe mille modis.
        Nec tellus eadem parit omnia: vitibus illa
           convenit, haec oleis; hic bene farra virent.
        Pectoribus mores tot sunt, quot in orbe figurae;
760   qui sapit, innumeris moribus aptus erit
        utque leves Proteus modo se tenuabit in undas,
           nunc leo, nunc arbor, nunc erit hirtus aper.
        Hic iaculo pisces, illic capiuntur ab hamis;
           hic cava contento retia fune trahunt.

---

755   **finio, -ire, -ivi (-ii), -itus,** *finish, come to an end,
      cease.* **diversus, -a, -um,** *different, dissimilar, various.*

756   **mille** (indecl. adj.), *a thousand.* **excipio, -ere, -cepi,
      -ceptus,** *take (out), capture, catch.*

757   **tellus, -uris,** f., *earth, land, ground, region.* **idem, eadem,
      idem,** *same.* **pario, -ere, peperi, paritus** and **partus,** *bring
      forth, bear, produce.* **vitis, -is,** f., *(grape)vine.* **illa: tellus**
      is understood.

758   **convenio, -ire, -veni, -ventus,** *come together, be suitable
      to, be adapted to.* **olea, -ae,** f., *olive (tree).* **far, far-
      ris,** n., *spelt, wheat.* **vireo, -ere, -ui,** *flourish, thrive.*

759   **tot,** *so many, (just) as many.* **orbis, -is,** m., *circle, earth,
      world.* **figura, -ae,** f., *form, shape, figure.*

760   **qui:** cf. 738. **sapio, -ere, -ivi (-ii),** *have sense, be wise.*
      innumerus, -a, -um, *countless, innumerable.*

761   **ut** (going with Proteus only) = 'like.' **Proteus, -ei (-eos),**
      m.: a god of the sea who was accustomed to turn himself into
      a variety of shapes. Here he is cited as a model for the lover,
      who must be ready to assume a variety of natures. **tenuo, -are,
      -avi, -atus,** *make thin, dilute, reduce, dissolve.*

762   **leo, -onis,** m., *lion.* **arbor, -oris,** f., *tree.* **hirtus, -a,
      -um,** *rough, hairy, shaggy.* **aper, apri,** m., *wild boar.*

763   The following lines declare that women, like fish, must be
      caught in different ways. **iaculum, -i,** n., *dart, javelin,*
      gig. **piscis, -is,** m., *fish.* **illic,** *in that place, there.* **hamus,
      -i,** m., *hook.*

764   **cavus, -a, -um,** *hollow, concave.* A picturesque adjective for
      describing nets weighed down with fish. **contentus, -a, -um**
      (from **contendo**), *stretched, strained, tense, tight.* **rete, -is,**
      n., *net.* **funis, -is,** m., *rope.* **traho, -ere, -xi, -ctus,** *drag,
      draw, draw in, draw up.* The subject of **trahunt** is **retia,** the ob-
      ject is 'them' (fish) understood.

Nec tibi conveniet cunctos modus unus ad annos: 765
   longius insidias cerva videbit anus;
si doctus videare rudi petulansve pudenti,
   diffidet miserae protinus illa sibi.
Inde fit, ut quae se timuit committere honesto,
   vilis in amplexus inferioris eat.   770

Here ends a part of Ovid's undertaking.

Pars superat coepti, pars est exhausta laboris.
   Hic teneat nostras ancora iacta rates.

---

765 **convenio, -ire, -veni, -ventus,** *come together, suit, be suit-
      able, be appropriate.* **cunctus, -a, -um,** *all.*

766 **longius** (comp. adv.), *from farther off, from a greater dis-
      tance.* **insidiae, -arum,** f., *ambush, snare.* **cerva, -ae,** f.,
hind, female deer. **anus, -us,** f. (but used here as adj.), *old
(woman), aged, mature.* --Ovid uses **cerva** . . . **anus** here to des-
ignate the more mature type of woman who does not fall into either
love or marriage as easily as a young girl.

767 **doctus, -a, -um,** *learned, intellectual.* **videare = videaris.**
      rudis, -e, *unpolished, uncultivated, ignorant, simple.* With
both **rudi** and **pudenti, puellae** is understood. **petulans, -antis,**
forward, wanton, bold. **-ve,** *or.* **pudens, -entis,** *bashful, shy,
modest.*

768 **diffido, -ere, -fisus sum** (with dat.), *distrust, lack confi-
      dence in.* **protinus** (adv.), *immediately, on the spot.*

769 **inde,** *thence, from that, in consequence.* **quae:** 'she who.'
      committo, -ere, -misi, -missus, *unite, give, entrust, commit.*
honestus, -a, -um, *honorable, respectable.* Understand **viro** here.

770 **vilis, -e,** *cheap, common, worthless, base, vile.* **amplexus,
      -us,** m., *embrace.* **inferior, -ius,** *inferior.* Used as noun
here.

771 **supero, -are, -avi, -atus,** *surpass, remain.* **coeptum, -i,** n.,
      work begun, undertaking. **exhaurio, -ire, -hausi, -haustus,**
empty, bring to an end, finish. **labor, -oris,** m., *labor, work.*

772 **ancora, -ae,** f., *anchor.* **iaceo, -ere, ieci, iactus,** *throw
      (out), cast.* **ratis, -is,** f., *raft, bark, boat, vessel.* Here
plur. for sing. Ovid speaks metaphorically of his poem as a ship.

Liber Secundus

Having recovered his breath, Ovid resumes his poetical treatise
with shouts of triumph. The girl has been won, he assumes. But
that is only the beginning. It requires even more skill to keep
her won, and for that Ovid's art is still needed.

Dicite 'Io Paean!' et 'Io' bis dicite 'Paean!'

Decidit in casses praeda petita meos;

laetus amans donat viridi mea carmina palma

praelata Ascraeo Maeonioque seni.

5   Talis ab armiferis Priameius hospes Amyclis

candida cum rapta coniuge vela dedit;

talis erat qui te curru victore ferebat,

vecta peregrinis Hippodamia rotis.

---

1   **io Paean:** a shout of triumphant joy: 'Hurrah! Victory!' **bis,**
twice.

2   **decido, -ere, decidi,** *fall (down).* **casses, -ium,** m., *(hunt-
ing) net, snare.* **praeda, -ae,** f., *booty, prey.*

3   **laetus, -a, -um,** *joyful, rejoicing, delighted.* **amans, aman-
tis,** m., *lover.* **dono, -are, -avi, -atus,** *give, present
(with).* Here the thing presented is in the abl., that to which it
is presented in the acc. **viridis, -e,** *green, fresh.* **carmen,
-inis,** n., *song, poem, verse.* **palma, -ae,** f., *palm, palm branch*
or *wreath, token of victory, prize.*

4   **praefero, -ferre, -tuli, -latus,** *place before, prefer.* **As-
craeus, -a, -um,** *Ascraean.* Ascra was the village in Boeotia
where the famous Greek poet Hesiod was born. **Maeonius, -a, -um,**
Maeonian, Lydian (referring here to the region in Asia Minor with
which Homer was associated). **senex, senis,** m., *old man.*

5   **talis, -e,** *such; (with such a feeling, feeling the same way).*
armifer, -fera, -ferum, *armed, warlike.* **Priameius, -a, -um,**
belonging to Priam (king of Troy), *(son) of Priam.* **hospes, -itis,**
m., *host, visitor, guest, stranger.* The reference is to Paris,
visiting Menelaus, husband of Helen. **Amyclae, -arum,** f.: a town
in Laconia and home of Helen.

6   **candidus, -a, -um,** *white, bright, beautiful.* Here neut. acc.
coniunx, -iugis, f. (m.), *spouse, wife, bride.* **velum, -i,**
n., *cloth, sail.* **vela dedit** = 'set sail.'

7   **talis:** 5. **qui:** 'he who.' **currus, -us,** m., *chariot.* **victor,
-oris,** m., *victor;* (in apposition as adj.) *victorious, con-
quering.*

8   **veho, -ere, -xi, -ctus,** *bear, carry, convey.* **peregrinus, -a,**

Quid properas, iuvenis? Mediis tua pinus in undis
    navigat, et longe, quem peto, portus abest.   10
Non satis est venisse tibi me vate puellam:
    arte mea capta est, arte tenenda mea est.
Nec minor est virtus, quam quaerere, parta tueri:
    casus inest illic, hoc erit artis opus.
  Ovid beseeches the proper divinities to favor his work.
Nunc mihi, siquando, puer et Cytherea, favete,   15
    nunc Erato (nam tu nomen amoris habes).
Magna paro, quas possit Amor remanere per artes,
    dicere, tam vasto pervagus orbe puer.

-um, *strange, foreign*. **Hippodamia**, -ae, f.: daughter of
Oenomaus, king of Elis. She was won from her father in a chariot
race by Pelops, who was a foreigner from Phrygia. She is not the
same Hippodamia whose wedding is referred to in Book I, 593. The
word is in the vocative case here, explaining who the **te** is. **ro-
ta**, -ae, f., *wheel*.

9   **propero**, -are, -avi, -atus, *hasten, hurry*. **pinus**, -us (-i),
f., *pine, ship, vessel, bark*.

10   **navigo**, -are, -avi, -atus, *sail*. **longe**, *a long way off, far
(off), at a distance*. **portus**, -us, m., *harbor, port*. **absum,
abesse, afui**, *be away from, be absent, be distant, be lacking*.

11   **satis**, *enough, sufficient*. **vates**, -is, m., f., *soothsayer,
poet*. Here used with **me** in an ablative absolute.

12   Here Ovid states his third topic of discussion, how to keep
the girl.

13   **minor**, -us, *less, smaller*. **virtus**, -utis, f., *manliness,
courage, excellence, virtue, merit*. **quam quaerere** should be
translated at the end of the line. **parta**, -orum, n., *what has
been won, acquisitions*. **tueor**, -eri, **tuitus**, *look at, maintain,
guard, preserve, defend, protect, retain*.

14   **casus**, -us, m., *falling, occurrence, accident, chance, mis-
fortune*. **insum**, -esse, -fui, *be in*. **illic**, *in that (place),
there*. Here refers to **quaerere**. **hoc** refers to **tueri**.

15   **siquando**, *if ever*. **puer** = Amor or Cupid, the son of Venus.
Cytherea, -ae, f.: a name for *Venus* derived from the island
of Cythera, celebrated for her worship. **faveo**, -ere, **favi, fau-
tus** (with dat.), *be favorable, be well disposed, favor*.

16   **Erato**, f.: the Muse of love poetry. **nam** (conj.), *for*.

17   **magna** ('great things') is either object of **paro**, with **dicere**
in apposition and the indirect question **quas** . . . **per artes**
as object of **dicere**; or else **magna** is object of **dicere**, with the
clause **quas** . . . **per artes** in apposition with **magna**. **paro**, -are,
-avi, -atus, *prepare, intend, be about to*. **remaneo**, -ere, -mansi,
remain, continue, abide, endure.

18   **vastus**, -a, -um, *empty, vast, immense, huge*. **pervagus**, -a,
-um, *wandering all about*. **orbis**, -is, m., *circle, earth,
world*. **puer**: in apposition with **Amor**.

Et levis est et habet geminas, quibus avolet, alas;
20   difficile est illis imposuisse modum.

The picture of Cupid flitting about the world suggests to Ovid's
nimble mind the story of Daedalus' escape from Minos through the
use of wings. If Minos could not stop a winged man, he despairing-
ly concludes, what chance have I to stop a winged god?

Hospitis effugio praestruxerat omnia Minos:
audacem pinnis repperit ille viam.
Daedalus ut clausit conceptum crimine matris
semibovemque virum semivirumque bovem,
25   'Sit modus exilio,' dixit 'iustissime Minos:
accipiat cineres terra paterna meos.

---

19   **geminus, -a, -um,** *twin, two.* **avolo, -are, -avi, -atus,** *fly
away.* **ala, -ae,** f., *wing.*

20   **difficilis, -e,** *hard, difficult, troublesome.* **impono, -ere,
-posui, -positus,** *place on, put on, set on, impose.*

21   **hospes, -itis,** m., *host, visitor, guest, stranger.* The refer-
ence is to Daedalus, an Athenian architect who had fled to
Crete. There at Minos' request he built the labyrinth for the Min-
otaur, a creature half man, half bull. When he wanted to return
home, Minos would not let him go. **effugium, -ii,** n., *flight, es-
cape.* **praestruo, -ere, -xi, -ctus,** *build up in front, block, put
in the way of.* **Minos, -ois,** m.: either of two great legendary
kings of Crete (here the grandson). The first European civiliza-
tion, the Minoan, was named by archaeologists for these rulers.

22   **audax, -acis,** *daring, bold.* **reperio, -ire, repperi, reper-
tus,** *find, hit upon, discover, invent.*

23   **Daedalus, -i,** m.: see note on 21. **claudo, -ere, -si, -sus,**
close, enclose, imprison. **concipio, -ere, -cepi, -ceptus,**
receive, conceive. **mater, -tris,** f., *mother.* Refers here to Pa-
siphaë, mother of the Minotaur, whose father was a bull. She was
also the mother of Minos' daughter Ariadne, whom we have met
earlier.

24   Concerning this peculiarly fascinating line the elder Seneca
relates an amusing anecdote. Ovid granted a group of his
friends the right to delete from his works any three lines of
which they particularly disapproved. However, he reserved the
right to write down privately three lines which were to be exempt
from this excision. When his friends had made their choices, the
lines picked were found to be exactly the same ones Ovid had set
down. This line was one of the three. The teaching: Ovid knew his
own faults and liked them just the same. **semibos, -bovis,** m.
(adj.), *half-bull.* **semivir, -viri,** m. (adj.), *half-man.* **bos,
bovis,** m., *bull.*

25   **exilium, -ii,** n., *exile.* **iustus, -a, -um,** *just, righteous.*
Minos: 21.

26   **cinis, -eris,** m., *ashes.* **terra, -ae,** f., *land, earth.* **pa-
ternus, -a, -um,** *of a father, father's, father-, ancestral.*

Et quoniam in patria, fatis agitatus iniquis,
    vivere non potui, da mihi posse mori.
Da reditum puero, senis est si gratia vilis;
    si non vis 'puero parcere, parce seni.'   30
Dixerat haec, sed et haec et multo plura licebat
    dicere: regressus non dabat ille viro.
Quod simul ut sensit,'Nunc, nunc, o Daedale,' dixit
    'materiam, qua sis ingeniosus, habes.
Possidet et terras et possidet aequora Minos;   35
    nec tellus nostrae nec patet unda fugae.
Restat iter caeli; caelo temptabimus ire!
    Da veniam coepto, Iuppiter alte, meo.

---

27   **quoniam,** *since.* **patria, -ae,** f., *fatherland, native country.*
    fatum, -i, n., *fate, destiny.* **agito, -are, -avi, -atus,**
drive, pursue, torment. **iniquus, -a, -um,** *unjust, hostile.*

28   **vivo, -ere, vixi, victus,** *live.* **morior, mori, mortuus,** *die.*

29   **reditus, -us,** m., *return.* **puero** = Icarus, young son of Daed-
    alus. **senex, senis,** m., *old man.* Here objective genitive:
'for . . .' or 'to . . .' **gratia, -ae,** f., *favor, regard, esteem,*
gratitude. **vilis, -e,** *cheap, of little value, worthless.*

30   **vis:** 2nd pers. sing. of **volo.** **parco, -ere, peperci (parsi),**
    parsurus (with dat.), *spare.* **seni:** 29.

31   **multo** (adv.), *by much, much.* **licebat dicere:** 'it was per-
    mitted to say' = 'he might have said.'

32   **regressus, -us,** m., *return.* **ille** = Minos.

33   **quod:** obj. of **sensit.** At the beginning of a sentence and re-
    ferring to the preceding sentence, 'which' = '(and . . .)
this.' **simul ut,** *as soon as.* **sentio, -ire, sensi, sensus,** *feel,*
perceive, observe, think. **o,** *O, oh!* **Daedale:** 23, 21. Daedalus is
talking to himself.

34   **materia, -ae,** f., *matter, material, subject, occasion, oppor-*
    tunity. **ingeniosus, -a, -um,** *clever, ingenious.*

35   **possideo, -ere, -sedi, -sessus,** *be master of, own, possess.*
    terra, -ae, f., *land, earth.* **aequor, -oris,** n., *sea.* --Note
how the repetition of **possidet** gives this line a delightful lilt
similar to that in 'Old King Cole' when the merry monarch calls
for various things. **Minos:** 21.

36   **tellus, -uris,** f., *earth, land.* **pateo, -ere, -ui,** *lie open,*
    be open. **fuga, -ae,** f., *flight, escape.*

37   **resto, -are, -stiti,** *be left, remain.* **iter, itineris,** n.,
    journey, way, path, road. **caelum, -i,** n., *sky, heaven.*
tempto, -are, -avi, -atus, *handle, try, attempt.*

38   **venia, -ae,** f., *pardon, forgiveness.* **coeptum, -i,** n., *work*
    begun, undertaking. **Iuppiter, Iovis,** m.: *Jupiter,* god of the
heavens, chief of the gods. **altus, -a, -um,** *high, exalted, lofty,*
great.

Non ego sidereas adfecto tangere sedes:
40   qua fugiam dominum, nulla, nisi ista, via est.
Per Styga detur iter, Stygias transnabimus undas!
Sunt mihi naturae iura novanda meae.'
Ingenium mala saepe movent: quis crederet umquam
aërias hominem carpere posse vias?
45   Remigium volucrum, disponit in ordine pinnas
et leve per lini vincula nectit opus,
imaque pars ceris adstringitur igne solutis,
finitusque novae iam labor artis erat.

---

39   **sidereus, -a, -um,** *starry, heavenly.* **adfecto, -are, -avi,**
-atus, *strive, aim, aspire, desire.* **tango, -ere, tetigi,**
tactus, *touch, reach, come to.* **sedes, -is,** f., *seat, residence,*
abode, dwelling.

40   **qua:** the antecedent is **via. dominus, -i,** m., *master.* **iste,**
-a, -ud, *that of yours, that, this.*

41   **Styx, Stygis** or **Stygos** (acc., **Styga**), f.: the famed and dread
river of the underworld. **detur:** either understand **si** with
this or translate: 'should (a way) be granted.' **iter, itineris,**
n., *journey, way, path, road.* **Stygius, -a, -um,** *of the Styx,*
Stygian. **transno, -are, -avi, -atus,** *swim across, swim through.*

42   **natura, -ae,** f., *nature.* **ius, iuris,** n., *right, law.* **novo,**
-are, -avi, -atus, *make new, change, alter.* --Daedalus means
that hitherto he has been restricted by the laws of nature to lo-
comotion on the ground; now he must adapt himself to flying
through the air.

43   The first part of this line is one way of saying 'Necessity
is the mother of invention.' **ingenium, -ii,** n., *nature, tal-*
ents, abilities, genius, invention, inventive qualities, wits.
malum, -i, n., *an evil, misfortune, calamity.* **umquam,** *ever.*

44   **aërius, -a, -um,** *of the air, aerial, airy, through the air.*
homo, -inis, m., f., *human being, man.* **carpo, -ere, -psi,**
-ptus, *pluck, use, pass along, navigate, sail through.* --In a way
Ovid shows imaginative kinship with Tennyson ('Locksley Hall') in
thus visualizing human flight. It has been well said that the aim
of science is to overtake mythology.

45   **remigium, -ii,** n., *rowing, oars, oarage.* Here in apposition
with **pinnas. volucris, -is,** f., *bird.* **dispono, -ere,**
-posui, -positus, *set in order, arrange.* **ordo, -inis,** m., *order.*

46   **linum, -i,** n., *flax, thread.* **vinculum, -i,** n., *bond, cord,*
fetter, fastening. **necto, -ere, -xui (-xi), -xus,** *bind, tie,*
fasten (together), connect.

47   **imus, -a, -um,** *lowest.* **cera, -ae,** f., *wax.* **adstringo, -ere,**
-inxi, -ictus, *bind* or *fasten together.* **solvo, -ere, solvi,**
solutus, *loosen, dissolve, melt.*

48   **finio, -ire, -ivi (-ii), -itus,** *finish.* **labor, -oris,** m.,
labor, work.

Tractabat ceramque puer pinnasque renidens,
    nescius haec umeris arma parata suis.   50
Cui pater 'His' inquit 'patria est adeunda carinis,
    hac nobis Minos effugiendus ope.
Aëra non potuit Minos, alia omnia clausit;
    quem licet, inventis aëra rumpe meis!
Sed tibi non virgo Tegeaea comesque Bootae,   55
    ensiger Orion, adspiciendus erit:
me pinnis sectare datis. Ego praevius ibo,
    sit tua cura sequi; me duce tutus eris.

---

49   This line shows a good knowledge of boy nature. His father
        probably told him to leave those things alone. **tracto, -are,**
-avi, -atus, *touch, handle.* **ceram:** 47. **renideo, -ere,** *shine,*
beam for joy, smile, laugh, grin.

50   **nescius, -a, -um,** *ignorant, unaware, not knowing.* The rest of
        the line is indirect statement depending on **nescius. umerus,**
-i, m., *shoulder.* **paro, -are, -avi, -atus,** *prepare, furnish,*
intend, design.

51   **inquam,** *say.* **patria, -ae,** f., *fatherland, native land.* **ad-**
        eo, -ire, -ivi (-ii), -itus, *go to, approach, reach.* **carina,**
-ae, f., *keel, vessel, boat, ship.* With mild humor Daedalus calls
the wings he had made ships, since they will have to take the
place of a ship.

52   **Minos:** 21. **effugio, -ere, -fugi,** *flee from, escape, avoid.*

53   **aër, aëris** (Gr. acc. **aëra**), m., *air.* **potuit:** supply **clau-**
        dere from **clausit. Minos:** 21. **alius, -a, -ud,** *other.* **clau-**
do, **-ere, -si, -sus,** *close, shut off, cut off.*

54   **quem:** object of **rumpere** understood, with **aëra** (54) as ante-
        cedent. **inventum, -i,** n., *device, contrivance, invention.*
aera: 53. **rumpo, -ere, rupi, ruptus,** *break, split, cleave.*

55   In the following lines Daedalus tells his son to keep his
        eyes fastened on him in their aerial journey, and not to ap-
proach or stare with curiosity at the various constellations they
will be passing; to fly neither too high nor too low. **virgo,**
-inis, f., *maiden, girl.* **Tegeaeus, -a, -um,** *Tegean, Arcadian.*
--This 'Arcadian maiden' is Callisto, who for certain good reasons
was turned into a bear and eventually placed in the sky as the con-
stellation of the Great Bear (which contains the Big Dipper). A
young boy could hardly be blamed for wanting to view such a curi-
osity close at hand. **comes, -itis,** m., f., *companion, comrade.*
Bootes, -ae, m., the constellation *Bootes, the Herdsman.*

56   **ensiger, -gera, -gerum,** *sword-bearing.* **Orion, -onis,** m.: a
        striking winter constellation; three of its stars form a
sword. **adspicio, -ere, -spexi, -spectus,** *behold, look at, see.*

57   **sector, -ari, -atus,** *follow continually.* **sectare:** imperative.
        praevius, -a, -um, *going before, leading the way.*

58   **sequor, sequi, secutus,** *follow.* **dux, ducis,** m., f., *leader,*
        guide. **tutus, -a, -um,** *safe, secure.*

Nam sive aetherias vicino sole per auras
60   ibimus, impatiens cera caloris erit;
sive humiles propiore freto iactabimus alas,
        mobilis aequoreis pinna madescet aquis.
Inter utrumque vola. Ventos quoque, nate, timeto,
        quaque ferent aurae, vela secunda dato.'
65   Dum monet, aptat opus puero monstratque moveri,
        erudit infirmas ut sua mater aves.
Inde sibi factas umeris accommodat alas
        perque novum timide corpora librat iter;
iamque volaturus parvo dedit oscula nato,
70   nec patriae lacrimas continuere genae.

---

59   **nam** (conj.), *for.* **sive . . . sive,** *if . . . or if.* **aethe-**
      rius, -a, -um, *of heaven, heavenly.* **vicinus, -a, -um,** *near,*
neighboring, in the vicinity. **sol, solis,** m., *sun.*

60   **impatiens, -entis** (with gen.), *impatient, incapable of endur-*
      ing. **cera, -ae,** f., *wax.* **calor, -oris,** m., *heat.*

61   **sive:** 59. **humilis, -e,** *low.* **propior, -ius,** *nearer, closer.*
      fretum, -i, n., *strait, sea.* **iacto, -are, -avi, -atus,**
throw, toss, shake, beat, flap. **ala, -ae,** f., *wing.*

62   **mobilis, -e,** *movable, pliant, flexible, nimble, swift.* **ae-**
      quoreus, -a, -um, *of the sea.* **madesco, -ere, -dui,** *become*
wet.

63   **inter** (with acc.), *between.* **uterque, utraque, utrumque,**
      each, one and the other, both. **volo, -are, -avi, -atus,** *fly.*
natus, -i, m., *son.* **timeto:** future imperative.

64   **velum, -i,** n., *cloth, sail.* **secundus, -a, -um,** *following,*
      favorable. **vela secunda dato:** 'give following sails' =
'spread your sails before the wind.' The expression is figurative
here; the two aviators had no sails, only wings.

65   **moneo, -ere, -ui, -itus,** *warn, advise, give instructions.*
      apto, -are, -avi, -atus, *fit, put on, adjust.* **monstro, -are,**
-avi, -atus, *show (how), teach (how).* **moveri:** either 'it is
moved' or (used as a middle voice) 'to move,' 'to fly.'

66   **erudio, -ire, -ivi (-ii), -itus,** *instruct, teach.* **infirmus,**
      -a, -um, *weak, feeble.* **sua:** 'their.' **avis, -is,** f., *bird.*

67   **inde,** *from that (place), after that, thereupon, then.* **umer-**
      us, -i, m., *shoulder.* **accommodo, -are, -avi, -atus,** *fit, put*
on, adjust. **ala, -ae,** f., *wing.*

68   **timide,** *fearfully, timidly, cautiously.* **corpora:** plural for
      singular, or may refer to the two of them. **libro, -are,**
-avi, -atus, *balance, poise.* **iter, itineris,** n., *journey, road.*

69   **volo, -are, -avi, -atus,** *fly.* **parvus, -a, -um,** *little,*
      small. **osculum, -i,** n., *kiss.* **natus, -i,** m., *son.*

70   **patrius, -a, -um,** *father's, of the father.* **contineo, -ere,**
      -tinui, -tentus, *hold back, restrain, check.* **continuere** =
continuerunt. gena, -ae, f., *cheek, eye.*

Monte minor collis, campis erat altior aequis:
  hinc data sunt miserae corpora bina fugae.
Et movet ipse suas et nati respicit alas
  Daedalus, et cursus sustinet usque suos.
Iamque novum delectat iter, positoque timore   75
  Icarus audaci fortius arte volat.
Hos aliquis, tremula dum captat harundine pisces,
  vidit, et inceptum dextra reliquit opus.
Iam Samos a laeva (fuerant Naxosque relictae
  et Paros et Clario Delos amata deo),   80
dextra Lebynthos erat silvisque umbrosa Calymne
  cinctaque piscosis Astypalaea vadis,

---

71   **mons, montis,** m., *mountain.* **minor, -us,** *less, smaller.* **collis, -is,** m., *hill.* **campus, -i,** m., *plain, field.* **altus, -a, -um,** *high.* **aequus, -a, -um,** *even, level, flat, equal, fair.*

72   **hinc,** *from this place, from here.* **bini, -ae, -a,** *two at a time, two, pair (of).* **fuga, -ae,** f., *flight.*

73   **nati:** 69. **respicio, -ere, -spexi, -spectus,** *look back at, regard.* **ala, -ae,** f., *wing.* **alas** is object of both verbs in this line.

74   **Daedalus:** 21, 23. **cursus, -us,** m., *course, journey, progress.* Here plural for singular. **sustineo, -ere, -tinui, -tentus,** *keep up, sustain, maintain.* **usque,** *all the way, without interruption, continuously, constantly.*

75   **delecto, -are, -avi, -atus,** *delight, please.* **iter, itineris,** n., *journey, road.* **timor, -oris,** m., *fear, timidity.*

76   **Icarus, -i,** m.: son of Daedalus. **audax, -acis,** *daring, bold.* **fortiter,** *strongly, vigorously, boldly, bravely.* **volo, -are, -avi, -atus,** *fly.*

77   **tremulus, -a, -um,** *shaking, quivering, trembling.* **capto, -are, -avi, -atus,** *try to catch, entice.* **harundo, -inis,** f., *reed, rod, fishing pole.* **piscis, -is,** m., *fish.*

78   **incipio, -ere, -cepi, -ceptus,** *take in hand, begin, commence.* **dextra, -ae,** f., *right hand.* Here nominative. --These last two lines present a bird's-eye view of a pretty and amusing little scene, pithily described.

79   **Samos, Naxos, Paros, Delos, Lebynthos, Calymne, Astypalaea** (all nom. and fem.): islands in the Aegean Sea, which is dotted with hundreds of these romantic specks. **a laeva,** *on the left.*

80   **Clarius, -a, -um,** *Clarian.* The Clarian god is Apollo, so called from the small town Claros where he had a temple and oracle. He was partial to Delos, where he was born.

81   **dextra,** *on the right.* **silva, -ae,** f., *forest, wood.* **umbrosus, -a, -um,** *shady.*

82   **cingo, -ere, cinxi, cinctus,** *surround, gird.* **piscosus, -a, -um,** *abounding in fish, fish-filled.* **vadum, -i,** n., *shallow water, shallow, shoal, sea.*

cum puer, incautis nimium temerarius annis,
    altius egit iter deseruitque patrem.
85 Vincla labant et cera deo propiore liquescit,
    nec tenues ventos bracchia mota tenent!
Territus a summo despexit in aequora caelo;
    nox oculis pavido venit oborta metu.
Tabuerant cerae! Nudos quatit ille lacertos
90   et trepidat nec, quo sustineatur, habet.
Decidit atque cadens 'Pater, o pater, auferor!' inquit:
    clauserunt virides ora loquentis aquae.
At pater infelix, nec iam pater, 'Icare!' clamat,
    'Icare,' clamat 'ubi es quoque sub axe volas?'

---

83   **incautus, -a, -um,** *incautious, heedless.* **nimium** (adv.), *too much, too.* **temerarius, -a, -um,** *rash, reckless, imprudent.*

84   **altius,** *higher.* **iter, itineris,** n., *journey, path, road.* **desero, -ere, deserui, desertus,** *leave, abandon, desert.*

85   **vinclum, -i,** n., *bond, cord, fetter, fastening.* **labo, -are, -avi, -atus,** *totter, give way, be loosened.* **cera, -ae,** f., *wax.* **deo:** here refers to the sun god; 'the sun.' **propior, -ius,** *nearer, closer.* **liquesco, -ere, licui,** *become liquid, melt.*

86   **bracchium, -ii,** n., *forearm, arm.*

87   **terreo, -ere, -ui, -itus,** *frighten, alarm, terrify.* **despicio, -ere, -spexi, -spectus,** *look down.* **aequor, -oris,** n., *sea.* **caelum, -i,** n., *sky, heaven.*

88   **pavidus, -a, -um,** *trembling, quaking, terrified.* **oborior, -iri, -ortus** (with dat.), *arise, appear before, spring up in front of.* **metus, -us,** m., *fear, dread.*

89   **tabesco, -ere, tabui,** *melt.* **cerae:** 85. **nudus, -a, -um,** *naked, bare.* **quatio, -ere, --, quassus,** *shake, flap.* **lacertus, -i,** m., *upper arm, arm.* --This line, here so full of pathos, in a less serious situation would seem funny.

90   **trepido, -are, -avi, -atus,** *tremble, shudder.* **quo:** 'anything by which.' **sustineo, -ere, -tinui, -tentus,** *hold up, keep up, support, sustain.*

91   **decido, -ere, -cidi,** *fall (down), drop.* **cado, -ere, cecidi, casus,** *fall.* **o, O, oh!** **aufero, auferre, abstuli, ablatus,** *carry away, destroy, kill.* **inquam,** *say.*

92   **claudo, -ere, -si, -sus,** *close, shut.* **viridis, -e,** *green.* **loquentis:** it is necessary, as often, to supply some obvious noun or pronoun with which the participle may be in agreement. --The suddenness of this line very vividly mirrors the swiftness of Icarus' fall.

93   **infelix, -icis,** *unfortunate, unhappy.* **nec iam pater:** a little twist of the sort Ovid delighted in: 'now no longer a father.' **Icarus, -i,** m.: son of Daedalus.

94   **quo:** modifies **axe.** **axis, -is,** m., *axle, axis, pole, heavens, part of the sky.* **volo, -are, -avi, -atus,** *fly.*

'Icare!' clamabat: pinnas adspexit in undis!   95
     Ossa tegit tellus; aequora nomen habent.
Non potuit Minos hominis compescere pinnas:
     ipse deum volucrem detinuisse paro!

The use of magic will be of no help in matters of love (99-107).
Neither are good looks so important. A good education and the
ability to talk are more effective. Ulysses is an outstanding ex-
ample of that.

     *   *   *   Ut ameris, amabilis esto,
     quod tibi non facies solave forma dabit.
Sit licet antiquo Nireus adamatus Homero,
     Naiadumque tener crimine raptus Hylas,   110
ut dominam teneas nec te mirere relictum,
     ingenii dotes corporis adde bonis.
Forma bonum fragile est,quantumque accedit ad annos,

---

95   adspicio, -ere, -spexi, -spectus, *behold, look at, see.*
      --Another line effective because of its suddenness.

96   os, ossis, n., *bone.* tego, -ere, -xi, -ctus, *cover, hide,*
      conceal. tellus, -uris, f., *earth.* aequor, -oris, n., *sea.*
--According to mythology, the Icarian sea (part of the Aegean)
received its name from this fall of Icarus. Observe how quickly
Ovid closes his story after his climax. This is one of the marks
of a good story-teller.

97   Minos, -ois, m.: king of Crete. homo, -inis, m., f., *human
      being, man.* compesco, -ere, -pescui, *check, curb, restrain.*

98   volucer, -ucris, -ucre, *flying, winged.* detineo, -ere,
      -tinui, -tentus, *keep back, detain, delay.* paro, -are, -avi,
-atus, *prepare, intend, be about (to), undertake.*

107   amabilis, -e, *worthy of love, lovable.* esto: fut. imperative
      of sum.

108   quod: 'a thing which' or 'and this.'   -ve, *or.*

109   antiquus, -a, -um, *old, ancient.* Nireus, -ei & -eos, m.:
      next to Achilles, the most handsome of the Greeks before
Troy, and so praised by Homer in the *Iliad.* adamo, -are, -avi,
-atus, *love deeply.* Homerus, -i, m., *Homer,* author of the *Iliad.*

110   Naias, -adis, f., *Naiad, water nymph.* Hylas, -ae, m.: a
      handsome youth who, while getting water, was drawn into the
spring by amorous water nymphs. --Nireus and Hylas, Ovid implies,
were loved for their beauty alone. It is safer, he goes on, to
equip oneself with more enduring qualities.

111   miror, -ari, -atus, *wonder, be astonished, be surprised, ad-
      mire.* mirere = mireris. relictum: supply esse.

112   ingenium, -ii, n., *native ability, genius, mind, intellect.*
      dos, dotis, f., *dowry, gift, talent.* addo, -ere, -didi,
-ditus, *add.* bonum, -i, n., *good thing, advantage, blessing.*

113   bonum: 112. fragilis, -e, *fragile, perishable, frail.* quan-
      tus, -a, -um, *how much, as much as.* accedo, -ere, -cessi,

fit minor et spatio carpitur ipsa suo.
115 Nec violae semper nec hiantia lilia florent,
et riget amissa spina relicta rosa;
et tibi iam venient cani, formose, capilli,
iam venient rugae, quae tibi corpus arent.
Iam molire animum, qui duret, et adstrue formae:
120 solus ad extremos permanet ille rogos.
Nec levis ingenuas pectus coluisse per artes
cura sit et linguas edidicisse duas;
non formosus erat, sed erat facundus, Ulixes
et tamen aequoreas torsit amore deas.

-cessus, *approach, be added.* **quantum accedit ad annos:** literally, 'as much as it approaches to the years' or 'as much as is added to the years,' i.e., 'the longer it exists' or 'the longer the years roll by.'

114 **minor, -us,** *less, smaller.* **spatium, -ii,** n., *space, space of time, length of existence.* **carpo, -ere, -psi, -ptus,** *pick, pluck, wear away, consume, devour, destroy.*

115 **viola, -ae,** f., *violet.* **hio, -are, -avi, -atus,** *open, gape.* **lilium, -ii,** n., *lily.* **floreo, -ere, -ui,** *bloom, blossom.*

116 **rigeo, -ere,** *be stiff, stand stiff.* **amitto, -ere, amisi, amissus,** *send away, let fall, drop, lose.* **spina, -ae,** f., *thorn.* **rosa, -ae,** f., *rose.* --**amissa** and **rosa** are ablative, **spina** and **relicta** are nominative. The whole line might be translated: 'and when the rose is lost, the stiff thorn is left behind.'

117 **canus, -a, -um,** *white, gray.*

118 **ruga, -ae,** f., *wrinkle.* **aro, -are, -avi, -atus,** *plow, make furrows over, wrinkle.*

119 **molior, -iri, -itus,** *endeavor, undertake, form, acquire.* **molire:** imperative. **animum:** object of both **molire** and **adstrue.** **duro, -are, -avi, -atus,** *harden, continue in existence, last, remain.* **adstruo, -ere, -struxi, -structus,** *add . . . to.*

120 **extremus, -a, -um,** *utmost, last, final, ultimate.* **permaneo, -ere, -mansi, -mansus,** *last, continue, endure, remain.* **ille** refers to **animum** (119). **rogus, -i,** m., *funeral pile, pyre.*

121 **levis** modifies **cura.** **ingenuus, -a, -um,** *worthy of a freeman, noble, liberal.* Here we see the ancestor of our expression, 'liberal arts.'

122 **lingua, -ae,** f., *tongue, language.* **edisco, -ere, edidici,** *learn (thoroughly), study.* **duo, -ae, -o,** *two.* --The two languages are Latin and Greek.

123 **facundus, -a, -um,** *eloquent.* **Ulixes, -is,** m., *Ulysses, Odysseus,* the crafty hero of Homer's *Odyssey.*

124 **aequoreus, -a, -um,** *of the sea.* **torqueo, -ere, torsi, tortus,** *twist, torment, torture.* **dea, -ae,** f., *goddess.* --Besides Calypso, there was the enchanting Circe, who turned men into pigs.

O quotiens illum doluit properare Calypso   125
   remigioque aptas esse negavit aquas!
Haec Troiae casus iterumque iterumque rogabat,
   ille referre aliter saepe solebat idem.
Litore constiterant: illic quoque pulchra Calypso
   exigit Odrysii fata cruenta ducis.   130
Ille levi virga (virgam nam forte tenebat)
   quod rogat, in spisso litore pingit opus.
'Haec' inquit 'Troia est' (muros in litore fecit);
   'hic tibi sit Simois; haec mea castra puta.

---

125   o, *O, oh!*   quotiens, *how often, how many times, as often as.*
     doleo, -ere, -ui, -itus, *grieve, lament, be sorry.*   propero,
-are, -avi, -atus, *hasten, be in a hurry.*   Calypso, -us, f.: a
nymph of the sea upon whose island Ogygia Ulysses, while on his
long way home from Troy, was cast. There he dallied pleasantly for
a time until, becoming homesick, he announced to the girl that he
must continue on his way. She was very distressed. According to
the way Ovid imagines it in the lines that follow, one of Ulysses'
great attractions was the entertaining and varied ways in which he
could describe his exploits, illustrating them on the sandy beach.

126   remigium, -ii, n., *rowing, oars.*   nego, -are, -avi, -atus,
say . . . not, deny, refuse.

127   haec = Calypso.   Troia, -ae, f., *Troy.*   casus, -us, m., *fall,
overthrow, destruction.* Here plur. for sing.   iterum, *again.*

128   aliter, *in another manner, differently, in different words.*
     idem, eadem, idem, *the same.* Here, 'the same thing,' 'the
same story.'

129   litus, -oris, n., *seashore, beach.*   consisto, -ere, -stiti,
     stand still, halt, stop, come to a halt.   illic, *in that
place, there.*   pulcher, pulchra, pulchrum, *beautiful, lovely.* Cal-
ypso: 125.

130   exigo, -ere, -egi, -actus, *drive out, demand, inquire into.*
     Odrysius, -a, -um, *Odrysian, Thracian.*   fatum, -i, n., *fate;*
(sing. & plur.) *death.*   cruentus, -a, -um, *bloody, cruel.*   dux,
ducis, m., f., *leader, ruler.* --The reference is to Rhesus, a
king of Thrace and an ally of the Trojans, who was killed by Dio-
medes and Ulysses while they were stealing his horses, the night
of his arrival at Troy. (It was said that Troy could not be taken
if once his horses had grazed on the Trojan plain.) Interestingly,
Ulysses here makes no mention of the part played by Diomedes.

131   virga, -ae, f., *branch, staff, stick.*   nam (conj.), *for.*
     forte, *by chance, accidentally.*

132   quod: the antecedent is opus.   spissus, -a, -um, *thick, com-
pact, dense, (deeply sanded).*   litore: 129.   pingo, -ere,
pinxi, pictus, *paint, draw, depict.*   opus: 'situation,' perhaps.

133   inquam, *say.*   Troia: 127.   murus, -i, m., *wall.*   litore: 129.

134   hic tibi sit might be translated 'imagine that this is.'   Si-
mois, -entis, m.: a small river near Troy.   castra, -orum,
n., *camp.*

48 P. OVIDI NASONIS

135 Campus erat' (campumque facit) 'quem caede Dolonis
sparsimus, Haemonios dum vigil optat equos.
Illic Sithonii fuerant tentoria Rhesi;
hac ego sum captis nocte revectus equis.'
Pluraque pingebat, subitus cum Pergama fluctus
140 abstulit et Rhesi cum duce castra suo.
Tum dea 'Quas' inquit 'fidas tibi credis ituro,
perdiderint undae nomina quanta, vides?'
Ergo age, fallaci timide confide figurae,
quisquis es, atque aliquid corpore pluris habe.

Avoid quarrels and fits of anger.

145 Dextera praecipue capit indulgentia mentes;

---

135 **campus, -i,** m., *plain, field.* **caedes, -is,** f., *slaughter, blood, gore.* **Dolo, -onis,** m., *Dolon* (a Trojan spy killed by Ulysses and Diomedes this same night while he was trying to capture the Thessalian horses of Achilles).

136 **spargo, -ere, -si, -sus,** *bestrew, sprinkle, wet, bespatter.* **Haemonius, -a, -um,** *Haemonian, Thessalian.* **vigil, -ilis,** *awake, watchful.* **opto, -are, -avi, -atus,** *wish for, desire.*

137 **illic,** *in that place, there.* **Sithonius, -a, -um,** *Sithonian, Thracian.* **tentorium, -ii,** n., *tent.* **Rhesus, -i,** m.: a king of Thrace, come to help the Trojans. (See note on line 130.)

138 **hac** (adv.), *in this place, this way, here.* **reveho, -ere, -xi, -ctus,** *carry back;* (pass.) *drive back, ride back.*

139 **pingo, -ere, pinxi, pictus,** *paint, draw.* **subitus, -a, -um,** *sudden, unexpected.* **Pergama, -orum,** n., *the citadel of Troy, Troy.* **fluctus, -us,** m., *wave.*

140 **aufero, auferre, abstuli, ablatus,** *take away, carry off, destroy.* **Rhesi:** 137. **dux, ducis,** m., f., *leader.* **castra, -orum,** n., *camp.*

141 For easier comprehension rearrange Calypso's words in this order: 'Vides quanta nomina undae, quas credis (esse) fidas tibi ituro, perdiderint?' **dea, -ae,** f., *goddess.* **inquam,** *say.* **fidus, -a, -um,** *faithful, trustworthy, safe.* **ituro:** future active participle of **eo.** Freely, 'as you prepare to leave.'

142 **perdo, -ere, -didi, -ditus,** *destroy.* **quantus, -a, -um,** *how great, as much as.*

143 Ovid's little story is ended. Only the moral remains to be hammered in. **ergo,** *therefore, then.* **fallax, -acis,** *deceitful, treacherous.* **timide,** *timidly, cautiously.* **confido, -ere, -fisus sum** (with dat.), *trust in, rely on, have confidence in.* **figura, -ae,** f., *form, figure, physical beauty, good looks.*

144 **pluris:** gen. of indef. value: 'of more value,' 'worth more.'

145 **dexter, -tera, -terum,** *right, skillful, clever, proper, fitting.* **praecipue,** *especially, particularly.* **indulgentia, -ae,** f., *gentleness, tenderness, indulgence.*

asperitas odium saevaque bella movet.
Odimus accipitrem, quia vivit semper in armis,
    et pavidum solitos in pecus ire lupos;
at caret insidiis hominum, quia mitis, hirundo,
    quasque colat turres, Chaonis ales habet.   150
Este procul, lites et amarae proelia linguae!
    Dulcibus est verbis mollis alendus amor.
Lite fugent nuptaeque viros nuptasque mariti,
    inque vicem credant res sibi semper agi.
Hoc decet uxores; dos est uxoria lites.   155
    Audiat optatos semper amica sonos.

          *   *   *   *   *   *   *

146 **asperitas, -atis,** f., *roughness, harshness, rudeness.* **odium,**
     -ii, n., *hatred, ill will, enmity, dislike.* **saevus, -a, -um,**
furious, fierce, savage. **bellum, -i,** n., *war, battle, fight.*

147 **odi, odisse,** *hate, dislike.* **accipiter, -tris,** m., *hawk.* **vi-**
     vo, -ere, vixi, victus, *live.*

148 **pavidus, -a, -um,** *trembling, timid, shy.* **pecus, pecoris,** n.,
     cattle, herd, flock. **lupus, -i,** m., *wolf.*

149 **careo, -ere, -ui, -itus** (with abl.), *be without, be free*
     from. **insidiae, -arum,** f., *ambush, snare(s), trap(s),*
plot(s). **homo, -inis,** m., f., *human being, man.* **mitis, -e,** *mild,*
soft, gentle, kind. **hirundo, -inis,** f., *swallow.*

150 **turris, -is,** f., *tower, dovecot.* Read **turres** as object of **ha-**
     bet and antecedent of **quas. Chaonis, -idis,** f. adj., *Chaoni-*
an, of Epirus. **ales, alitis,** m., f., *bird.* --The 'Chaonian bird'
is the dove, so called from a region in Epirus (northwest Greece)
whose forests contained famous doves having the gift of prophecy.

151 **procul,** *at a distance, far off, far away.* **lis, litis,** f.,
     strife, dispute, quarrel. **amarus, -a, -um,** *bitter, biting,*
sarcastic. **proelium, -ii,** n., *battle.* **lingua, -ae,** f., *tongue.*

152 **dulcis, -e,** *sweet, pleasant, soft.* **alo, -ere, alui, altus &**
     alitus, *feed, nourish, maintain, strengthen.*

153 **lite:** 151. **fugo, -are, -avi, -atus,** *cause to flee, put to*
     flight, drive away. **nupta, -ae,** f., *bride, wife.* **maritus,**
-i, m., *married man, husband.*

154 **in vicem,** *by turns, alternately, mutually.* **res, rei,** f.,
     thing, affair, matter. **res sibi agi:** legal phraseology:
'that their cases are on trial,' i.e., 'that things are at a
critical stage.'

155 **uxor, -oris,** f., *wife.* **dos, dotis,** f., *dowry, gift.* **uxo-**
     rius, -a, -um, *of or belonging to a wife.* **lites:** 151. --It
is apparent from these lines that marriages of the Maggie and
Jiggs or running skirmish type were just as common in Rome as in
America.

156 **audio, -ire, -ivi (-ii), -itus,** *hear.* **optatus, -a, -um,** *de-*
     sired, pleasing, pleasant. **sonus, -i,** m., *sound, word.*

Blanditias molles auremque iuvantia verba
160   adfer, ut adventu laeta sit illa tuo.
Non ego divitibus venio praeceptor amandi:
    nil opus est illi, qui dabit, arte mea;
secum habet ingenium,qui,cum libet,'Accipe' dicit.
Cedimus! Inventis plus placet ille meis.
165 Pauperibus vates ego sum, quia pauper amavi;
    cum dare non possem munera, verba dabam.
Pauper amet caute, timeat maledicere pauper
    multaque divitibus non patienda ferat.
Me memini iratum dominae turbasse capillos:
170   haec mihi quam multos abstulit ira dies!

---

159 **blanditia, -ae,** f., *flattery.* **auris, -is,** f., *ear.*

160 **adfero, adferre, attuli, adlatus,** *bring to, bring, bring along.* **adventus, -us,** m., *coming, approach, arrival.* **laetus, -a, -um,** *joyful, glad, happy, delighted.*

161 **dives, -itis,** *rich, wealthy.* Used here as substantive. **praeceptor, -oris,** m., *teacher, instructor.*

162 **nil,** *nothing, not at all, not.* **nil opus est illi** (with abl.): 'he has no need at all of.' **dabit** refers, of course, to the giving of gifts.

163 The meaning of this line is that the fellow who can hand out presents on every occasion has no need of any other talents or qualities of character or intellect. **secum** freely = 'of his own' or 'in his pocket.' **ingenium, -ii,** n., *nature, talents, abilities, cleverness, genius.* **libet, -ere, libuit & libitum est,** *it pleases, it is pleasing.*

164 **cedo, -ere, cessi, cessus,** *go, withdraw, yield, give up.* **inventum, -i,** n., *device, invention, discovery.*

165 **pauper, -eris,** m., f., *poor man, (the) poor.* **vates, -is,** m., f., *soothsayer, poet.*

166 **verba dabam:** This is a Latin pun. On the surface it means that he gave words, i.e., poetry, as his gifts. But **verba dare** is also an idiom which means 'to deceive.' Perhaps the best we can do is to translate cumbersomely 'I was accustomed to give poetry and deception,' or with some obscurity but more in Ovid's spirit 'I was accustomed to give verses and reverses.'

167 **pauper:** 165. **caute,** *cautiously, with caution.* **maledico, -ere, -xi, -ctus,** *abuse, revile, speak roughly.*

168 **dives, -itis,** *rich, wealthy.* **patior, pati, passus,** *suffer, bear, endure, undergo, allow.*

169 **memini, -isse,** *remember.* **iratus, -a, -um,** *enraged, angry.* **turbo, -are, -avi, -atus,** *disturb, disorder, disarrange, rumple, muss.* **turbasse** = turbavisse.

170 **mihi:** 'from me' is here more idiomatic than 'for me.' **aufero, auferre, abstuli, ablatus,** *carry away, take away.* **ira,**

Nec puto nec sensi tunicam laniasse, sed ipsa
  dixerat, et pretio est illa redempta meo.
At vos, si sapitis, vestri peccata magistri
  effugite et culpae damna timete meae.
Proelia cum Parthis, cum culta pax sit amica   175
  et iocus et causas quidquid amoris habet.

If your girl is not very sweet to you, persevere. Be patient and
agreeable. Do everything you can to put her in a good humor. Com-
ply with all her whims.

Si nec blanda satis nec erit tibi comis amanti,
  perfer et obdura: postmodo mitis erit.
Flectitur obsequio curvatus ab arbore ramus;
  frangis, si vires experiere tuas.   180

-ae, f., *anger, rage.* dies: i.e., days when he was permitted to
have dates with the girl. She probably told Ovid she never wanted
to see him again, undoubtedly with mental reservations.

171 sentio, -ire, -si, -sus, *feel, perceive, notice, think.* tu-
    nica, -ae, f., *tunic, (dress).* lanio, -are, -avi, -atus,
tear. --The present tense of puto shows that Ovid is still uncon-
vinced of his guilt. But the man always pays.

172 pretium, -ii, n., *money, price, cost, expense.* redimo, -ere,
    -emi, -emptus, *buy back, redeem, pay for.*

173 sapio, -ere, -ivi (-ii), *have sense, be prudent, be wise.*
    vester, -tra, -trum, *your.* peccatum, -i, n., *fault, error,*
mistake, sin. magister, -tri, m., *master, teacher, instructor.*

174 effugio, -ere, -fugi, *flee from, avoid, shun.* culpa, -ae,
    f., *fault, error, blame, offence, misbehavior.* damnum, -i,
n., *harm, damage, loss, penalty.*

175 proelium, -ii, n., *battle.* As its verb, supply sint from sit.
    Parthi, -orum, m., *the Parthians* (a warlike people of Asia,
Rome's most annoying enemy). cultus, -a, -um, *cultivated, cul-*
tured, refined, polished, elegant. pax, pacis, f., *peace.*

176 iocus, -i, m., *jest, joke, joking, mirth.*

177 blandus, -a, -um, *pleasant, agreeable, sweet.* satis, *enough,*
    sufficient(ly). comis, -e, *courteous, kind, friendly.* aman-
ti: either a participle modifying tibi or a substantive ('lover')
in apposition with tibi.

178 perfero, -ferre, -tuli, -latus, *bear through, endure (to the*
    end), put up with (it), submit. obduro, -are, -avi, -atus,
be hard, hold out, persist, endure. postmodo, *afterwards, soon,*
in a little while. mitis, -e, *mild, soft, gentle, kind.*

179 flecto, -ere, -xi, -xus, *bend.* obsequium, -ii, n., *compli-*
    ance, yielding, flexibility, (patience, gentle perseverance).
curvo, -are, -avi, -atus, *curve, bend.* arbor, -oris, f., *tree.*
ramus, -i, m., *branch, bough.*

180 frango, -ere, fregi, fractus, *break.* experior, -iri, exper-
    tus, *try.*

Obsequio tranantur aquae, nec vincere possis
    flumina, si contra, quam rapit unda, nates.
Obsequium tigresque domat Numidasque leones;
184   rustica paulatim taurus aratra subit.
        *   *   *   *   *   *   *

Cede repugnanti: cedendo victor abibis;
    fac modo, quas partes illa iubebit, agas.
Arguet: arguito; quidquid probat illa, probato;
200   quod dicet, dicas; quod negat illa, neges;
    riserit: adride; si flebit, flere memento.
Imponat leges vultibus illa tuis.
Seu ludet numerosque manu iactabit eburnos,

---

181 obsequio: 179. **trano, -are, -avi, -atus,** *swim across.*

182 flumen, -inis, n., *river.* **contra** (adv.), *against, opposite,
    in an opposite direction.* **quam,** *than* (after the comparison
implied in **contra**). **contra quam rapit unda:** 'against the force of
the current.' **nato, -are, -avi, -atus,** *swim.*

183 obsequium: 179. **tigris, -is,** m., f., *tiger.* **domo, -are,
    -avi, -atus,** *tame, subdue.* **Numidae, -arum** (adj.), *Numidian.*
Numidia was a section of northern Africa (now Algeria), noted for
its lions. **leo, -onis,** m., *lion.*

184 rusticus, -a, -um, *rural, rustic, provincial.* **paulatim,** *lit-
    tle by little, by degrees, gradually.* **taurus, -i,** m., *bull.*
aratrum, -i, n., *plow.* **subeo, -ire, -ii, -itus,** *go under, submit
to.*

197 cedo, -ere, cessi, cessus, *go, yield, submit.* **repugno, -are,
    -avi, -atus,** *fight back, resist.* With **repugnanti** understand
puellae or the like. **victor, -oris,** m., *victor;* (as adj.) *victo-
rious.* **abeo, -ire, -ivi (-ii), -itus,** *go away, depart, come off.*

199 arguo, -ere, -ui, -utus, *prove, blame, accuse, find fault.*
    arguet really implies a supposition ('suppose') or a condi-
tion ('if') rather than a statement of fact. **-to:** fut. imperative
sing. ending. It appears on several verbs in this passage. **probo,
-are, -avi, -atus,** *test, approve, commend.*

200 dicas . . . neges: subjunctives used as imperatives. **nego,
    -are, -avi, -atus,** *say no, deny.*

201 rideo, -ere, risi, risus, *laugh.* **adrideo, -ere, -risi, -ri-
    sus,** *laugh at, or with, laugh too.* **memini, -isse,** *remember.*

202 impono, -ere, -posui, -positus, *place . . . on, impose . . .
    on.* **lex, legis,** f., *law.* **vultus, -us,** m., *expression, coun-
tenance, face.* Here plur. for sing. --Some authorities (female)
doubt the validity of Ovid's psychology in this passage. Too much
agreement, they say, will rub a woman the wrong way. Of course,
the individual and the particular stage of the friendship must be
taken into account. In general, it is safer to say Yes than No to
a woman, which is Ovid's contention.

203 seu . . . seu . . . sive, *if . . . or if . . . or if.* **ludo,
    -ere, lusi, lusus,** *play, play games.* **numerus, -i,** m.,

tu male iactato, tu male iacta dato;

seu iacies talos, victam ne poena sequatur, 205

damnosi facito stent tibi saepe canes;

sive latrocinii sub imagine calculus ibit,

fac pereat vitreo miles ab hoste tuus.

Ipse tene distenta suis umbracula virgis,

ipse fac in turba, qua venit illa, locum 210

nec dubita tereti scamnum producere lecto

et tenero soleam deme vel adde pedi.

Saepe etiam dominae, quamvis horrebis et ipse,

---

number, die (plur. *dice*). **iacto, -are, -avi, -atus,** *throw, cast.*
eburnus, -a, -um, *of ivory, ivory.*

204 **iactato:** 203; 199. **iacio, -ere, ieci, iactus,** *throw.* **iacta
dato:** 'move your throws.' This expression shows that the ref-
erence in these two lines is not to a game like craps (as in the
next two), but to a game resembling backgammon.

205 **seu:** 203. **iacies:** 204. **talus, -i,** m., *anklebone, die,
'bone.' Tesserae,* probably alluded to in 203, were cubes like
our own dice. *Tali* were oblong, rounded at the ends, and marked on
only four sides. **victam:** 'her, defeated' = 'her defeat.' **poena,
-ae,** f., *punishment, penalty.* **sequor, sequi, secutus,** *follow.*
victam ne poena sequatur: freely, 'to avoid punishment for beat-
ing her.'

206 **damnosus, -a, -um,** *hurtful, injurious, damaging, ruinous.*
sto, -are, steti, status, *stand, (turn up).* **canis, -is,** m.,
f., *dog.* This term was employed for the worst throw in dicing,
when, if *tali* were being used, the same number turned up on each
of the four dice. The best throw - a different number on each of
the four - was termed, not badly, 'Venus.'

207 **sive:** 203. **latrocinium, -ii,** n., *robbery.* **imago, -inis,** f.,
likeness, form, semblance. **latrocinii sub imagine** refers to
a popular game resembling chess or checkers in which the men, usu-
ally made of glass, represented bandits or soldiers. **calculus,
-i,** m., *pebble, piece, man* (in a board game).

208 **vitreus, -a, -um,** *of glass, glassy.* **miles, -itis,** m., f.,
soldier. **hostis, -is,** m., f., *enemy, foe.*

209 **distendo, -ere, -di, -tus,** *stretch out, extend, distend.* **um-
braculum, -i,** n., *parasol, umbrella.* **virga, -ae,** f., *branch,
rod, rib* (of a parasol).

210 **turba, -ae,** f., *turmoil, crowd, throng.*

211 **dubito, -are, -avi, -atus,** *doubt, hesitate.* **teres, -etis,**
round, smooth, polished, elegant. **scamnum, -i,** n., *stool.*
produco, -ere, -xi, -ctus, *bring forth, bring out, produce.* **lec-
tus, -i,** m., *couch, dining couch.*

212 **solea, -ae,** f., *slipper, sandal.* These were removed before
reclining at meals. **demo, -ere, dempsi, demptus,** *take off,
remove.* **vel,** *or.* **addo, -ere, addidi, additus,** *add, put . . . on.*

213 **quamvis,** *though.* **horreo, -ere, -ui,** *bristle, shake, shiver.*

　　　algenti manus est calfacienda sinu;
215　nec tibi turpe puta (quamvis sit turpe, placebit)
　　　ingenua speculum sustinuisse manu.
　　　Ille, fatigata praebendo monstra noverca,
　　　　qui meruit caelum quod prior ipse tulit,
　　　inter Ioniacas calathum tenuisse puellas
220　creditur et lanas excoluisse rudes.
　　　Paruit imperio dominae Tirynthius heros:
　　　　i nunc et dubita ferre quod ille tulit!
　　　Iussus adesse foro, iussa maturius hora

214　**algeo, -ere, alsi,** *be cold, freeze.* **calfacio, -ere, -feci,
　　-factus,** *warm.*

215　**quamvis:** 213.

216　**ingenuus, -a, -um,** *freeborn.* Emphasized because mirror-hold-
　　ing was usually a slave's job. **speculum, -i,** n., *looking
glass, mirror.* **sustineo, -ere, -tinui, -tentus,** *hold up, support.*
--For better or for worse, the compact seems to have done away
with this chore.

217　Translate the following four lines in this order: **noverca fa-
　　tigata** (abl. abs.) **praebendo monstra, ille qui meruit caelum
quod prior ipse tulit, creditur tenuisse calathum inter Ioniacas
puellas et excoluisse rudes lanas. ille =** Hercules. Ovid points
out that even this mightiest of the he-men once stooped to sissy
tasks. The story is of his servitude to Queen Omphale of Lydia,
who compelled him to exchange clothes with her and to do the spin-
ning. **fatigo, -are, -avi, -atus,** *tire out, weary.* **praebeo,
-ere, -ui, -itus,** *offer, furnish, supply.* **monstrum, -i,** n., *por-
tent, monster.* **noverca, -ae,** f., *stepmother* (i.e., Juno, who did
all she could to destroy Hercules. Among other things, she sent
two snakes while he was still in his cradle. He strangled them).

218　**mereo, -ere, -ui, -itus,** *deserve, earn, win.* **caelum, -i,** n.,
　　sky, heaven. **prior, prius,** *former(ly), previous(ly), first.*
--Hercules, substituting for Atlas, once held up the heavens. At
his death he was received into heaven as a god.

219　**inter** (with acc.), *among, in the midst of.* **Ioniacus, -a,
　　-um,** *of Ionia, Ionian.* Ionia was a region of western Asia
Minor, roughly equivalent to Lydia here. **calathus, -i,** m., *wicker
basket, wool basket.*

220　**lana, -ae,** f., *wool.* **excolo, -ere, -colui, -cultus,** *work
　　carefully, spin fine.* **rudis, -e,** *unworked, rough, raw.*

221　**pareo, -ere, -ui, -itus** (with dat.), *obey, submit to.* **impe-
　　rium, -ii,** n., *command, rule.* **Tirynthius, -a, -um,** *Tirynthi-
an, of Tiryns* (where Hercules was brought up). **heros, -ois,** m.,
demigod, hero.

222　**i:** imperative of **eo. dubito, -are, -avi, -atus,** *doubt, hesi-
　　tate.*

223　**forum, -i,** n., *market place, forum.* **mature** (adv.), *early,
　　quickly, soon.* **hora, -ae,** f., *hour, time.*

fac semper venias nec nisi serus abi.

Occurras aliquo, tibi dixerit: omnia differ;   225
curre, nec inceptum turba moretur iter.

Nocte domum repetens epulis perfuncta redibit:
tunc quoque pro servo, si vocat illa, veni.

Rure erit et dicet 'Venias' (Amor odit inertes):
si rota defuerit, tu pede carpe viam,   230

nec grave te tempus sitiensque Canicula tardet
nec via per iactas candida facta nives.

Militiae species amor est: discedite, segnes!

---

224   **serus, -a, -um,** *late.* **abeo, -ire, -ivi (-ii), -itus,** *go away, come away, depart.*

225   **occurro, -ere, -curri, -cursus,** *run to meet, meet.* The sub-junctive here is an indirect command after **dixerit.** 'Her' should be understood as the object. **aliquo** (adv.), *to some place, somewhere.* **differo, differre, distuli, dilatus,** *scatter, put off, postpone.*

226   **curro, -ere, cucurri, cursus,** *run.* **incipio, -ere, -cepi, -ceptus,** *begin, commence.* **turba, -ae, f.,** *turmoil, crowd, throng.* **moror, -ari, -atus,** *delay, retard, hinder.* **iter, itineris, n.,** *journey, trip, road, path.*

227   **domus, -us, f.,** *house, home.* **repeto, -ere, -ivi (-ii), -itus,** *seek again, go back (to), return (to).* **epulae, -arum, f.,** *banquet, dinner party.* **perfungor, -i, -functus** (with abl.), *perform, endure, enjoy.* **redeo, -ire, -ii, -itus,** *come back, return.*

228   **tunc,** *then.* **pro** (with abl.), *before, for, in place of.* **servus, -i,** m., *slave, servant.* Here probably the servant who escorted his mistress home with a torch. **voco, -are, -avi, -atus,** *call, summon.* **veni:** imperative.

229   **rus, ruris, n.,** *country.* **venias:** subjunctive used as imper-ative. **odi, odisse,** *hate, dislike.* **iners, -ertis,** *idle, sluggish, lazy.* Here used substantively.

230   **rota, -ae, f.,** *wheel, carriage, chariot.* **desum, -esse, -fui,** *be absent, be lacking, be not at hand.* **carpo, -ere, -psi, -ptus,** *pick;* (with **viam**) *go, make one's way, make the journey.*

231   **gravis, -e,** *heavy, severe, disagreeable, unpleasant.* **sitiens, -entis,** *thirsty, dry, parching.* **Canicula, -ae, f.,** *small dog; the Dog Star* (whose heliacal rising coincides with the sultry days of July and August, whence the term 'dog days'). **tardo, -are, -avi, -atus,** *make slow, hinder, delay, retard.*

232   **iactus, -a, -um** (part. of **iacio**), *thrown, cast, fallen, driven.* **candidus, -a, -um,** *(shining) white, bright, beautiful.* **nix, nivis, f.,** *snow.*

233   **militia, -ae, f.,** *military service, warfare.* **species, -ei, f.,** *form, sort, kind.* **discedo, -ere, -cessi, -cessus,** *go away, depart, leave.* **segnis, -e,** *slow, sluggish, lazy.*

Non sunt haec timidis signa tuenda viris.
235   Nox et hiems longaeque viae saevique dolores
         mollibus his castris et labor omnis inest.

Be pleasant and courteous to the lady's servants, even to the extent of giving them small presents (251-260). This suggests the delicate subject of gifts to the object of your affections. They need not be expensive, but merely well chosen; e.g., fruit from your estate, even if you have to buy it downtown. Some of your own poetry is a possibility, but only a few women would appreciate that.

Nec dominam iubeo pretioso munere dones:
        parva, sed e parvis callidus apta dato.
Dum bene dives ager, dum rami pondere nutant,
        adferat in calatho rustica dona puer.
265   Rure suburbano poteris tibi dicere missa,
        illa vel in Sacra sint licet empta via.
        Adferat aut uvas, aut quas Amaryllis amabat—

---

234   **timidus, -a, -um,** *timid, cowardly.* **signum, -i,** n., *sign, standard, banner.* **tueor, -eri, tuitus,** *watch, guard, defend.*

235   **hiems, -emis,** f., *winter, stormy weather.* **saevus, -a, -um,** *savage, cruel, severe.* **dolor, -oris,** m., *pain, grief, trouble, vexation.*

236   **castra, -orum,** n., *camp.* **labor, -oris,** m., *labor, exertion, hardship, trouble.* **insum, -esse, -fui** (with dat.), *be in, be contained in, belong to.* **inest,** though singular, has five subjects in these two lines.

261   **pretiosus, -a, -um,** *valuable, costly, expensive.* **dono, -are, -avi, -atus,** *present* (someone with something), *give.*

262   **parvus, -a, -um,** *little, small.* Supply **munera,** as with **apta. callidus, -a, -um,** *skillful, clever, shrewd, cunning, sly.* **dato:** future imperative.

263   **dives, -itis,** *rich, fertile, fruitful.* **ager, agri,** m., *land, field.* Subject of **est** understood. **ramus, -i,** m., *branch, bough.* **pondus, -eris,** n., *weight.* **nuto, -are, -avi, -atus,** *nod, sway to and fro, (bend).*

264   **adfero, adferre, attuli, adlatus,** *bring (to).* **calathus, -i,** m., *wicker basket.* **rusticus, -a, -um,** *of (from) the country, rural, rustic.* **donum, -i,** n., *gift, present.* **puer, -eri,** m., *boy, slave, servant.*

265   **rus, ruris,** n., *country, farm, estate.* **suburbanus, -a, -um,** *near the city, suburban.* **missa (esse)** agrees with **dona** (understood).

266   **vel,** *or, even.* **sacer, sacra, sacrum,** *holy, sacred.* **Sacra . . via:** Rome's 'Main Street,' leading past the Forum to the Capitol. **licet** ('though') introduces the entire clause here. **emo, -ere, emi, emptus,** *buy.* --Many an unsuccessful fisherman has performed the same trick.

267   **adferat:** 264. **uva, -ae,** f., *grape.* **quas** refers to **castaneas**

at nunc castaneas non amat illa nuces!
Quin etiam turdoque licet missaque corona
  te memorem dominae testificere tuae.   270
Turpiter his emitur spes mortis et orba senectus.
A! Pereant, per quos munera crimen habent!
Quid tibi praecipiam teneros quoque mittere versus?
Ei mihi! Non multum carmen honoris habet.
Carmina laudantur, sed munera magna petuntur: 275
  dummodo sit dives, barbarus ipse placet.
Aurea sunt vere nunc saecula: plurimus auro
  venit honos, auro conciliatur amor.

. . . **nuces. Amaryllis, -idis (-idos),** f.: name used by
classical poets to denote a shepherdess or rustic maiden. Ovid has
in mind Vergil's second 'Eclogue,' line 52: 'castaneasque nuces,
mea quas Amaryllis amabat.'

268 **castanea, -ae,** f., *chestnut.* This either is used as an adjec-
tive here or is in apposition with **nuces,** which is superflu-
ous so far as translation is concerned. **nux, nucis,** f., *nut.*

269 **quin etiam,** *nay even, moreover, what is more.* **turdus, -i,**
m., *thrush.* **mitto, -ere, misi, missus,** *send.* **corona, -ae,**
f., *garland, wreath, corsage, bouquet.*

270 **te:** subject of **esse** understood. **memor, -oris** (with gen.),
mindful of, remembering. **testificor, -ari, -atus,** *give evi-
dence, show, demonstrate.* **testificere** is second person singular
and the subjunctive depends on **licet.**

271 In the next two lines Ovid is referring to the practice of
giving presents to the childless in the hope of being includ-
ed in their wills. **turpiter,** *shamefully, disgracefully.* **emo,
emere, emi, emptus,** *buy.* **spes, -ei,** f., *hope.* **mors, mortis,** f.,
death. **orbus, -a, -um,** *bereaved, childless.* **senectus, -utis,** f.,
old age.

272 **a,** *ah!*

273 **praecipio, -ere, -cepi, -ceptus,** *anticipate, advise, in-
struct, bid.* **mittere:** 269. **versus, -us,** m., *line, verse.*

274 **ei,** *oh! ah!* **carmen, -inis,** n., *song, poem, poetry.* **honos,
-oris,** m., *honor, esteem.* **honoris** is partitive genitive with
multum; English would omit the 'of.'

275 **carmina:** 274. **laudo, -are, -avi, -atus,** *praise.*

276 **dummodo,** *so long as, provided that, if only.* **dives, -itis,**
rich, wealthy. **barbarus, -i,** m., *foreigner, barbarian.*

277 A sarcastic reference to the Golden Age of mythology, when
life and men were flawless. **aureus, -a, -um,** *of gold, gold-
en.* **vere,** *truly.* **saeculum, -i,** n., *generation, age.* Here probab-
ly plural for singular. **plurimus, -a, -um,** *most, very much.* **au-
rum, -i,** n., *gold.*

278 **honos:** 274. **auro:** 277. **concilio, -are, -avi, -atus,** *unite,
acquire, win, gain.*

Ipse licet venias Musis comitatus, Homere,
280   si nihil attuleris, ibis, Homere, foras.
Sunt tamen et doctae, rarissima turba, puellae,
altera non doctae turba, sed esse volunt.
Utraque laudetur per carmina; carmina lector
commendet dulci qualiacumque sono.
285   His ergo aut illis vigilatum carmen in ipsas
forsitan exigui muneris instar erit.

Feed the girl's vanity. See to it that she shall ask you to do
whatever you have already decided to do; you lose nothing, she
feels important. Always praise her clothes and appearance.

At quod eris per te facturus et utile credis,
id tua te facito semper amica roget.
Libertas alicui fuerit promissa tuorum:
290   hanc tamen a domina fac petat ille tua;

279 **Musa, -ae, f.,** *a Muse* (one of the nine patron goddesses of
poetry and other arts and sciences). **comito, -are, -avi,
-atus,** *accompany, attend.* **Homerus, -i, m.,** *Homer,* famous Greek
epic poet.

280 **nihil** (indecl.), n., *nothing.* **adfero, adferre, attuli, adla-
tus,** *bring (to).* **Homere:** 279. **foras** (adv.), *out through the
door, out of doors, out.* With **ire** this comes close to the expres-
sion 'to be given the gate' or 'to be shown the door.'

281 **doctus, -a, -um,** *learned, well educated, cultivated, intel-
lectual.* **rarus, -a, -um,** *scattered, rare, scanty, uncommon,
scarce.* **turba, -ae, f.,** *crowd, group.*

282 **doctae:** 281. Predicate nominative, plural since **turba** is a
collective noun and refers to girls. The verb is understood
from **sunt** above. **turba:** 281.

283 **uterque, utraque, utrumque,** *each, one as well as the other,
both.* **laudo, -are, -avi, -atus,** *praise.* **carmen, -inis, n.,**
song, poem, poetry. **lector, -oris, m.,** *reader.*

284 **commendo, -are, -avi, -atus,** *recommend, procure favor for,
make agreeable, set off.* **dulcis, -e,** *sweet, delightful,
pleasant, charming.* **qualiscumque, qualecumque,** *of whatever sort
or quality, no matter what sort.* **sonus, -i, m.,** *sound, voice.*

285 **his** refers to the **non doctae, illis** to the **doctae. ergo,**
consequently, therefore. **vigilo, -are, -avi, -atus,** *stay
awake; make while watching.* **vigilatum** = 'worked on during the
night,' 'written in the wee hours of the night.' **carmen:** 283. **in**
= 'in honor of.'

286 **forsitan,** *perhaps.* **exiguus, -a, -um,** *small, little.* **instar**
(with gen.), *like, the equivalent of.*

287 **quod:** the antecedent is **id. per te:** 'of yourself,' 'of your
own accord.' **utilis, -e,** *useful, profitable, advantageous.*

289 **libertas, -atis, f.,** *freedom, liberty.* **promitto, -ere, pro-
misi, promissus,** *promise.* **fuerit promissa:** 'suppose that . .
has been promised.' **tuorum:** 'of your slaves.'

si poenam servo, si vincula saeva remittis,
    quod facturus eras, debeat illa tibi.
Utilitas tua sit, titulus donetur amicae;
    perde nihil, partes illa potentis agat.
Sed te, cuicumque est retinendae cura puellae,   295
    attonitum forma fac putet esse sua.
Sive erit in Tyriis, Tyrios laudabis amictus;
    sive erit in Cois, Coa decere puta.
Aurata est: ipso tibi sit pretiosior auro;
    gausapa si sumit, gausapa sumpta proba;   300
adstiterit tunicata: 'Moves incendia!' clama,
    sed timida, caveat frigora, voce roga.

---

291 **poena, -ae,** f., *punishment.* **servus, -i,** m., *slave, servant.*
vinculum, -i, n., *fetter, rope, chain.* **saevus, -a, -um,** *savage, cruel.* **remitto, -ere, -misi, -missus,** *send back, relax, remove, remit, put an end to.*

292 **quod:** 'what' or 'that which.' The clause it introduces is object of **debeat. debeo, -ere, -ui, -itus,** *owe, ought, must.*

293 **utilitas, -atis,** f., *benefit, profit, advantage.* **titulus, -i,** m., *title, glory, credit.* **dono, -are, -avi, -atus,** *give, present, bestow, confer.*

294 **perdo, -ere, -didi, -ditus,** *destroy, lose.* **nihil** (indecl.), n., *nothing.* **potens, -entis,** *powerful, having the mastery, influential.* Here used as a substantive in the sense of 'the person in power,' 'boss.'

295 **retineo, -ere, -ui, -tentus,** *retain, keep.*

296 **attonitus, -a, -um,** *thunderstruck, stunned, spellbound, enthralled.*

297 **sive . . . sive,** *if . . . or if.* **Tyrius, -a, -um,** *Tyrian, purple* (Tyre being noted for its purple dye, which was quite expensive). **laudo, -are, -avi, -atus,** *praise, compliment.* **amictus, -us,** m., *garment, dress, clothes.*

298 **sive:** 297. **Coa, -orum,** n., *Coan garments, dress from Cos, silk garments.* Cos was a Greek island noted for its silk, and clothes from there were very fine and transparent.

299 **auratus, -a, -um,** *ornamented with gold, dressed in gold.* **pretiosus, -a, -um,** *valuable, precious.* **aurum, -i,** n., *gold.*

300 **gausapa, -orum,** n., *woolen clothes.* **sumo, -ere, sumpsi, sumptus,** *take (up), put on.* **probo, -are, -avi, -atus,** *test, approve, commend.*

301 **adsto, -are, -stiti,** *stand near, stand by.* **tunicatus, -a, -um,** *clothed in a tunic; wearing shorts (?).* **incendium, -ii,** n., *burning, fire, flame.*

302 **timidus, -a, -um,** *fearful, timid.* **caveo, -ere, cavi, cautus,** *beware of, guard against.* The subjunctive represents an indirect command after **roga. frigus, -oris,** n., *cold, chill.* Note

Compositum discrimen erit: discrimina lauda;
     torserit igne comam: torte capille, place!
305 Bracchia saltantis, vocem mirare canentis,
     et, quod desierit, verba querentis habe.
       *   *   *   *   *   *   *

     Ut fuerit torva violentior illa Medusa,
310   fiet amatori lenis et aequa suo.
     Tantum, ne pateas verbis simulator in illis,
        effice nec vultu destrue dicta tuo.
     Si latet ars, prodest; adfert deprensa pudorem
        atque adimit merito tempus in omne fidem.

If your girl should fall ill, though Ovid hopes not, show your
sympathy and do everything for her that you can. This does not,
however, include administering medicine. Let your rival do that.

---

the play on words: **incendia** and **frigora**.

303 **compono, -ere, -posui, -positus,** *arrange, set in order, ad-
     just.* **discrimen, -inis,** n., *division, part in the hair.*
laudo, -are, -avi, -atus, *praise, compliment.*

304 **torqueo, -ere, torsi, tortus,** *twist, curl.*

305 **bracchium, -ii,** n., *(fore)arm.* **salto, -are, -avi, -atus,**
     dance. With **saltantis,** as with **canentis,** some such word as
puellae is understood. **miror, -ari, -atus,** *wonder at, admire.*
cano, -ere, cecini, cantus, *sing.*

306 **queror, -i, questus,** *complain.* The participle here should be
     translated 'of one who . . . .'

309 **ut** = *even if, though.* **torvus, -a, -um,** *grim, savage, fierce.*
     violens, -entis, *furious, violent.* **Medusa, -ae,** f.: the no-
torious and dangerous snake-haired female who could turn men to
stone. Here ablative.

310 **amator, -oris,** m., *lover, sweetheart.* **lenis, -e,** *soft, gen-
     tle, mild.* **aequus, -a, -um,** *even, calm, reasonable, kind.*

311 **tantum** (adv.), *only.* **ne** . . .: this clause depends on **effi-
     ce.** **pateo, -ere, -ui,** *lie open, be exposed, be discovered,
be plain(ly).* **simulator, -oris,** m., *pretender, hypocrite.*

312 **efficio, -ere, -feci, -fectus,** *bring (it) to pass, see to it,
     take care.* **vultus, -us,** m., *countenance, looks, expression,
face.* **destruo, -ere, -xi, -ctus,** *destroy, ruin, weaken.* **dictum,
-i,** n., *what has been said, word.*

313 **lateo, -ere, -ui,** *lie hid, be concealed.* **prosum, prodesse,
     profui,** *be useful, be of use, profit.* **adfero, adferre, attu-
li, adlatus,** *bring (to).* **deprendo, -ere, -di, -sus,** *catch, de-
tect, find out, discover, perceive.* **pudor, -oris,** m., *shame, em-
barrassment, disgrace, modesty.*

314 **adimo, -ere, -emi, -emptus,** *take away, remove.* **merito**
     (adv.), *deservedly, rightly, justly.* **fides, -ei,** f., *trust,
faith, confidence, belief, credibility.*

Saepe sub autumnum, cum formosissimus annus,   315
  plenaque purpureo subrubet uva mero,
cum modo frigoribus premitur, modo solvitur aestu,
  aëre non certo corpora languor habet.
Illa quidem valeat, sed si male firma cubabit
  et vitium caeli senserit aegra sui,   320
tunc amor et pietas tua sit manifesta puellae;
  tum sere, quod plena postmodo falce metas.
Nec tibi morosi veniant fastidia morbi,
  perque tuas fiant, quae sinet ipsa, manus,
et videat flentem, nec taedeat oscula ferre,   325

---

315 **autumnus, -i,** m., *autumn.* **annus:** supply **est.**

316 **plenus, -a, -um,** *full, ripe, mature.* **purpureus, -a, -um,**
     purple. **subrubeo, -ere,** *become reddish, blush.* **uva, -ae,**
f., *grape.* **merum, -i,** n., *(pure) wine.*

317 **frigus, -oris,** n., *cold.* **premo, -ere, pressi, pressus,**
     press, oppress, overwhelm, (pinch, benumb). **premitur** and **sol-**
vitur are probably used impersonally. In translating it is neces-
sary to supply some subject such as 'one,' 'we,' or 'nature.'
Otherwise, **uva** must be the subject. **solvo, -ere, solvi, solutus,**
loosen, dissolve, weaken, enervate. **aestus, -us,** m., *heat.*

318 **aër, aëris,** m., *air, weather.* **certus, -a, -um,** *certain, set-*
     tled. **languor, -oris,** m., *faintness, weariness, lassitude,*
languor, sluggishness.

319 **quidem** (adv.), *indeed, at least, certainly.* **valeo, -ere,**
     -ui, -itus, *be strong, be well, be healthy.* The subjunctive
here is optative, expressing a wish. **firmus, -a, -um,** *firm,*
strong. **male firma** is a roundabout way of saying 'infirm,' 'ail-
ing,' or 'ill.' Such usage is called *litotes.* **cubo, -are, -ui,**
-itus, *lie down, go to bed.*

320 **caelum, -i,** n., *sky, climate, weather.* **sentio, -ire, sensi,**
     sensus, *feel, feel the effects of, perceive.* **aeger, -gra,**
-grum, *ill, sick, suffering.*

321 **tunc,** *then.* **pietas, -atis,** f., *sense of duty; affection, de-*
     votion. **manifestus, -a, -um,** *clear, evident, manifest.*

322 **sero, -ere, sevi, satus,** *sow.* **plenus, -a, -um,** *full.* **post-**
     modo, *afterwards, presently, soon.* **falx, falcis,** f., *sickle,*
scythe. **meto, -are, -avi, -atus,** *reap.*

323 **morosus, -a, -um,** *peevish, fretful.* **fastidium, -ii,** n.,
     loathing, dislike, disgust. **morbus, -i,** m., *sickness, dis-*
ease, ailment, illness, malady.

324 **quae** = 'the things which,' 'whatever.' **sino, -ere, sivi,**
     situs, *allow, permit.*

325 **flentem** modifies **te** understood. **taedet, -ere, -duit (-sum**
     est), *it disgusts, it wearies.* **osculum, -i,** n., *kiss.* **nec**
taedeat oscula ferre: 'and don't grow weary of giving her kisses.'

et sicco lacrimas combibat ore tuas.

Multa vove, sed cuncta palam; quotiensque libebit,
    quae referas illi, somnia laeta vide;
et veniat quae lustret anus lectumque locumque,
330   praeferat et tremula sulpur et ova manu.
Omnibus his inerunt gratae vestigia curae;
    in tabulas multis haec via fecit iter.
Nec tamen officiis odium quaeratur ab aegra:
    sit suus in blanda sedulitate modus.
335   Neve cibo prohibe nec amari pocula suci
    porrige: rivalis misceat illa tuus!

---

326 **siccus, -a, -um,** *dry, parched.* **combibo, -ere, -bibi,** *drink up, absorb.* --One shudders to think what a physician would say about this treatment. Fortunately, the Romans had not heard about germs.

327 **voveo, -ere, vovi, votus,** *vow, make a vow.* **cunctus, -a, -um,** *all.* **palam,** *openly, plainly, (aloud).* A typical Ovidian touch: he sees no use in making vows on the girl's behalf if she does not know about it. **quotiens,** *how often, as often as.* **libet, -ere, libuit (libitum est),** *it is pleasing, it is agreeable.*

328 **somnium, -ii,** n., *dream.* **laetus, -a, -um,** *happy, cheerful, pleasant.* --The dreams, of course, would be on pertinent subjects, such as the girl's recovery. The implication is that you make them up when necessary.

329 The subject of **veniat** is **anus.** **quae** introduces a relative clause of purpose. **lustro, -are, -avi, -atus,** *purify.* **anus, -us,** f., *old woman.* **lectus, -i,** m., *couch, bed.*

330 **praefero, -ferre, -tuli, -latus,** *carry in front, carry along.* **et:** translate before **praeferat. tremulus, -a, -um,** *shaking, trembling.* **sulpur, -uris,** n., *sulphur.* **ovum, -i,** n., *egg.* --Sick rooms were purified (disinfected?) with sulphur and eggs. Ovid may also have in mind their use in cases of unrequited love.

331 **insum, -esse, -fui** (with dat.), *be in, be contained in.* **gratus, -a, -um,** *pleasing, agreeable, dear, grateful, deserving thanks.* **vestigium, -ii,** n., *footstep, sign, token, evidence.*

332 **tabula, -ae,** f., *tablet, will.* **iter, itineris,** n., *way, journey, road, path.* --This line means roughly: 'this method has provided many people with a way into the wills of the rich.'

333 **officium, -ii,** n., *service, kindness, duty.* **odium, -ii,** n., *hatred, ill will, dislike, annoyance.* **aeger, aegra, aegrum,** *ill, sick, suffering.*

334 **suus:** 'its own,' i.e., 'a proper.' **blandus, -a, -um,** *flattering, pleasant, agreeable.* **sedulitas, -atis,** f., *zeal, earnestness, attentiveness.*

335 **neve,** *and . . . not, and that not.* **cibus, -i,** m., *food.* **prohibeo, -ere, -ui, -itus,** *hold back, keep (back), restrain, forbid.* Supply 'her' as the object. **amarus, -a, -um,** *bitter.* **poculum, -i,** n., *cup, goblet.* **sucus, -i,** m., *juice, medicine, dose.*

336 **porrigo, -ere, -rexi, -rectus,** *hold forth, reach out, offer,*

A change of tactics is advisable after you have become well es-
tablished. When you are sure you will be missed, absent yourself.
But it is dangerous to stay away too long: out of sight, out of
mind.

Sed non, quo dederas a litore carbasa, vento
   utendum, medio cum potiere freto.
Dum novus errat amor, vires sibi colligat usu;
   si bene nutrieris, tempore firmus erit.   340
Quem taurum metuis, vitulum mulcere solebas;
   sub qua nunc recubas arbore, virga fuit;
nascitur exiguus sed opes adquirit eundo,
   quaque venit, multas accipit amnis aquas.
Fac tibi consuescat: nil adsuetudine maius;   345
   quam tu dum capias, taedia nulla fuge.
Te semper videat, tibi semper praebeat aures,

---

present. **rivalis, -is,** m., *rival.* **misceo, -ere, -ui, mix-
tus,** *mix, mingle, blend.*

337 **quo** (adv.), *whither, where, to which.* The antecedent is **ven-
to. litus, -oris,** n., *shore.* **carbasa, -orum,** n., *sails.*

338 **utor, uti, usus** (with abl.), *use.* **utendum (erit)** is the im-
personal form of the second periphrastic. It should be trans-
lated either '(the wind) should be used' or, better, 'you should
use (the wind).' **potior, -iri, -itus** (with abl.), *get possession
of, obtain, gain, reach.* **fretum, -i,** n., *strait, sea.*

339 **erro, -are, -avi, -atus,** *wander, move uncertainly, err.* **col-
ligo, -ere, -legi, -lectus,** *gather, collect.* **usus, -us,** m.,
use, experience.

340 **nutrio, -ire, -ii (-ivi), -itus,** *nourish, feed, foster,
nurse.* **firmus, -a, -um,** *firm, strong.*

341 **taurus, -i,** m., *bull.* **metuo, -ere, -ui,** *fear, be afraid of.*
vitulus, -i, m., *calf.* **mulceo, -ere, mulsi, mulsus,** *stroke,
caress.*

342 **recubo, -are,** *lie back, recline.* **arbor, -oris,** f., *tree.*
arbore should really be translated as the subject of **fuit** and
the antecedent of **qua. virga, -ae,** f., *green sprout, twig.*

343 The subject of all the verbs in this sentence is **amnis. nas-
cor, nasci, natus,** *be born, rise, spring forth, begin.* **exi-
guus, -a, -um,** *small, tiny.* **adquiro, -ere, -quisivi, -quisitus,**
acquire, gain. **eundo:** gerund of **eo.**

344 **amnis, -is,** m., *river.*

345 **consuesco, -ere, -suevi, -suetus,** *become accustomed* or *used
to.* The subject here is 'she.' **nil** (indecl.), n., *nothing.*
Subject of **est** understood. **adsuetudo, -inis,** f., *custom, habit.*

346 The antecedent of **quam** is **adsuetudine;** here it is best trans-
lated 'this' or 'that.' **taedium, -ii,** n., *weariness, tire-
some task.*

347 **praebeo, -ere, -ui, -itus,** *offer, furnish, give, lend.* **au-
ris, -is,** f., *ear.*

exhibeat vultus noxque diesque tuos.
Cum tibi maior erit fiducia posse requiri,
350   cum procul absenti cura futurus eris,
da requiem: requietus ager bene credita reddit,
terraque caelestes arida sorbet aquas.
Phyllida Demophoon praesens moderatius ussit;
exarsit velis acrius illa datis.
355   Penelopen absens sollers torquebat Ulixes;
Phylacides aberat, Laodamia, tuus.
Sed mora tuta brevis; lentescunt tempore curae,
vanescitque absens et novus intrat amor.

---

348   **exhibeo, -ere, -ui, -itus,** *present, show, display, exhibit, reveal.* **vultus, -us,** m., *face, countenance.*

349   **fiducia, -ae,** f., *confidence.* **posse:** indirect statement depending on **fiducia,** with **te** understood as subject. **requiro, -ere, -sivi (-sii), -situs,** *seek for, want, miss.*

350   **procul,** *far (off).* **absens, -entis,** *absent, away.* **absenti** modifies **puellae** understood. **futurus eris:** first periphrastic of **sum.**

351   **requies, -etis** (acc. **requiem**), f., *rest.* **requietus, -a, -um,** *rested.* **ager, agri,** m., *field.* **credita** (acc. pl.): 'what has been entrusted (to it).'

352   **terra, -ae,** f., *land, ground.* **caelestis, -e,** *of heaven, coming from heaven.* **aridus, -a, -um,** *dry, parched.* **sorbeo, -ere, -ui,** *drink up, absorb.*

353   **Phyllis, -idis & -idos** (acc. **-ida**), f.: princess of Thrace who hanged herself because of the failure of her lover Demophoön to return. **Demophoon, -ontis,** m.: a son of Theseus and Phaedra who fought at Troy. **praesens, -entis,** *(when) present.* **moderate,** *moderately, to a moderate degree.* **uro, -ere, ussi, ustus,** *burn, inflame, arouse the glow of love in.*

354   **exardesco, -ere, -arsi, -arsus,** *catch fire, become inflamed (with love).* **velum, -i,** n., *cloth, sail.* **velis . . . datis** (abl. abs.) = 'after he had set sail.' **acriter,** *sharply, strongly, violently, passionately.*

355   **Penelope, -es** (acc. **-en**), f.: faithful wife of Ulysses. **absens:** 350. **sollers, -tis,** *skillful, clever, crafty.* **torqueo, -ere, torsi, tortus,** *twist, torture, torment.*

356   **Phylacides, -ae,** m., *Phylacides,* i.e., *Protesilaus* (the first Greek to be killed at Troy). **absum, abesse, afui,** *be (far) away, be absent.* **Laodamia, -ae,** f.: Protesilaus' wife who, from her deep love, followed him to the underworld after his death. --The implication of this line is that it was Protesilaus' absence which was the cause of Laodamia's great longing and love.

357   **mora** almost = 'absence.' **tutus, -a, -um,** *safe.* **brevis, -e,** *short, brief.* **lentesco, -ere,** *slacken, relax, dwindle.*

358   **vanesco, -ere,** *pass away, disappear, vanish.* **absens:** 350. **intro, -are, -avi, -atus,** *enter.*

Helen eloped with Paris simply because Menelaus stayed away too
long (359-372). Neither wild boar nor lioness nor viper (not to
mention hell) has a fury like a woman scorned. So if your fancy
strays elsewhere, don't get caught (373-424). But often exactly
the opposite tactics should be used (425-434). With some girls the
prick of jealousy is necessary, just so you do not overdo it. All
the recriminations, quarrels, and tantrums are justified in the
sweet moments of reconciliation.

Sunt quibus ingrate timida indulgentia servit   435

et, si nulla subest aemula, languet amor.

Luxuriant animi rebus plerumque secundis,

nec facile est aequa commoda mente pati.

Ut levis, absumptis paulatim viribus, ignis

ipse latet, summo canet in igne cinis,   440

sed tamen extinctas admoto sulpure flammas

invenit, et lumen, quod fuit ante, redit:

sic, ubi pigra situ securaque pectora torpent,

---

435   **sunt quibus:** 'there are some (girls) whom.'   **ingrate,** *un-
gratefully; without thanks, without appreciation.*   **timidus,**
-a, -um, *faint-hearted, timid.*   **indulgentia, -ae,** f., *indulgence,
gentleness, tenderness, fondness, devotion.*   **servio, -ire, -ivi
(-ii), -itus** (with dat.), *serve.*   --The meaning is that some girls
give you no thanks or credit for unwavering devotion.

436   **subsum, subesse,** *be under, be near, be at hand.*   **aemula, -ae,**
f., *rival.*   **langueo, -ere,** *be weak, languish.*

437   **luxurio, -are, -avi, -atus,** *run riot, lose control of one-
self, become conceited.*   **res, rei,** f., *thing, circumstance.*
plerumque, *generally, very often.*   **secundus, -a, -um,** *following,
favorable, prosperous.*

438   **facilis, -e,** *easy.*   **aequus, -a, -um,** *even, unruffled, calm.*
commodum, -i, n., *advantage, good thing;* (plur.) *good for-
tune, prosperity.*   **patior, pati, passus,** *bear, suffer, endure,
experience, allow.*

439   **ut** ('as') introduces the next four lines; then **sic** introduces
the conclusion of the comparison.   **absumo, -ere, -mpsi,
-mptus,** *take away, diminish, consume.*   **paulatim,** *little by little,
gradually.*

440   **lateo, -ere, -ui,** *lie hid, be concealed.*   **caneo, -ere, -ui,**
be gray, be white.   **cinis, -eris,** m., *ashes.*

441   **extinguo, -ere, -nxi, -nctus,** *extinguish.*   **admoveo, -ere,
-movi, -motus,** *bring to, apply.*   **sulpur, -uris,** n., *sulphur.*
flamma, -ae, f., *flame.*

442   **invenio, -ire, -veni, -ventus,** *come upon, find.* The subject
is probably **ignis,** rather than **cinis.**   **lumen, -inis,** n.,
light.   **redeo, -ire, -ii, -itus,** *come back, return.*

443   **piger, -gra, -grum,** *reluctant, dull, sluggish, lazy.*   **situs,
-us,** m., *situation, idleness, inactivity.*   **securus, -a, -um,**
free from care, untroubled, careless, confident, safe.   **torpeo,
-ere,** *be inactive, torpid, sluggish, dull, listless.*

acribus est stimulis eliciendus amor.

445   Fac timeat de te tepidamque recalface mentem;
palleat indicio criminis illa tui.

O quater et quotiens numero comprendere non est
felicem, de quo laesa puella dolet,

quae, simul invitas crimen pervenit ad aures,

450   excidit, et miserae voxque colorque fugit!

Ille ego sim, cuius laniet furiosa capillos;
ille ego sim, teneras cui petat ungue genas,

quem videat lacrimans, quem torvis spectet ocellis,
quo sine non possit vivere, posse velit!

455   Si spatium quaeras, breve sit, quod laesa queratur,

---

444   **acer, acris, acre,** *sharp, keen.* **stimulus, -i,** m., *goad, in-*
centive, stimulus. **elicio, -ere, elicui,** *draw out, entice*
out, *lure forth.*

445   **tepidus, -a, -um,** *lukewarm, cooled, faint, languid.* **recal-**
facio, -ere, -feci, *make warm again, warm.*

446   **palleo, -ere, -ui,** *grow pale, be anxious.* **indicium, -ii,** n.,
discovery, disclosure, indication, proof.

447   **o, O,** *oh!* **quater,** *four times.* **quotiens,** *how many times, as*
often as. **numerus, -i,** m., *number.* **comprendo, -ere, -di,**
-sus, *grasp, comprehend.* **et quotiens numero comprendere non est:**
freely, 'no, a million times'; literally, 'and how many times it
is not (possible) to comprehend in number.'

448   **felix, -icis,** *lucky, fortunate, happy.* **felicem** is accusative
of exclamation: 'happy is the man.' **doleo, -ere, -ui, -itus,**
suffer, pain, grieve.

449   **simul,** *at the same time, as soon as.* **invitus, -a, -um,** *un-*
willing, reluctant. **pervenio, -ire, -veni, -ventus,** *come to,*
reach. **auris, -is,** f., *ear.*

450   **excido, -ere, -cidi,** *fall down, collapse, faint.* **miserae:**
supply **puellae.**

451   **sim:** optative subjunctive, expressing a wish. **lanio, -are,**
-avi, -atus, *tear.* **furiosus, -a, -um,** *mad, raging, furious.*

452   **cui =** a genitive in translation. **unguis, -is,** m., *(finger)*
nail. Here singular for plural. **gena, -ae,** f., *cheek.*

453   **lacrimo, -are, -avi, -atus,** *shed tears, weep, cry.* **torvus,**
-a, -um, *wild, fierce, savage.* **ocellus, -i,** m., *(dear) (lit-*
tle) eye. The amusing use of the diminutive here indicates Ovid's
affection for the girl in spite of her tantrum, and also his en-
joyment of the situation.

454   **quo sine = sine quo.** **vivo, -ere, vixi, victus,** *live.* **velit:**
'(but) would like.'

455   **spatium, -ii,** n., *space, interval, period of time.* **spatium**
. . . **quod =** 'how long.' **brevis, -e,** *short, brief.* **laesa:**
supply **puella.** **queror, queri, questus,** *complain, make complaint,*
lament.

ne lenta vires colligat ira mora;
candida iamdudum cingantur colla lacertis,
    inque tuos flens est accipienda sinus.
Oscula da flenti. . . .
    Pax erit! Hoc uno solvitur ira modo.   460
    *   *   *   *   *   *   *

Quae modo pugnarunt,iungunt sua rostra columbae,   465
    quarum blanditias verbaque murmur habet.

Since the beginning of things all creatures have paired off,
male and female. Men and women are no exception (467-492). Apollo
now appears with the famous precept 'Know thyself'; i.e., know
your strengths and weaknesses and act accordingly.

Haec ego cum canerem, subito manifestus Apollo
    movit inauratae pollice fila lyrae.
In manibus laurus, sacris induta capillis   495
    laurus erat; vates ille videndus adit.
Is mihi 'Lascivi' dixit 'praeceptor Amoris,

---

456   **lentus, -a, -um,** *slow, lingering, long lasting.* Here abla-
       tive, modifying **mora. colligo, -ere, -legi, -lectus,** *gather,*
collect.   **ira, -ae,** f., *anger, rage.*

457   **candidus, -a, -um,** *white, beautiful.* **iamdudum,** *long since,*
       without delay, immediately. **cingo, -ere, -xi, -nctus,** *encir-*
cle.   **collum, -i,** n., *neck.* Here plural for singular. **lacertus,**
-i, m., *(upper) arm.*

459   **osculum, -i,** n., *kiss.*

460   **pax, pacis,** f., *peace.* **solvo, -ere, solvi, solutus,** *loosen,*
       remove, soothe, dissolve, dispel. **ira, -ae,** f., *anger, rage.*

465   **pugno, -are, -avi, -atus,** *fight, quarrel.* **pugnarunt : pugna-**
       verunt. iungo, -ere, -nxi, -nctus, *join.* **rostrum, -i,** n.,
beak, bill.   **columba, -ae,** f., *dove, pigeon.*

466   **quarum** goes with **murmur. blanditia, -ae,** f., *flattery, sweet*
meaning.   **murmur, -uris,** n., *murmur, murmuring, cooing.*

493   **cano, -ere, cecini, cantus,** *sing, proclaim in verse.* **subito,**
       suddenly, unexpectedly. **manifestus, -a, -um,** *evident, mani-*
fest, visible.   **Apollo, -inis,** m.: god of, among other things,
poetry and music.

494   **inauro, -are, -avi, -atus,** *cover with gold, gild.* **pollex,**
       -icis, m., 'thumb. **filum, -i,** n., *thread, string.* **lyra, -ae,**
f., *lyre.*

495   **laurus, -i,** f., *laurel* (sacred to Apollo; emblem of poetic
       distinction and of victory). **sacer, -cra, -crum,** *holy, sa-*
cred.   **induo, -ere, -ui, -utus,** *put on* or *in, place on* or *in.*

496   **laurus:** 495. **vates, -is,** m., f., *prophet, poet.* **adeo, -ire,**
       -ivi or **-ii, -itus,** *go to, approach.*

497   **is, ea, id,** *this, that; he, she, it.* **lascivus, -a, -um,**
       playful, frolicsome, roguish. **praeceptor, -oris,** m., *teach-*
er, instructor.

duc, age, discipulos ad mea templa tuos,
  est ubi diversum fama celebrata per orbem
500   littera, cognosci quae sibi quemque iubet.
Qui sibi notus erit, solus sapienter amabit
  atque opus ad vires exiget omne suas.
Cui faciem natura dedit, spectetur ab illa;
  cui color est, umero saepe patente cubet;
505 qui sermone placet, taciturna silentia vitet;
    qui canit arte, canat: qui bibit arte, bibat.
Sed neque declament medio sermone diserti,
  nec sua non sanus scripta poeta legat!'
Sic monuit Phoebus: Phoebo parete monenti;

---

498 **duco, -ere, duxi, ductus,** *lead, conduct.* **discipulus, -i,** m., *pupil.* **templum, -i,** n., *temple.* Here plural for singular.

499 **est:** the subject is **littera. diversus, -a, -um,** *diverse, separate, remote, (whole wide).* **fama, -ae,** f., *renown, fame.* Here ablative. **celebratus, -a, -um,** *known, celebrated, famous.* **orbis, -is,** m., *circle, earth, world.*

500 **littera, -ae,** f., *letter, line, inscription.* Refers here to the maxim 'Know thyself,' inscribed in gold letters on the temple of Apollo at Delphi. **cognosco, -ere, -gnovi, -gnitus,** *become acquainted with, learn, know.*

501 **notus, -a, -um,** *known.* **sapienter,** *wisely, sensibly.*

502 **exigo, -ere, -egi, -actus,** *drive out, demand, complete, weigh, measure, adjust, estimate.*

503 **natura, -ae,** f., *nature.* **ab** (with abl.), *from, by, with regard to, on account of, in consequence of.*

504 **color** = 'good complexion,' 'handsome skin.' **umerus, -i,** m., *shoulder.* **pateo, -ere, -ui,** *lie open, be exposed.* **cubo, -are, -ui, -itus,** *lie down, recline (at the table).* --The modern equivalent would be to appear frequently in a bathing suit.

505 **sermo, -onis,** m., *talk, conversation.* **taciturnus, -a, -um,** *quiet, still, wordless.* **silentium, -ii,** n., *silence.* **vito, -are, -avi, -atus,** *shun, avoid.*

506 **cano, -ere, cecini, cantus,** *sing.* --To drink with 'art' or 'skill' might imply grace (little finger curled?), or else the ability to drink a great deal without ill effect.

507 **declamo, -are, -avi, -atus,** *declaim, speak oratorically.* **sermone:** 505. **diserti, -orum,** m., *the fluent, the eloquent.*

508 **sanus, -a, -um,** *sound, sane.* **non sanus** is litotes again (cf. II, 319 and note). It is a less impolite (litotes!) way of saying 'insane.' Genius has always been considered akin to madness. Anyway Ovid, being a poet, should have known what he was talking about. **scriptum, -i,** n., *writing, composition, work.* **poeta, -ae,** m., *poet.*

509 **moneo, -ere, -ui, -itus,** *warn, advise.* **Phoebus, -i,** m., *Phoebus, Apollo.* **pareo, -ere, -ui** (with dat.), *obey, be obedient to.*

certa dei sacro est huius in ore fides.   510

If Ovid's rules are followed, success is certain, though not al-
ways immediate. A lover will have to endure many things from his
sweetheart; worst of all, a rival.

Ad propiora vocor. Quisquis sapienter amabit,
    vincet et, e nostra quod petet arte, feret.
Credita non semper sulci cum foenore reddunt,
    nec semper dubias adiuvat aura rates;
quod iuvat,exiguum,plus est,quod laedat amantes: 515
    proponant animo multa ferenda suo.
Quot lepores in Atho,quot apes pascuntur in Hybla,
    caerula quot bacas Palladis arbor habet,
litore quot conchae, tot sunt in amore dolores.
    Quae patimur, multo spicula felle madent.   520
Dicta erit isse foras, quam tu fortasse videbis:

---

510   **certus, -a, -um,** *sure, reliable, unerring.* **sacer, -cra,
      -crum,** *holy, sacred.* **fides, -ei,** f., *trust, faith, truth.*

511   **propior, -us** (gen. **-oris**), *nearer.* **propiora:** 'nearer things,'
      'more immediate concerns.' **sapienter,** *wisely, sensibly.*

513   **credita** (acc. plur.): 'the things which have been entrusted
      (to them),' referring to sown seed. **sulcus, -i,** m., *furrow.*
foenus, -oris, n., *interest.*

514   **dubius, -a, -um,** *doubtful, uncertain, veering.* **adiuvo, -are,
      -iuvi, -iutus,** *help, aid, assist.* **ratis, -is,** f., *raft,*
boat, ship, vessel.

515   In full this line would read: Id *(that)* **quod iuvat amantes
      est exiguum; id quod laedat amantes est plus.** **exiguus, -a,
-um,** *small, little, tiny.* **amans, -antis,** m., f., *lover.*

516   **propono, -ere, -posui, -positus,** *set before, propose, imag-
      ine, conceive.*

517   **lepus, -oris,** m., *hare.* **Athos,** m.: a mountain in Macedonia
      which projects into the sea. **apis, -is,** f., *bee.* **pascor,
-i, pastus,** *feed.* **Hybla, -ae,** f.: a mountain in Sicily noted for
its flowers and bees.

518   **caerulus, -a, -um,** *dark blue, dark green.* **baca, -ae,** f.,
      berry, olive. **Pallas, -adis,** f.: another name for *Athene
(Minerva),* to whom the olive tree was sacred. **arbor, -oris,** f.,
tree.

519   **litus, -oris,** n., *seashore, beach.* **concha, -ae,** f., *shell-
      fish, shell.* **tot** (indecl. adj.), *so many.* **dolor, -oris,** m.,
pain, ache, grief, sorrow, trouble.

520   **patior, pati, passus,** *bear, suffer, endure, allow.* **spiculum,
      -i,** n., *dart, arrow.* **fel, fellis,** n., *poison.* **madeo, -ere,
-ui,** *be wet, drip.*

521   The implied subject of **dicta erit** is **puella** or **ea** *(she),* to
      be understood also as the antecedent of **quam.** **foras** (adv.),
out of doors, out. **fortasse,** *perhaps.*

522 isse foras et te falsa videre puta!
   *   *   *   *   *   *   *

    Cum volet, accedes: cum te vitabit, abibis:
530   dedecet ingenuos taedia ferre sui.
    'Effugere hunc non est' quare tibi possit amica
      dicere? Non omni tempore sensus obest.
    Nec maledicta puta nec verbera ferre puellae
      turpe nec ad teneros oscula ferre pedes.
535 Quid moror in parvis? Animus maioribus instat;
      magna canam: toto pectore, vulgus, ades!
    Ardua molimur; sed nulla, nisi ardua, virtus:
      difficilis nostra poscitur arte labor.

---

522 **isse:** supply **eam** as subject. **foras:** 521. **te falsa** ('false things') **videre** = 'that your eyes deceive you.'

529 **accedo, -ere, -cessi, -cessus,** *go to, approach.* **vito, -are, -avi, -atus,** *shun, avoid.* **abeo, -ire, -ivi (-ii), -itus,** *go away, depart.*

530 **dedecet, -ere, -cuit,** *it is unseemly, it is unbecoming.* **ingenuus, -i,** m., *free-born man, man of good breeding, gentleman.* **taedium, -ii,** n., *weariness.* **taedia ferre sui:** 'to bear wearinesses of themselves' = either 'to endure becoming bores' or 'to cause boredom.'

531 **effugio, -ere, -fugi,** *flee from, escape, avoid.* **est:** 'it is possible.' **quare,** *why.* **tibi:** hardly 'to you' here; probably 'your,' 'of you,' or 'for you to overhear.'

532 **sensus, -i,** m., *feeling, sense, good sense, discretion, tact.* **obsum, -esse, -fui,** *hinder, hurt, be a hindrance.* --The understatement (litotes again; cf. II, 319, 508) in this line seems to imply that discretion is sometimes the better part of valor.

533 **maledictum, -i,** n., *abusive word.* **puta . . . turpe:** 'think (it) disgraceful.' **verber, -eris,** n., *blow, slap.*

534 **osculum, -i,** n., *kiss.*

535 **moror, -ari, -atus,** *delay, tarry, linger.* **parvus, -a, -um,** *little, small, insignificant, trifling.* **insto, -are, -stiti** (with dat.), *stand on, approach, press on (to), pursue.*

536 **cano, -ere, cecini, cantus,** *sing, proclaim (in verse).* **totus, -a, -um,** *all, whole.* **vulgus, -i,** n., *people, crowd.* **ades:** imperative singular of **adsum.**

537 **arduus, -a, -um,** *high, lofty, hard, difficult.* **molior, -iri, molitus,** *endeavor, undertake, attempt.* The second **ardua** may be either feminine nominative or neuter accusative (object of **molimur** understood). **virtus, -utis,** f., *manliness, courage, merit, excellence, virtue.*

538 **difficilis, -e,** *hard, difficult.* **posco, -ere, poposci,** *demand, require.* **labor, -oris,** m., *labor, toil, work.*

Rivalem patienter habe: victoria tecum

    stabit; eris magni victor in arte Iovis.   540

Haec tibi non hominem, sed quercus crede Pelasgas

    dicere; nil istis ars mea maius habet.

Innuet illa: feras; scribet: ne tange tabellas;

    unde volet, veniat, quoque libebit, eat.

But after giving such good and important advice, Ovid admits that he himself has often been unable to live up to it. Nevertheless he still insists it is good advice (545-600). People who kiss and tell, or who don't and tell anyway, should be ashamed of themselves (601-640). Treat a woman's faults and blemishes as attractions. Soon you will become accustomed to them and no longer notice them.

Parcite praecipue vitia exprobrare puellis,   641

    utile quae multis dissimulasse fuit.

Nec suus Andromedae color est obiectus ab illo,

---

539   **rivalis, -is,** m., *rival.* **patienter,** *patiently, with patience.* **victoria, -ae,** f., *victory.*

540   **sto, -are, steti, status,** *stand, remain, abide, rest.* **victor, -oris,** m., *conqueror, victor.* **Iuppiter, Iovis,** m., *Jupiter, Jove* (noted for his dexterity in the art of love).

541   **homo, -inis,** m., f., *human being, man.* **quercus, -us,** f., *oak.* **Pelasgus, -a, -um,** *Pelasgian, Grecian.* --The reference is to the talking oaks of Dodona, where was an oracle sacred to Pelasgian Zeus or Jupiter. In this way Ovid emphasizes the importance of that which he is setting forth.

542   **nil** (indecl.), n., *nothing.* **iste, -a, -ud,** *that, this.* **istis** refers to the same things as **haec** (541).

543   With both **innuet** and **scribet** understand **rivali** (539). **innuo, -ere, -ui, -utus,** *nod (to), give a sign.* **feras:** the subjunctive = an imperative. **scribo, -ere, scripsi, scriptus,** *write.* **tango, -ere, tetigi, tactus,** *touch.* **tabella, -ae,** f., *(writing) tablet;* (plur.) *letter.*

544   **unde** (adv.), *from what (which) place, whence.* **quo** (adv.), *to what (which) place, whither, where.* **libet, -ere, libuit (libitum est),** *it pleases, it is pleasing, it is agreeable.*

641   **parco, -ere, peperci, parsus,** *spare, forbear, refrain (from), cease, omit.* **praecipue,** *especially, particularly.* **exprobro, -are, -avi, -atus** (with acc. of the thing and dat. of the person), *upbraid with, reproach with.*

642   **utilis, -e,** *useful, advantageous.* **dissimulo, -are, -avi, -atus,** *pretend not to exist* or *notice; conceal.* **dissimulasse** = **dissimulavisse.**

643   **Andromeda, -ae,** f.: princess of Ethiopia rescued from a sea monster by Perseus, who swooped down from the sky on winged feet. He soon married her. Being Ethiopian (cf. later heroine Aida), Andromeda may well have been dusky. **obicio, -ere, obieci, obiectus,** *throw up against, reproach, make a reproach against.*

mobilis in gemino cui pede pinna fuit.
645   Omnibus Andromache visa est spatiosior aequo:
unus, qui modicam diceret, Hector erat.
Quod male fers,adsuesce: feres bene;multa vetustas
lenit, at incipiens omnia sentit amor.
Dum novus in viridi coalescit cortice ramus,
650   concutiat tenerum quaelibet aura, cadet;
mox etiam ventis spatio durata resistet
firmaque adoptivas arbor habebit opes.
Eximit ipsa dies omnes e corpore mendas,
quodque fuit vitium, desinit esse mora.
655   Ferre novae nares taurorum terga recusant;

---

644 **mobilis, -e,** *movable, swift, fleet.* **geminus, -a, -um,** *twin, two, either, each.*

645 **Andromache, -es,** f.: tall and heroic wife of Hector. **spatiosus, -a, -um,** *ample, large, long, tall.* **aequum, -i,** n., *right; (what is) proper* or *reasonable.*

646 **unus** (stronger than just our 'one'): 'the one person,' 'the only one.' **modicus, -a, -um,** *moderate, moderate-sized.* **Hector, -oris,** m.: Trojan prince and outstanding hero.

647 **adsuesco, -ere, -evi, -etus,** *accustom oneself to, become accustomed to.* **vetustas, -atis,** f., *age, long existence, long duration, passage of time.*

648 **lenio, -ire, -ivi (-ii), -itus,** *soften, alleviate, moderate, render less objectionable, make endurable.* **incipio, -ere, -cepi, -ceptus,** *begin.* **sentio, -ire, -si, -sus,** *feel, perceive, observe, notice.*

649 **viridis, -e,** *green.* **coalesco, -ere, -alui, -alitus,** *grow together, unite, become strong.* **cortex, -icis,** m., *bark.* **ramus, -i,** m., *branch, bough.* --The reference is to grafting.

650 **concutio, -ere, -cussi, -cussus,** *shake.* Note the subjunctive; translate as condition or with 'let.' **tenerum:** understand **ramum. quilibet, quaelibet, quodlibet,** *any . . . at all, any . . whatsoever.* **cado, -ere, cecidi, casus,** *fall.*

651 **mox,** *soon, presently.* **spatium, -ii,** n., *space, interval, lapse of time.* **duro, -are, -avi, -atus,** *harden, strengthen.* **resisto, -ere, -stiti** (with dat.), *withstand, resist.*

652 **firmus, -a, -um,** *strong, firm.* **adoptivus, -a, -um,** *acquired by adoption, adoptive, adopted.* **arbor, -oris,** f., *tree.*

653 **eximo, -ere, -emi, -emptus,** *take away, remove.* **menda, -ae,** f., *fault, defect, blemish.*

654 **mora** may be construed as either nominative or ablative here, according to the meaning used.

655 **naris, -is,** f., *nostril.* **taurus, -i,** m., *bull.* **tergum, -i,** n., *back, skin, hide.* **recuso, -are, -avi, -atus,** *refuse, be unwilling.*

adsiduo domitas tempore fallit odor.
Nominibus mollire licet mala: fusca vocetur,
  nigrior Illyrica cui pice sanguis erit;
si paeta est, Veneri similis, si rava, Minervae;
  sit gracilis, macie quae male viva sua est;   660
dic habilem, quaecumque brevis, quae turgida, plenam
  et lateat vitium proximitate boni.
Nec quotus annus eat nec quo sit nata, require,
  consule, quae rigidus munera censor habet;

---

656 **adsiduus, -a, -um,** *continual.* **adsiduo . . . tempore** = 'by
     the long passage of time.' **domo, -are, -ui, -itus,** *tame, sub-*
due. With **domitas** understand **nares. odor, -oris,** m., *smell, odor,*
stench, stink.

657 **mollio, -ire, -ivi (-ii), -itus,** *soften, lighten, render more*
     pleasant, render less disagreeable. **malum, -i,** n., *a bad*
thing, an evil, a fault. **fuscus, -a, -um,** *dark, swarthy, tawny,*
brunette. **voco, -are, -avi, -atus,** *call.* **vocetur:** supply **puella**
as the subject and as the antecedent of **cui.**

658 **niger, -gra, -grum,** *black, dark.* **Illyricus, -a, -um,** *Illyr-*
     ian. Illyria was a country on the Adriatic corresponding
roughly to Yugoslavia and Albania. **pix, picis,** f., *pitch, tar.*
sanguis, -inis, m., *blood.*

659 **paetus, -a, -um,** *leering, with a cast in the eyes, blinking,*
     winking, blink-eyed. This adjective was often applied to Ve-
nus. As she was a very beautiful woman, in her case it must refer
to some more attractive attribute, such as a flirtatious wink or a
provocative sidewise glance through half-closed eyelids. **similis,**
-e (with gen. or dat.), *like, resembling.* **ravus, -a, -um,** *gray-*
yellow, (yellowish, washed-out), gray, tawny. Ovid is usually con-
sidered to be speaking of hair here; if so, he means a nonde-
script, drab color. But it might refer to eyes, for Minerva was
known as the gray-eyed goddess. **Minerva, -ae,** f.: goddess of wis-
dom, etc.

660 **sit:** 'let her be' = 'she should be called.' **gracilis, -e,**
     slight, slender, slim. **macies, -ei,** f., *leanness, thinness,*
skinniness. **male:** 'badly' = 'scarcely.' **vivus, -a, -um,** *alive.*

661 **habilis, -e,** *light, nimble, cute (?).* **brevis, -e,** *short,*
     little, small. **turgidus, -a, -um,** *swollen, inflated, big and*
fat. **plenus, -a, -um,** *full, stout, corpulent, (pleasingly) plump.*

662 **lateo, -ere, -ui,** *lie hidden, be concealed.* **proximitas,**
     -atis, f., *nearness, proximity, similarity, resemblance.*
bonum, -i, n., *good (thing), what is favorable, what is pleasant,*
good quality. The genitive might here be rendered by 'to' rather
than 'of.'

663 **quotus, -a, -um,** *which (in number),* the 'how manyeth,' how
     many (with sing. as plur.). **quotus annus eat** = 'how old she
is.' **quo . . . consule:** 'under what consul' - a Roman method of
dating years. **nascor, nasci, natus,** *be born.* **requiro, -ere,**
-sivi (-sii), -situs, *seek for, ask, inquire.*

664 **consul, -ulis,** m., *consul.* **rigidus, -a, -um,** *stiff, stern.*

665   praecipue si flore caret, meliusque peractum
            tempus, et albentes iam legit illa comas.

The greater experience and sophistication of older women often make them especially attractive (667-702). Love should be a thing of pleasure, mutual and equal (703-732). Ovid's task is now finished. He graciously acknowledges that he is the master teacher of those who love, and promises the girls that his next work will be for them.

        Finis adest operi: palmam date, grata iuventus,
            sertaque odoratae myrtea ferte comae.
735   Quantus apud Danaos Podalirius arte medendi,
            Aeacides dextra, pectore Nestor erat,
        quantus erat Calchas extis, Telamonius armis,
            Automedon curru, tantus amator ego!
        Me vatem celebrate, viri, mihi dicite laudes,

---

censor, -oris, m., *censor,* a high Roman magistrate whose duties included prying into people's private affairs. He was a combined financial officer, census-taker, and censor of morals.

665 praecipue, *especially, particularly.* flos, floris, m., *flower, bloom of youth.* careo, -ere, -ui, -itus (with abl.), *be without, lack, (be past).* melior, melius, *better.* perago, -ere, -egi, -actus, *carry through, finish.*

666 albens, -entis, *white.*

733 finis, -is, m., *end.* palma, -ae, f., *palm, palm branch, palm wreath* (token of victory). gratus, -a, -um, *pleasing, grateful.* iuventus, -utis, f., *youth* (in collective sense), *young people, youths, young men.*

734 serta, -orum, n., *wreaths, garlands.* odoratus, -a, -um, *sweet-smelling, fragrant.* myrteus, -a, -um, *of myrtle.*

735 quantus, -a, -um, *how great, as great as.* apud (with acc.), *with, among, in the opinion of.* Danai, -orum, m., *the Danai, the Greeks.* Podalirius, -ii, m.: a celebrated physician, present at the siege of Troy. medeor, -eri, *heal, cure.*

736 Aeacides, -ae, m., *descendant of Aeacus, Achilles* (grandson of Aeacus). dextra, -ae, f., *right hand, (strength, combat).* Nestor, -oris, m.: oldest and wisest of the Greeks before Troy.

737 quantus: 735. Calchas, -antis, m.: priest of Apollo, prophet of the Greek army before Troy. exta, -orum, n., *internal organs, vital organs* (of animals, from which prognostications were drawn); *soothsaying, prophecy.* Telamonius, -ii, m., *son of Telamon, Ajax* (mighty Greek warrior in Trojan War).

738 Automedon, -ontis, m.: the charioteer of Achilles (cf. I, 5). currus, -us, m., *chariot.* tantus, -a, -um, *so great.* amator, -oris, m., *lover.*

739 vates, -is, m., f., *prophet, poet.* celebro, -are, -avi, -atus, *attend, honor, praise, celebrate.* laus, laudis, f., *praise.*

cantetur toto nomen in orbe meum!   740
Arma dedi vobis; dederat Vulcanus Achilli:
    vincite muneribus, vicit ut ille, datis.
Sed quicumque meo superarit Amazona ferro,
    inscribat spoliis 'NASO MAGISTER ERAT.'

Ecce, rogant tenerae,sibi dem praecepta,puellae.   745
    Vos eritis chartae proxima cura meae!

---

740   **canto, -are, -avi, -atus,** *sing.* **totus, -a, -um,** *all, whole,*
      entire. **orbis, -is,** m., *circle, world, earth.*

741   **Vulcanus, -i,** m., *Vulcan* (god of fire and metal working, who
      made a famous set of armor for Achilles). **Achilles, -is,** m.:
outstanding Greek hero of Trojan War.

743   **supero, -are, -avi, -atus,** *overcome, subdue, conquer.* **supera-
      rit** = **superaverit. Amazon, -onis** (acc. **-ona**), f., *an (the)*
Amazon (one of a warlike tribe of women; used here of any woman
engaged in the war of love). **ferrum, -i,** n., *iron, weapon, sword.*

744   **inscribo, -ere, -psi, -ptus,** *write on, inscribe on.* **spolium,
      -ii,** n., *booty, plunder, spoil.* **Naso, -onis,** m.: family name
(cognomen) of Publius Ovidius Naso. **magister, -tri,** m., *master,
teacher, instructor.*

745   **ecce,** *lo! see! behold!* **dem:** subjunctive depending on **rogant;**
      the omission of **ut** perhaps emphasizes the idea of wishing.
praeceptum, -i, n., *rule, precept, direction.*

746   **charta, -ae,** f., *paper, writing, poem.* **proximus, -a, -um,**
      next.

Liber Tertius

Ovid now prepares to arm women for the War of Love. He points out that the sinister reputation of that sex is due merely to a few famed sinners. Men, not women, are the usual deceivers. The latter have lacked only instruction, and Venus has ordered Ovid to remedy this deficiency.

> Arma dedi Danais in Amazonas; arma supersunt
>> quae tibi dem et turmae, Penthesilea, tuae.
> Ite in bella pares; vincant, quibus alma Dione
>> faverit et, toto qui volat orbe, puer.
> 5   Non erat armatis aequum concurrere nudas;
>> sic etiam vobis vincere turpe, viri.
> Dixerit e multis aliquis 'Quid virus in angues
>> adicis et rabidae tradis ovile lupae?'

---

1   **Danai, -orum,** m., *the Danai, the Greeks.* **Amazones, -um** (acc. **-as**), f., *the Amazons* (a warlike race of women who fought against the Greeks; here they typify the female sex, as the Greeks do the male). **supersum, -esse, -fui,** *be left, remain, abound.*

2   **quae . . . dem** (relative clause of purpose): 'for me to give.' **turma, -ae,** f., *troop, crowd, throng, band.* **Penthesilea, -ae,** f.: a queen of the Amazons, killed by Achilles while she was fighting for the Trojans against the Greeks. Here vocative.

3   **bellum, -i,** n., *war, battle.* **par, paris,** *equal, on equal terms.* The antecedent of **quibus** is the subject of **vincant.** **almus, -a, -um,** *nourishing, kind, propitious.* **Dione, -es,** f., *Dione; Venus* (as daughter of Dione).

4   **faveo, -ere, favi, fautus** (with dat.), *be favorable to, favor.* **totus, -a, -um,** *all, whole, entire.* **volo, -are, -avi, -atus,** *fly.* **orbis, -is,** m., *circle, world, earth.* **puer**: second subject of **faverit** and antecedent of **qui.** Obviously Cupid.

5   **armatus, -i,** m., *armed man.* **aequus, -a, -um,** *equal, fair, just.* **concurro, -ere, -curri, -cursus** (with dat.), *run together, engage in combat with, fight.* **nudus, -a, -um,** *naked, unclothed, unarmed, unprotected.* Note gender here and supply noun.

7   **dixerit**: 'may say.' **virus, -i,** n., *poison, venom.* **anguis, -is,** m., f., *serpent, snake.*

8   **adicio, -ere, -ieci, -iectus,** *throw to, add to.* **rabidus, -a, -um,** *savage, fierce.* **trado, -ere, -didi, -ditus,** *hand over, deliver, surrender.* **ovile, -is,** n., *sheepfold.* **lupa, -ae,** f., *she-wolf.*

Parcite paucarum diffundere crimen in omnes;
   spectetur meritis quaeque puella suis.   10
Si minor Atrides Helenen, Helenesque sororem
   quo premat Atrides crimine maior habet,
*   *   *   *   *   *   *

est pia Penelope, lustris errante duobus   15
   et totidem lustris bella gerente viro.
*   *   *   *   *   *   *

Saepe viri fallunt, tenerae non saepe puellae;   31
   paucaque, si quaeras, crimina fraudis habent.
Phasida, iam matrem, fallax dimisit Iaso;
   venit in Aesonios altera nupta sinus.

---

9   **parco, -ere, peperci, parsus,** *spare, forbear; refrain from*
    (with Lat. inf. translated as Eng. ger.). **paucus, -a, -um,**
few. **diffundo, -ere, -fudi, -fusus,** *pour out, extend, spread.*

10   **meritum, -i,** n., *merit.*

11   Rearrange 11-12 as follows: **Si minor Atrides crimen habet quo
    Helenen premat, Atridesque maior crimen habet quo Helenes so-
rorem premat** . . . . **minor, minus,** *lesser, smaller, younger.*
Atrides, -ae, m., *son of Atreus;* i.e., *Agamemnon* or *Menelaus* (his
younger brother). **Helene, -es** (acc. **-en**), f., *Helen* (runaway wife
of Menelaus; her sister was Clytemnestra, who was faithless to her
husband Agamemnon and later murdered him). **soror, -oris,** f., *sis-
ter.*

12   **premo, -ere, pressi, pressus,** *press, overwhelm, accuse.*
    Atrides: 11. **maior, maius,** *greater, elder.*

15   **pius, -a, -um,** *dutiful, devout, good, loyal, devoted, faith-
    ful.* **Penelope, -es,** f.: famed for her faithfulness to her
husband Ulysses, though he was away from her fighting in the Tro-
jan War for ten years and it took him another ten years to get
back home. **lustrum, -i,** n., *period of five years.* **erro, -are,
-avi, -atus,** *wander.* **errante** and **gerente** modify **viro** (abl. abs.).
duo, -ae, -o, *two.*

16   **totidem** (indecl. adj.), *just as many, the same number of.*
    lustris: 15. **bellum, -i,** n., *war, battle.* **gero, -ere, ges-
si, gestus,** *bear, wear, wage.*

32   **paucus, -a, -um,** *few.* **fraus, fraudis,** f., *deceit.*

33   **Phasis, -idis** (acc. **-ida**), f., *the Phasian, the Colchian
    girl;* i.e., *Medea* (princess of Colchis who assisted Jason in
stealing the Golden Fleece from her father; having run off with
Jason, she was later repudiated by him for another wife). **mater,
-tris,** f., *mother.* **fallax, -acis,** *deceitful.* **dimitto, -ere, di-
misi, dimissus,** *send away, let go, dismiss, abandon, forsake.*
Iaso, -onis, m., *Jason* (son of Aeson, the king of Thessaly).

34   **Aesonius, -a, -um,** *Aesonian; of Jason, Jason's.* **nupta, -ae,**
    f., *bride, wife.* **sinus:** plur. for sing.; or translate *arms.*

35   Quantum in te, Theseu, volucres Ariadna marinas
          pavit, in ignoto sola relicta loco.
          *   *   *   *   *   *   *

        Et famam pietatis habet, tamen hospes et ensem
40   praebuit et causam mortis, Elissa, tuae.
        Quid vos perdiderit, dicam: nescistis amare;
          defuit ars vobis; arte perennat amor.
        Nunc quoque nescirent, sed me Cytherea docere
          iussit et ante oculos constitit ipsa meos.
45   Tum mihi 'Quid miserae' dixit 'meruere puellae?
          Traditur armatis vulgus inerme viris.
        Illos artifices gemini fecere libelli:
          Haec quoque pars monitis erudienda tuis. . . .'

---

35   **quantus, -a, -um**, *how much, as much as.* **quantum in te:** 'so
       far as you were concerned.' **Theseus, -ei & -eos** (voc. **-eu**):
son of Aegeus, king of Athens; he killed the Minotaur with the
help of Ariadne, eloped with her, and immediately abandoned her on
an island. Cf. I, 527-564. **volucris, -is,** f., *bird.* **Ariadna,
-ae,** f., *Ariadne,* daughter of Minos, the king of Crete. **marinus,
-a, -um,** *of the sea, sea-.*

36   **pasco, -ere, pavi, pastus,** *feed.* **ignotus, -a, -um,** *unknown,
strange.*

39   **fama, -ae,** f., *report, rumor, reputation.* **pietas, -atis,** f.,
       sense of duty, dutiful conduct, loyalty, faithfulness. **hos-
pes, -itis,** m., f., *host, guest, visitor, stranger.* The reference
is to Aeneas. Hospitably entertained and loved by Dido, queen of
Carthage, he deserted her to follow the call of empire. She killed
herself with a sword he had given her. **ensis, -is,** m., *sword.*

40   **praebeo, -ere, -ui, -itus,** *offer, give, furnish, supply.*
       mors, -tis, f., *death.* **Elissa, -ae,** f., *Elissa, Dido.*

41   **vos** refers to all these unlucky-in-love women Ovid has men-
       tioned. **perdo, -ere, -didi, -ditus,** *destroy, ruin.* **nescio,
-ire, -ii (-ivi), -itus,** *not know (how), be ignorant.*

42   **desum, -esse, -fui,** *be absent, be lacking.* **perenno, -are,
-avi, -atus,** *last for many years, endure.*

43   **nescirent:** 41. **Cytherea, -ae,** f., *Cytherea, Venus* (because
       she rose from the sea near the island of Cythera).

44   **consisto, -ere, -stiti,** *stand, halt.*

45   **mereo, -ere, -ui, -itus,** *deserve, merit.*

46   **trado, -ere, -didi, -ditus,** *hand over, deliver, surrender.*
       armatus, -a, -um, *armed.* **vulgus, -i,** n., *mass, crowd, multi-
tude, throng.* **inermis, -e,** *unarmed, without weapons, defenceless.*

47   **artifex, -ficis,** m., *artist, expert;* (adj.) *skillful, clever.*
       geminus, -a, -um, *twin, two.* **libellus, -i,** m., *little book.*
--The 'twin books' are the first two books of the *Ars Amatoria.*

48   **pars** refers to womankind. **monitum, -i,** n., *advice, counsel,
       instruction.* **erudio, -ire, -ivi (-ii), -itus,** *teach, in-*

Never forget that old age is approaching. 'Gather ye rosebuds while ye may' (Ovid happens to mention violets).

Dum facit ingenium,petite hinc praecepta,puellae!   57
*   *   *   *   *   *   *

Venturae memores iam nunc estote senectae:
   sic nullum vobis tempus abibit iners.   60
Dum licet et vernos etiamnum degitis annos,
   ludite: eunt anni more fluentis aquae;
nec quae praeteriit, iterum revocabitur unda,
   nec quae praeteriit, hora redire potest.
Utendum est aetate: cito pede labitur aetas   65
   nec bona tam sequitur, quam bona prima fuit.
Hos ego, qui canent, frutices violaria vidi;
   hac mihi de spina grata corona data est.

---

struct, educate.

57   **ingenium, -ii,** n., *nature, ability, genius.* **dum facit ingenium**: 'while (Venus) inspires me.' **hinc,** *from this place, hence, from this source.* **praeceptum, -i,** n., *rule, precept, direction, instruction.*

59   **venturae**: fut. part. of **venio,** modifying **senectae. memor, -oris,** *mindful of.* **iam nunc,** *already now, even now, at this very time.* **estote**: fut. imperat. plur. of **sum. senecta, -ae,** f., *old age.*

60   **abeo, -ire, -ivi (-ii), -itus,** *go away, depart, vanish, slip away.* **iners, -ertis,** *unskilled, inactive, idle, wasted.*

61   **vernus, -a, -um,** *of spring, spring-; of youth's springtime, youthful.* **etiamnum,** *still, even now.* **dego, -ere, degi,** *pass, spend.*

62   **ludo, -ere, -si, -sus,** *play, have fun, have a good time.* **more** (abl. of **mos**; with gen.), *in the manner of, like.* **fluo, -ere, fluxi, fluxus,** *flow.*

63   **praetereo, -ire, -ii (-ivi), -itus,** *go by, pass by.* **iterum** (adv.), *again, a second time.* **revoco, -are, -avi, -atus,** *call back, recall.*

64   **praeteriit**: 63. **hora, -ae,** f., *hour, time, season.* **redeo, -ire, -ii, -itus,** *come back, return.*

65   **utor, uti, usus** (with abl.), *use, make use of.* **utendum est**: supply **vobis**: 'you must make use of.' **aetas, -atis,** f., *time of life, life, time, age, youth.* **citus, -a, -um,** *quick, swift, rapid.* **labor, labi, lapsus,** *glide along, slip away.*

66   **bonus, -a, -um,** *good, pleasant.* With **bona** supply **aetas. sequor, sequi, secutus,** *follow, succeed, come next.*

67   **hos** modifies **frutices,** which is antecedent of **qui. caneo, -ere, -ui,** *be gray, be white, grow old, wither.* **frutex, -icis,** m., *shrub, bush, plant.* **violarium,-ii,** n., *bed of violets.*

68   **spina, -ae,** f., *thorn, thorny bush.* **gratus, -a, -um,** *pleas-*

*   *   *   *   *   *   *

Quam cito (me miserum!) laxantur corpora rugis,
     et perit, in nitido qui fuit ore, color;
75   quasque fuisse tibi canas a virgine iuras,
     spargentur subito per caput omne comae.
Anguibus exuitur tenui cum pelle vetustas,
     nec faciunt cervos cornua iacta senes.
Nostra sine auxilio fugiunt bona: carpite florem,
80   qui, nisi carptus erit, turpiter ipse cadet.

Cultivation of one's appearance is of primary importance. Natural beauty is a gift of God, and not many girls possess it. But such a lack may be offset by careful grooming. In this sophisticated era there is no place for primitive simplicity.

101   Ordior a cultu: cultis bene Liber ab uvis
          provenit, et culto stat seges alta solo.

---

ing. **corona, -ae,** f., *garland, chaplet, wreath, crown.* --Ovid is simply illustrating how quickly the beautiful is succeeded by the ugly.

73   **cito,** *quickly, soon.* **me:** acc. of exclamation. **laxo, -are, -avi, -atus,** *slacken, relax, make flabby.* **ruga, -ae,** f., *wrinkle.*

74   **nitidus, -a, -um,** *shining, bright, lovely, handsome, beautiful.*

75   Antecedent of **quas** is **comae** (76). **canus, -a, -um,** *white, gray.* **a virgine:** 'from girlhood.' **iuro, -are, -avi, -atus,** *swear.*

76   **spargo, -ere, sparsi, sparsus,** *scatter, sprinkle.* **subito,** *suddenly.* **caput, -itis,** n., *head.*

77   **anguis, -is,** m., f., *serpent, snake.* **exuo, -ere, -ui, -utus,** *strip off, put off, lay aside.* **pellis, -is,** f., *skin.* **vetustas, -atis,** f., *old age, age.*

78   **cervus, -i,** m., *stag, deer.* **cornu, -us,** n., *horn, antler.* **iacio, -ere, ieci, iactus,** *throw, cast, shed.* **senex, senis,** (adj.), *old, aged.*

79   **auxilium, -ii,** n., *help, aid.* **bonum, -i,** n., *good thing, blessing, charm.* **carpo, -ere, -psi, -ptus,** *pick, pluck, enjoy.* **flos, floris,** m., *flower, blossom.*

80   **carptus erit:** 79. **turpiter,** *in an ugly manner, shamefully, basely.* **cado, -ere, cecidi, casus,** *fall, perish, wither.*

101   **ordior, -iri, orsus,** *begin.* **a:** English would say 'with (the subject of).' **cultus, -us,** m., *care or cultivation* (of the land or of one's person), *grooming, style of dress, attire, adornment.* **Liber, -eri,** m., *Liber, Bacchus, wine.* **uva, -ae,** f., *grape.*

102   **provenio, -ire, -veni, -ventus,** *come forth, originate, arise, be produced.* **sto, -are, steti, status,** *stand.* **seges, -etis,** f., *grainfield, crop, grain.* **altus, -a, -um,** *high, deep.* **solum, -i,** n., *ground, soil.*

Forma dei munus. Forma quota quaeque superbit?
Pars vestrum tali munere magna caret.
Cura dabit faciem: facies neglecta peribit,   105
Idaliae similis sit licet illa deae.
Corpora si veteres non sic coluere puellae,
nec veteres cultos sic habuere viros.
Si fuit Andromache tunicas induta valentes,
quid mirum? Duri militis uxor erat.   110
Scilicet Aiaci coniunx ornata venires,
cui tegumen septem terga fuere boum!
Simplicitas rudis ante fuit, nunc aurea Roma est

---

103   **quotus, -a, -um,** *how many;* (with **quisque**) *how few.* **superbio,**
-ire, *be proud, take pride in.*

104   **vestrum:** gen. plur. of **tu.** **talis, -e,** *such (a).* **careo,**
-ere, -ui, -itus (with abl.), *be without, lack.*

105   **facies,** in this passage contrasted with **forma** ('natural beau-
ty'), is perhaps best translated 'attractive appearance.'
neglectus, -a, -um, *neglected.*

106   **Idalius, -a, -um,** *Idalian, Cyprian, of Idalium* (a city in
Cyprus sacred to Venus). **similis, -e** (with gen. or dat.),
like, resembling.

107   **vetus, -eris,** *old, of old, of former times, earlier, ancient.*

108   **veteres** (supply **puellae**): 107.   **habuere = habuerunt.**

109   **Andromache, -es,** f.: wife of Hector, the Trojan hero. Ovid
never seemed to care much for her type; cf. II, 645.   **tunica,**
-ae, f., *tunic, (under)garment.* **induo, -ere, indui, indutus** (also
in the passive forms), *put on, dress (oneself) in, wear.* **valens,**
-entis, *strong, stout, thick, coarse.*

110   **mirus, -a, -um,** *wonderful, surprising, strange.* **miles,**
-itis, m., f., *soldier.* **uxor, -oris,** f., *wife.*

111   This line is sarcastic, meaning that if you were the wife of
an uncouth warrior like Ajax, you would *not* feel very much
like dressing up for him. **scilicet,** *of course, no doubt.* **Aiax,**
Aiacis, m., *Ajax,* beefy Greek hero who fought against the Trojans.
coniunx, -iugis, m., f., *spouse, wife.* **ornatus, -a, -um,** *adorned,
ornamented, bedecked, elaborately dressed.* **venires:** potential
subjunctive: 'you would have come.'

112   **cui . . . fuere:** 'to whom were' = 'who had.' **tegumen, teg-
minis,** n., *covering, shield.* Here in apposition with **terga.**
Ajax had a shield made of seven bulls' hides. **septem** (indecl.
adj.), *seven.* **tergum, -i,** n., *back, hide.* **bos, bovis** (gen. plur.
boum; dat. plur. **bubus**), m., f., *ox, bull, cow.*

113   **simplicitas, -atis,** f., *simplicity, plainness.* **rudis, -e,**
rough, rude, unpolished, uncultivated. **aureus, -a, -um,**
golden. **Roma, -ae,** f., *Rome.*

et domiti magnas possidet orbis opes.
115 Adspice quae nunc sunt Capitolia, quaeque fuerunt:
alterius dices illa fuisse Iovis.
Curia consilio nunc est dignissima tanto:
de stipula, Tatio regna tenente, fuit.
Quae nunc sub Phoebo ducibusque Palatia fulgent,
120 quid nisi araturis pascua bubus erant?
Prisca iuvent alios, ego me nunc denique natum
gratulor: haec aetas moribus apta meis,
non quia nunc terrae lentum subducitur aurum,
lectaque diverso litore concha venit,

---

114 **domo**, **-are**, **-ui**, **-itus**, *tame, subdue, conquer.* **possideo**, **-ere**, **-sedi**, **-sessus**, *possess, be master of.* **orbis**, **-is**, m., *circle, world.*

115 **adspicio**, **-ere**, **-spexi**, **-spectus**, *look at, see, consider.* **Capitolium**, **-ii**, n. (sing. and plur.), *the Capitol, the temple of Jupiter* (at Rome).

116 **illa** = 'that earlier Capitol.' **fuisse** (with gen.) = 'belonged to.' **Iuppiter**, **Iovis**, m., *Jupiter, Jove*, chief of the Roman gods.

117 **curia**, **-ae**, f., *the senate house.* **consilium**, **-ii**, n., *counsel, plan, advice, council, deliberative body.* **dignus**, **-a**, **-um** (with abl.), *worthy of.* **tantus**, **-a**, **-um**, *so great.*

118 **de . . . fuit**: 'it was (made) of.' **stipula**, **-ae**, f., *straw.* **Tatius**, **-ii**, m.: one of the earliest kings of Rome, having reigned jointly with Romulus. **regnum**, **-i**, n., *kingship, royal power, rule.* Here plural for singular.

119 Rearrange these two lines as follows: **Quid erant Palatia, quae nunc sub Phoebo ducibusque fulgent, nisi pascua araturis bubus?** Reference is to the fact that a temple of Apollo and the residences of the chief men of Rome, including Augustus, were on the Palatine hill. **Phoebus**, **-i**, m., *Phoebus, Apollo.* **dux**, **ducis**, m., f., *leader, chief (man).* **Palatium**, **-ii**, n. (sing. and plur.), *the Palatine hill* (first of the seven to be settled). **fulgeo**, **-ere**, **fulsi**, *flash, gleam, glisten, shine.*

120 **aro**, **-are**, **-avi**, **-atus**, *plow.* **pascuum**, **-i**, n., *pasture.* **bos**, **bovis** (dat. plur. **bubus**), m., f., *ox, bull, cow.*

121 **prisca**, **-orum**, n., *ancient things, olden times.* **alius**, **-a**, **-ud**, *another; other.* **denique**, *finally, at last.* **nascor**, **nasci**, **natus**, *be born.* **nunc denique natum**: 'that I was not born until now.'

122 **gratulor**, **-ari**, **-atus**, *congratulate.* **aetas**, **-atis**, f., *life, age, period of time, time.*

123 **terra**, **-ae**, f., *earth, ground.* Terrae is a dative of separation. **lentus**, **-a**, **-um**, *pliant, flexible, tough, tenacious, obstinate.* **subduco**, **-ere**, **-duxi**, **-ductus**, *draw from under, take away from, remove from.* **aurum**, **-i**, n., *gold.*

124 **lectus**, **-a**, **-um**, *gathered, collected; choice.* **diversus**, **-a**,

nec quia decrescunt effosso marmore montes,   125
    nec quia caeruleae mole fugantur aquae,
sed quia cultus adest,nec nostros mansit in annos
    rusticitas priscis illa superstes avis.

But avoid the excessive use of jewelry and ornamentation. Such
display may drive away the very men whose attentions are sought.
Careful grooming is much more important. The hair should be taste-
fully arranged; there is a variety of styles. German hair dyes and
bought hair are sometimes used.

Vos quoque non caris aures onerate lapillis
    quos legit in viridi decolor Indus aqua,   130
nec prodite graves insuto vestibus auro.
    Per quas nos petitis, saepe fugatis, opes.
Munditiis capimur: non sint sine lege capilli;
    admotae formam dantque negantque manus.

   -um, *different, remote, far distant.* **litus, -oris**, n.,
shore, beach. **concha, -ae,** f., *shellfish, shell, pearl.*

125 **decresco, -ere, -crevi, -cretus,** *grow less, decrease, dimin-*
    ish. **effodio, -ere, effodi, effossus,** *dig out.* **marmor,**
-oris, m., *marble.* **mons, montis,** m., *mountain.*

126 **caeruleus, -a, -um,** *dark blue, dark green, azure.* **moles,**
    -is, f., *mass, dike, pier, mole, breakwater.* **fugo, -are,**
-avi, -atus, *put to flight.* --The Romans were adept at protecting
or extending their beaches with moles.

127 **cultus, -us,** m., *cultivation, culture, elegance, civiliza-*
    tion, refinement, good grooming, ornament. **maneo, -ere, man-**
si, mansus, *remain, continue.*

128 **rusticitas, -atis,** f., *rustic behavior, rusticity; rudeness,*
    boorishness. **priscus, -a, -um,** *old, ancient, primitive.* **su-**
perstes, -itis (with dat.), *surviving.* **avus, -i,** m., *grandfather,*
forefather, ancestor. --It is refreshing to find a poet who does
not yearn for the good old days when life was simple.

129 **carus, -a, -um,** *dear, precious, costly.* **auris, -is,** f., *ear.*
    onero, -are, -avi, -atus, *load, burden.* **lapillus, -i,** m.,
pebble, precious stone, gem, jewel.

130 **viridis, -e,** *green.* **decolor, -oris,** *discolored, dusky, dark.*
    Indus, -i, m., *Indian.*

131 **prodeo, -ire, -ii, -itus,** *go or come forth, appear.* **gravis,**
    -e, *heavy, loaded, important.* **insuo, -ere, -ui, -utus** (with
dat.), *sew on, embroider on.* **vestis, -is,** f., *clothing, clothes.*
aurum, -i, n., *gold.*

132 The following is awkward Latin but easier to translate: Saepe
    nos fugatis per opes per quas nos petitis. **fugo, -are, -avi,**
-atus, *put to flight, drive away.*

133 **munditia, -ae,** f., *cleanliness, neatness, elegance, careful*
    grooming. **lex, legis,** f., *law, order.*

134 **admoveo, -ere, admovi, admotus,** *move to, apply.* **nego, -are,**
    -avi, -atus, *say no, deny, refuse.*

135   Nec genus ornatus unum est: quod quamque decebit
    eligat, et speculum consulat ante suum.
    Longa probat facies capitis discrimina puri:
    sic erat ornatis Laodamia comis.
    Exiguum summa nodum sibi fronte relinqui,
140   ut pateant aures, ora rotunda volunt.
    Alterius crines umero iactentur utroque:
    talis es adsumpta, Phoebe canore, lyra.
    Altera succinctae religetur more Dianae,
    ut solet, attonitas cum petit illa feras.
145   Huic decet inflatos laxe iacuisse capillos,

---

135   **genus, -eris,** n., *race, kind, sort.* **ornatus, -us,** m., *preparation, arrangement, adornment.* **quod quamque decebit eligat:** 'let each girl choose that which will be becoming to her.'

136   **eligo, -ere, elegi, electus,** *choose.* **speculum, -i,** n., *looking glass, mirror.* **consulo, -ere, -lui, -ltus,** *consult, take counsel, reflect, deliberate.*

137   The line means that smoothly-combed hair parted in the middle goes well with an oval (long) face. **probo, -are, -avi, -atus,** *test, approve, recommend, (harmonize with).* **caput, -itis,** n., *head.* **discrimen, -inis,** n., *division, parting* or *part of the hair.* **purus, -a, -um,** *pure, unadorned.*

138   **ornatus, -a, -um,** *adorned, arranged.* **Laodamia, -ae,** f.: an ancient heroine who followed her husband Protesilaus in death. Cf. II, 356. **comis:** ablative of description.

139   **exiguus, -a, -um,** *small, little, tiny.* **nodus, -i,** m., *knot.* **sibi:** 'for themselves,' but may be omitted in translation. **frons, frontis,** f., *forehead, brow, front.*

140   **pateo, -ere, -ui,** *lie open, be exposed.* **auris, -is,** f., *ear.* **rotundus, -a, -um,** *round.*

141   **crinis, -is,** m., *hair, lock, tress.* **umerus, -i,** m., *shoulder.* **iacto, -are, -avi, -atus,** *throw, toss.* **uterque, utraque, utrumque,** *each, either, both.*

142   **talis, -e,** *such, of such appearance.* **adsumo, -ere, -mpsi, -mptus,** *take up.* **Phoebus, -i,** m., *Phoebus, Apollo.* He was the god of music, among other things, and was often depicted with flowing locks - the prototype of the familiar long-haired musician. **canorus, -a, -um,** *melodious, tuneful.* **lyra, -ae,** f., *lyre.*

143   **succinctus, -a, -um,** *girt-up, with skirt tucked up.* **religo, -are, -avi, -atus,** *bind back* or *up, fasten up.* **more** (abl. of **mos;** with gen.), *in the manner of, like.* **Diana, -ae,** f.: goddess of the moon, the hunt, etc.

144   **attonitus, -a, -um,** *stunned, terrified, frightened.* **fera, -ae,** f., *wild animal, wild beast.*

145   **inflatus, -a, -um,** *inflated, wind-blown, hanging loose, floating.* **laxe,** *loosely.*

illa sit adstrictis impedienda comis;
hanc placet ornari testudine Cyllenea,
  sustineat similes fluctibus illa sinus.
Sed neque ramosa numerabis in ilice glandes,
  nec quot apes Hyblae, nec quot in Alpe ferae,   150
nec mihi tot positus numero comprendere fas est:
  adicit ornatus proxima quaeque dies.
Et neglecta decet multas coma: saepe iacere
  hesternam credas; illa repexa modo est.
Ars casu similis: sic capta vidit ut urbe   155
  Alcides Iolen, 'Hanc ego' dixit 'amo!'

---

146 **adstringo, -ere, -inxi, -ictus,** *draw together, bind tight.*
     impedio, -ire, -ivi, -itus, *hinder, encircle.*

147 **orno, -are, -avi, -atus,** *equip, ornament, adorn, embellish.*
     testudo, -inis, f., *tortoise, tortoise shell, lyre.* Here re-
ferring to some form of hairdress resembling a lyre, which instru-
ment was first made out of a tortoise shell by Mercury (born on
Mt. Cyllene). **Cylleneus, -a, -um,** *Cyllenian, Mercury's.*

148 **sustineo, -ere, -tinui, -tentus,** *hold up, support, bear.* **si-
     milis, -e** (with gen. or dat.), *like, resembling, similar to.*
fluctus, -us, m., *wave, billow.*

149 **ramosus, -a, -um,** *branchy, branching.* **numero, -are, -avi,
     -atus,** *count.* **ilex, ilicis,** f., *holm oak* (an evergreen oak).
glans, glandis, f., *acorn.*

150 Supply **sint** in each clause of this line. **apis, -is,** f., *bee.*
     Hybla, -ae, f.: a mountain in Sicily noted for its bees.
Alpis, -is, f., *the Alps.* **fera, -ae,** f., *wild animal, wild beast.*

151 **tot** (indecl. adj.), *so many.* **positus, -us,** m., *position,
     arrangement.* **numero comprendere:** 'to comprehend in number' =
'to enumerate.' **fas** (indecl.), n., *right, possible.*

152 **adicio, -ere, -ieci, -iectus,** *add, contribute.* **ornatus, -us,**
     m., *preparation, arrangement, style.* **proximus, -a, -um,**
nearest, next, successive.

153 **neglectus, -a, -um,** *neglected, (tousled).*

154 **hesternus, -a, -um,** *yesterday's, from* or *since yesterday.*
     Here modifies **comam** understood. **repecto, -ere, --, -xus,** *comb
(again).*

155 **casus, -us** (dat. sometimes **-u**), m., *chance, accident.* **simi-
     lis, -e** (with gen. or dat.), *like, similar to.* **urbs, urbis,**
f., *city.*

156 **Alcides, -ae,** m., *descendant of Alceus; Hercules* (his grand-
     son). **Iole, -es** (acc. **-en**), f.: princess of Oechalia, whom
Hercules carried off after taking the city and killing her father.
In the confusion it was natural that Iole's hair should become
tousled. Ovid feels that such accidental but charming disarray
might well be imitated by art.

Talem te Bacchus, satyris clamantibus 'euhoe!',
    sustulit in currus, Gnosi relicta, suos.

    O quantum indulget vestro natura decori,
160   quarum sunt multis damna pianda modis!
Nos male detegimur, raptique aetate capilli,
    ut Borea frondes excutiente, cadunt.
Femina canitiem Germanis inficit herbis,
    et melior vero quaeritur arte color;
165   femina procedit densissima crinibus emptis
    proque suis alios efficit aere suos.

---

157 **talis, -e,** *such, of such appearance.* **Bacchus, -i,** m.: god of
    wine. Finding Ariadne deserted by Theseus on an island, he
married her. See I, 527-564. **talem te Bacchus . . . sustulit:**
'that's the way you looked when Bacchus lifted you.' **satyrus, -i,**
m., *satyr* (a goat-footed forest deity, associated with Bacchus).
euhoe: a shout of joy at the festivals of Bacchus.

158 **tollo, -ere, sustuli, sublatus,** *lift, lift up, raise.* **cur-
    rus, -us,** m., *chariot.* **Gnosis, -idis** (voc. **-si**), f., *Cnos-
sian girl, Cretan girl;* i.e., *Ariadne* (daughter of Minos, king of
Crete).

159 **o,** *O, oh!* **quantum indulget . . . natura =** 'how kind nature
    is to.' **quantum,** *how much, to how great an extent, as much
as.* **indulgeo, -ere, indulsi, indultus,** *be kind, be indulgent,
grant, allow.* **vester, -tra, -trum,** *your* (plur.). **natura, -ae,**
f., *nature.* **decor, -oris,** m., *beauty, charms.*

160 **quarum:** 'you whose.' The antecedent is in **vestro. damnum,
    -i,** n., *harm, loss, misfortune, defect.* **pio, -are, -avi,
-atus,** *appease, make good, cover up.*

161 **nos =** 'we men.' **detego, -ere, -texi, -tectus,** *uncover, lay
    bare, unroof.* A vivid way of saying 'grow bald'! **aetas,
-atis,** f., *life, age, time.*

162 **ut:** with the abl. abs., 'as when'; or with **frondes,** 'as.'
    Boreas, -ae, m., *Boreas; the north wind.* **frons, frondis,** f.,
leafy branch, foliage, leaf. **excutio, -ere, -cussi, -cussus,**
shake off. **cado, -ere, cecidi, casus,** *fall.*

163 **canities, -ei,** f., *grayness, gray hair.* **Germanus, -a, -um,**
    German. **inficio, -ere, -feci, -fectus,** *dye.* **herba, -ae,** f.,
herb, plant, grass.

164 **melior, melius,** *better.* **verus, -a, -um,** *true, real, genuine.*
    With **vero** understand **colore.**

165 **procedo, -ere, -cessi, -cessus,** *go forth, proceed, walk
    along, appear.* **densus, -a, -um,** *thick, dense, thickly cov-
ered with.* **crinis, -is,** m., *hair, lock, tress.* **emo, -ere, emi,
emptus,** *buy.*

166 **pro** (with abl.), *before, for, in place of, instead of.* With
    suis and **alios** understand **crinibus** and **crines. alius, -a,
-ud,** *another, other.* **alios . . . suos:** 'another person's hair her
own.' **efficio, -ere, -feci, -fectus,** *bring about, cause, make,
render.* **aes, aeris,** n., *copper, bronze, money.*

Nec rubor est emisse; palam venire videmus
Herculis ante oculos virgineumque chorum.

Clothes may be colorful and attractive without being expensive.
Among the hues suggested are sky-blue, gold, aquamarine, saffron,
myrtle-green, amethyst, white rose, crane-gray, chestnut-brown,
almond, wax-yellow. Dark clothes are best suited to blondes;
white is becoming to brunettes.

Quid de veste loquar? Nec nunc segmenta requiro,
　　nec quae de Tyrio murice, lana, rubes.　　　　　170
Cum tot prodierint pretio leviore colores,
　　quis furor est census corpore ferre suos!
Aëris ecce color, tum cum sine nubibus aër,
　　nec tepidus pluvias concitat Auster aquas.
　*　　　*　　　*　　　*　　　*　　　*　　　*

Quot nova terra parit flores, cum vere tepenti　　185
　　vitis agit gemmas pigraque fugit hiems,

167　**rubor, -oris,** m., *blush, shame, disgrace, cause of embarrass-
　　ment.* **emisse:** 165. **palam,** *openly, publicly, undisguisedly.*
veneo, -ire, -ivi (-ii), -itus, *be sold.* Subject of **venire** is **cri-
nes** understood.

168　**Hercules, -is,** m.: the strong man of mythology. **virgineus,
　　-a, -um,** *of the maiden(s), maidenly.* **chorus, -i,** m., *chorus,
band, troop.* --Hercules and the Muses **(virgines)** had a temple in
the vicinity of the wig-makers' shops.

169　**vestis, -is,** f., *clothes, clothing, attire.* **segmentum, -i,**
　　n., *strip, strip of brocade, flounce, purfle* (!). **requiro,
-ere, requisivi (-ii), requisitus,** *ask (for), demand, need, want,
require.*

170　**nec (te requiro), lana** (voc.), **quae** . . . . **de:** 'from' =
　　'with.' **Tyrius, -a, -um,** *Tyrian.* Tyre was celebrated for its
purple dye. **murex, -icis,** m., *purple (dye).* **lana, -ae,** f., *wool.*
rubeo, -ere, *be red, turn red, blush.*

171　**tot** (indecl. adj.), *so many.* **prodeo, -ire, -ii, -itus,** *come
　　forth, appear.* **pretium, -ii,** n., *value, price.*

172　**furor, -oris,** m., *madness, folly.* **census, -us,** m., *census,
　　wealth, riches, property, fortune.* **suos:** 'one's.'

173　**aër, aëris,** m., *air, sky.* **ecce,** *lo! see! behold!* **nubes,
　　-is,** f., *cloud.*

174　**tepidus, -a, -um,** *(luke)warm, tepid.* **pluvius, -a, -um,**
　　rainy, rain-. **concito, -are, -avi, -atus,** *stir up, arouse.*
Auster, -tri, m., *the south wind.*

185　**terra, -ae,** f., *earth, land, ground, soil.* **pario, -ere, pe-
　　peri, paritus & partus,** *bring forth, produce.* **flos, -oris,**
m., *flower, blossom.* **ver, veris,** n., *spring, springtime.* **tepens,
-entis,** *(luke)warm, tepid.*

186　**vitis, -is,** f., *vine.* **gemma, -ae,** f., *bud, gem.* **piger,
　　-gra, -grum,** *slow, dull, lazy, sluggish.* **hiems, hiemis,** f.,
winter.

> lana tot aut plures sucos bibit. Elige certos,
>   nam non conveniens omnibus omnis erit.
> Pulla decent niveas: Briseida pulla decebant;
> 190   cum rapta est, pulla tum quoque veste fuit.
> Alba decent fuscas: albis, Cephei, placebas;
>   sic tibi vestitae pressa Seriphos erat.

Civilized girls should need no instructions as to care of the
person. Make-up is important; Ovid has already written a little
book on the subject. But the paint and powder should not be ap-
plied publicly. Your boy friends should see only the finished
product. There are a lot of things it is better for a man not to
know.

> Quam paene admonui, ne trux caper iret in alas,
>   neve forent duris aspera crura pilis!
> 195   Sed non Caucasea doceo de rupe puellas,

---

187 **lana, -ae,** f., *wool.* **tot** (indecl. adj.), *so many.* **sucus,**
    -i, m., *juice, dye.* **eligo, -ere, elegi, electus,** *choose, se-*
lect. **certus, -a, -um,** *certain, particular, specified, definite.*

188 **conveniens, -entis,** *harmonious, appropriate, suitable, be-*
    coming. With **omnibus** supply **feminis,** with **omnis** supply **sucus**
or **color.**

189 **pullum, -i,** n., *dark* or *dark gray garment.* **niveus, -a, -um,**
    snowy, snow-white, fair-complexioned, blonde. Here supply
puellas. **Briseis, -idos** (acc. **-ida**), f.: a captive girl in the
Trojan War, over whom Achilles and Agamemnon quarreled.

190 **pullus, -a, -um,** *dark gray, dark.* **vestis, -is,** f., *clothes,*
    clothing, garment.

191 **album, -i,** n., *whiteness, white garment.* **fuscus, -a, -um,**
    dark, tawny, brunette. **Cepheis, -idis** (voc. **-i**), f., *daugh-*
ter of Cepheus; i.e., *Andromeda* (princess of Ethiopia and decided-
ly brunette).

192 **tibi:** dat of agent. **vestio, -ire, -ivi (-ii), -itus,** *dress,*
    clothe. **premo, -ere, pressi, pressus,** *press, oppress, walk,*
upon, tread. **Seriphos, -i,** f.: a small, rocky island in the Aege-
an Sea; here, where his mother was living, Perseus first brought
his bride Andromeda after having rescued her from the sea monster.

193 **paene,** *nearly, almost.* **admoneo, -ere, -ui, -itus,** *advise,*
    warn. **trux, trucis,** *rough, rude, unpleasant.* **caper, capri,**
m., *goat,* used by the Romans to symbolize the same thing as B. O.
(body odor) in twentieth-century advertising. **ala, -ae,** f., *wing,*
armpit.

194 **-ve,** *or, and.* **forent = essent.** **asper, -era, -erum,** *rough,*
    prickly, bristling. **crus, -uris,** n., *leg.* **pilus, -i,** m.,
hair.

195 **Caucaseus, -a, -um,** *Caucasian, of Caucasus* (a wild mountain
    range in southern Russia). **rupes, -is,** f., *rock, cliff.*

quaeque bibant undas, Myse Caice, tuas.
Quid si praecipiam ne fuscet inertia dentes,
　　oraque suscepta mane laventur aqua?
Scitis et inducta candorem quaerere creta;
　　sanguine quae vero non rubet, arte rubet.　　　　200
＊　　　＊　　　＊　　　＊　　　＊　　　＊　　　＊

Est mihi, quo dixi vestrae medicamina formae,　　　205
　　parvus, sed cura grande, libellus, opus:
hinc quoque praesidium laesae petitote figurae;
　　non est pro vestris ars mea rebus iners.
Non tamen expositas mensa deprendat amator
　　pyxidas: ars faciem dissimulata iuvat.　　　　　210
＊　　　＊　　　＊　　　＊　　　＊　　　＊　　　＊

196　**quaeque:** 'and those who.' **Mysus, -a, -um,** *Mysian.* **Caicus,
-i,** m.: a river in Mysia, a country in northwest Asia Minor.

197　**Quid:** 'What?' 'What would you say?' **praecipio, -ere, -cepi,
-ceptus,** *advise, warn, instruct, bid.* **fusco, -are, -avi,
-atus,** *make dark, darken, blacken, stain.* **inertia, -ae,** f., *idle-
ness, laziness.* **dens, dentis,** m., *tooth.*

198　**suscipio, -ere, -cepi, -ceptus,** *take up.* **suscepta** modifies
　　aqua. mane, *in the morning.* **lavo, -are, lavi, lautus**
(**lotus, lavatus**), *wash.*

199　**scio, -ire, -ivi, -itus,** *know (how).* **induco, -ere, -duxi,
-ductus,** *bring in, put on, spread over, overlay, apply.* **can-
dor, -oris,** m., *whiteness, fair complexion, beauty.* **creta, -ae,**
f., *chalk, powder.*

200　**sanguis, -inis,** m., *blood.* **quae:** 'she who.' **verus, -a, -um,**
true, real, actual. **rubeo, -ere,** *be red (pink), blush.*

205　This couplet is easier to understand thus: **Est mihi** (dat. of
　　poss.) **libellus parvus, sed (est) opus grande cura** (abl. of
specif.), **quo . . . . vester, -tra, -trum,** *your* (plur.). **medica-
men, -inis,** n., *drug, paint, cosmetic.*

206　**parvus, -a, -um,** *small, little.* **grandis, -e,** *large, great.*
　　libellus, -i, m., *little book, treatise.* --A portion of
Ovid's 'little book,' *Medicamina Faciei Femineae,* still survives.

207　**hinc,** *from this (place), hence, from this source.* **praesi-
dium, -ii,** n., *protection, help, aid.* **petitote:** fut. imper-
ative plur. **figura, -ae,** f., *form, figure, appearance, beauty.*

208　**pro** (with abl.), *before, for, in behalf of.* **vestris:** 205.
　　res, rei, f., *thing, affair, interest.* **iners, -ertis,** *inac-
tive, idle, sluggish, inert.*

209　**expono, -ere, -posui, -positus,** *set out, expose.* **mensa, -ae,**
　　f., *table.* **deprendo, -ere, -di, -sus,** *catch, detect, dis-
cover.* **amator, -oris,** m., *lover, sweetheart, boy friend.*

210　**pyxis, -idis,** f., *(cosmetic) box.* **dissimulo, -are, -avi,
-atus,** *disguise, hide, conceal.*

215   Nec coram mixtas cervae sumpsisse medullas
          nec coram dentes defricuisse probem;
       ista dabunt formam, sed erunt deformia visu,
          multaque, dum fiunt, turpia, facta placent.
       Quae nunc nomen habent operosi signa Myronis,
220   pondus iners quondam duraque massa fuit;
       anulus ut fiat, primo conliditur aurum;
          quas geritis vestes, sordida lana fuit;
       cum fieret, lapis asper erat: nunc, nobile signum,
          nuda Venus madidas exprimit imbre comas.
225   Tu quoque dum coleris, nos te dormire putemus:

215 **coram,** *in the presence of* (a person), *openly, publicly.* **mis-**
     ceo, -ere, miscui, mixtus, *mix, blend.* **cerva, -ae,** f., *hind,*
deer. **sumo, -ere, sumpsi, sumptus,** *take, use, apply.* The infini-
tive here (as in 216) is the object of **probem,** and might be trans-
lated as a gerund: 'your applying' (i.e., as a beauty aid). **me-**
dulla, -ae, f., *marrow.*

216 **coram:** 215. **dens, dentis,** m., *tooth.* **defrico, -are, -cui,**
     -c(a)tus, *rub, scour, brush.* **probo, -are, -avi, -atus,**
approve (of), recommend.

217 **iste, ista, istud,** *that, that of yours, such.* **deformis, -e,**
     ugly, disgusting. **visu:** supine of **video:** 'to see.'

219 **signa** is the antecedent of **quae** and the subject of **fuit;**
     fuit, which has been attracted into the singular by its pred-
icate noun **pondus,** must be translated as a plural, 'were.' **opero-**
sus, -a, -um, *painstaking, busy, industrious.* **signum, -i,** n.,
sign, statue. **Myron, -onis,** m.: a celebrated Greek sculptor; he
produced the bronze Discus Thrower, copies of which abound.

220 **pondus, -eris,** n., *weight, mass.* **iners, -ertis,** *idle, slug-*
     gish, inert. **quondam,** *at one time, once, formerly.* **massa,**
-ae, f., *lump, mass.*

221 **anulus, -i,** m., *ring.* **primo** (adv.), *at first, first.* **con-**
     lido, -ere, -lisi, -lisus, *strike together, beat.* **aurum, -i,**
n., *gold.*

222 **gero, -ere, gessi, gestus,** *bear, wear.* **vestis, -is,** f.,
     clothes, garment. **sordidus, -a, -um,** *dirty, filthy.* **lana,**
-ae, f., *wool.* **fuit** actually should be plural, with **vestes** used
as subject.

223 **lapis, -idis,** m., *stone.* **asper, -era, -erum,** *rough.* **nobi-**
     lis, -e, *famous, renowned, noble, excellent.* **signum:** 219.

224 **nudus, -a, -um,** *naked, nude.* **Venus:** reference is to a famous
     statue by Praxiteles of Venus rising from the sea. **madidus,**
-a, -um, *wet, drenched, dripping, soaked.* **exprimo, -ere, -pressi,**
-pressus, *squeeze out, wring.* **imber, -bris,** m., *rain, water.*
Translate after **madidas.**

225 **coleris:** 'you are putting on your make-up.' **dormio, -ire,**

aptius a summa conspiciere manu.
Cur mihi nota tuo causa est candoris in ore?
Claude forem thalami! Quid rude prodis opus?
Multa viros nescire decet; pars maxima rerum
    offendat, si non interiora tegas.   230
Aurea quae splendent ornato signa theatro,
    inspice, quam tenuis brattea ligna tegat;
sed neque ad illa licet populo, nisi facta, venire,
    nec nisi summotis forma paranda viris.
At non pectendos coram praebere capillos,   235
    ut iaceant fusi per tua terga, veto.

     *   *   *   *   *   *   *

    -ivi (-ii), -itus, *sleep.*

226 **apte,** *fitly, suitably, properly, rightly.* **a summa . . . manu:** 'after the final touch.' **conspicio, -ere, -spexi, -spectus,** *look at, observe, see.* **conspiciere** is 2nd person singular future passive.

227 **cur,** *why.* **notus, -a, -um,** *known.* **candor, -oris,** m., *whiteness, fair complexion, beauty.*

228 **claudo, -ere, -si, -sus,** *shut, close.* **foris, -is,** f., *door.* **thalamus, -i,** m., *chamber, bedroom.* **rudis, -e,** *rough, unfinished.* **prodo, -ere, -didi, -ditus,** *bring forth, reveal, expose.*

229 **nescio, -ire, -ivi (-ii), -itus,** *not to know, be ignorant of.* **maximus, -a, -um,** *greatest.* **res, rei,** f., *thing.*

230 **offendo, -ere, -di, -sus,** *be offensive, offend, shock.* **interior, -ius,** *inner, more secret, more intimate.* **tego, -ere, -xi, -ctus,** *cover, hide, conceal.*

231 **aureus, -a, -um,** *of gold, golden, gilded.* **splendeo, -ere,** *shine, gleam, glisten.* **ornatus, -a, -um,** *decorated, handsome, ornate.* **signum, -i,** n., *sign, statue.* **signa** is the antecedent of **quae.** **theatrum, -i,** n., *theater.*

232 **inspicio, -ere, -spexi, -spectus,** *look at, inspect, consider, examine.* **brattea, -ae,** f., *gold leaf.* **lignum, -i,** n., *wood.* **tegat:** 230.

233 **populus, -i,** m., *people.* **facta:** 'when finished.'

234 **nisi:** with **summotis viris. summoveo, -ere, -movi, -motus,** *send away, remove.* **paro, -are, -avi, -atus,** *get ready, prepare, work on.* With **paranda** supply **est.**

235 **non:** with **veto. pecto, -ere, pexi, pexus,** *comb.* **coram,** *in the presence of (men), openly, publicly.* **praebeo, -ere, -ui, -itus,** *offer, furnish, cause, allow, permit.* Supply **te** as subject of **praebere.**

236 **fusus, -a, -um,** *spread out, flowing.* **tergum, -i,** n., *back.* **veto, -are, -ui, -itus,** *forbid.*

Quae male crinita est, custodem in limine ponat
    orneturve Bonae semper in aede Deae.
245 Dictus eram subito cuidam venisse puellae:
    turbida perversas induit illa comas.
Hostibus eveniat tam foedi causa pudoris,
    inque nurus Parthas dedecus illud eat!
Turpe pecus mutilum, turpis sine gramine campus
250   et sine fronde frutex et sine crine caput.

Beautiful girls do not have much need of Ovid's advice.   But
perfect beauty is rare. Learn to conceal your defects.

Non mihi venistis, Semele Ledeve, docendae,
    perve fretum falso Sidoni vecta bove,

---

243 **quae:** antecedent is subject of **ponat. crinitus, -a, -um,**
    provided with hair. **custos, -odis,** m., f., *guard, attendant.*
limen, -inis, n., *threshold, doorway, entrance.*

244 **orno, -are, -avi, -atus,** *get ready, ornament, adorn, deck,*
    embellish. **-ve,** *or.* **Bona Dea, Bonae Deae,** f., *the Good God-*
dess (worshipped by the women of Rome as the goddess of fertility
and chastity; no man was permitted to enter her temple). **aedis** or
aedes, -is, f., *temple.*

245 **dictus eram subito . . . venisse:** 'I had been said suddenly
    to have come' = 'my unexpected arrival was announced.' **subi-**
to, *suddenly, unexpectedly.* **quidam, quaedam, quoddam,** *a certain.*

246 **turbidus, -a, -um,** *confused, disordered.* **perversus, -a, -um,**
    turned the wrong way, askew, backward. **induo, -ere, -ui,**
-utus, *put on.*

247 **hostis, -is,** m., f., *(public) enemy.* **evenio, -ire, eveni,**
    eventus (with dat.), *happen to, befall.* **foedus, -a, -um,**
foul, horrible, disgraceful, shameful. **pudor, -oris,** m., *shame ,*
disgrace, embarrassment.

248 **nurus, -us,** f., *daughter-in-law, young woman.* **Parthus, -a,**
    -um, *Parthian.* The Parthians, inhabiting a part of what is
now Iran, were the current enemies of Rome. **dedecus, -oris,** n.,
disgrace, infamy, shame.

249 **pecus, pecoris,** n., *cattle, herd, flock, animal, bull.* **muti-**
    lus, -a, -um, *mutilated, without horns.* **gramen, -inis,** n.,
grass. **campus, -i,** m., *plain, field.*

250 **frons, -dis,** f., *foliage, leaves.* **frutex, -icis,** m., *shrub,*
    bush. **crinis, -is,** m., *hair.* **caput, -itis,** n., *head.*

251 **Semele, -es,** f.: sweetheart of Jupiter, and by him mother of
    Bacchus. **Lede, -es,** f., *Leda* (wooed by Jupiter in the guise
of a swan; mother of Castor and Pollux, Helen and Clytemnestra).

252 **-ve,** *or.* **fretum, -i,** n., *strait, sea.* **falsus, -a, -um,** *pre-*
    tended, feigned, deceitful, false. **Sidonis, -idis** (voc. **-i**),
f., *Sidonian (Phoenician) girl;* i.e., *Europa* (carried off to Crete
by Jupiter, who took the form of a bull). **veho, -ere, -xi, -ctus,**
bear, carry, convey. **bos, bovis,** m., f., *ox, bull, cow.*

aut Helene, quam non stulte, Menelae, reposcis,
    tu quoque non stulte, Troice raptor, habes.
Turba docenda venit,pulchrae turpesque puellae,   255
    pluraque sunt semper deteriora bonis.
Formosae non artis opem praeceptaque quaerunt:
    est illis sua dos, forma sine arte potens;
cum mare compositum est, securus navita cessat;
    cum tumet, auxiliis adsidet ille suis.   260
Rara tamen mendo facies caret: occule mendas,
    quaque potes, vitium corporis abde tui.
Si brevis es, sedeas, ne stans videare sedere,

---

253 **Helene, -es,** f., *Helen* (wife of Menelaus; she eloped to Troy
    with Paris. She and the other girls mentioned belong to that
alluring and desirable group who, Ovid feels, need none of his ad-
vice). **stulte,** *foolishly.* **Menelaus, -i,** m.: king of Sparta,
brother of Agamemnon, and a leader of the Greeks against Troy.
reposco, -ere, *demand back.*

254 **stulte:** 253. **Troicus, -a, -um,** *Trojan.* **raptor, -oris,** m.,
    robber, abductor, ravisher.

255 **turba, -ae,** f., *crowd, throng, multitude.* **pulcher, -chra,**
    -chrum, *beautiful.* **puellae:** nom. plur. in app. with **turba.**

256 **deterior, -ius,** *worse.* **deteriora** (as noun, subject of **sunt**):
    'worse things,' 'the worse,' 'the inferior.' **bonum, -i,** n.,
good thing, the good.

257 **praeceptum, -i,** n., *rule, instruction, precept.*

258 **illis:** dat of possession. **dos, dotis,** f., *dowry, gift.*
    potens, -entis, *powerful, mighty, potent.*

259 The meaning of this couplet is that beautiful girls, like a
    sailor on a calm sea, can take things easy; the plain, like a
sailor on a stormy sea, had better get busy. **mare, -is,** n., *sea.*
compositus, -a, -um, *well arranged, quiet, peaceful, calm.* **secu-
rus, -a, -um,** *free from care, unconcerned, untroubled.* **navita,
-ae,** m., *sailor, mariner.* **cesso, -are, -avi, -atus,** *loiter, be at
leisure, do nothing, rest.*

260 **tumeo, -ere,** *swell, be violent, become violent.* **auxilium,
    -ii,** n., *help, aid, assistance.* **adsideo, -ere, adsedi, ad-
sessus** (with dat.), *sit down to, attend to, apply oneself to.*

261 **rarus, -a, -um,** *rare, few, here and there; seldom, rarely,*
    mendum, -i, n., *fault, blemish, defect.* **careo, -ere, -ui,
-itus** (with abl.), *be without, lack.* **occulo, -ere, -cului, -cul-
tus,** *cover (up), hide, conceal.* **menda, -ae,** f., *fault, defect,
blemish.*

262 **abdo, -ere, abdidi, abditus,** *hide, conceal, keep secret.*

263 **brevis, -e,** *short, small, low.* **sedeas** and **iaceas:** subjunc-
    tives used for imperatives. **sto, -are, steti, status,** *stand.*
videare = videaris.

inque tuo iaceas quantulacumque toro;
265   hic quoque, ne possit fieri mensura cubantis,
          iniecta lateant fac tibi veste pedes.
        Quae nimium gracilis, pleno velamina filo
          sumat, et ex umeris laxus amictus eat;
        pallida purpureis tangat sua corpora virgis;
270   nigrior, ad Pharii confuge piscis opem.
        Pes malus in nivea semper celetur aluta,
          arida nec vinclis crura resolve suis.
        Conveniunt tenues scapulis analectrides altis;

---

264   **quantuluscumque, quantulacumque, quantulumcumque,** *however*
      small, however insignificant. **torus, -i,** m., *couch, sofa,*
bed.

265   **mensura, -ae,** f., *measurement, measure, estimation of size.*
      cubo, -are, -avi, -atus, *lie down, recline.* **cubantis** modifies
tui ('of you') understood.

266   **inicio, -ere, inieci, iniectus,** *throw over.* **lateo, -ere,**
      -ui, *be* or *lie hidden* or *concealed.* **vestis, -is,** f.,
clothes, garment, robe.

267   The antecedent of **quae** is the subject of **sumat. nimium,** *too,*
      too much. **gracilis, -e,** *thin, slender, lean.* **plenus, -a,**
-um, *full, bulky, thick.* **velamen, -inis,** n., *covering, clothing,*
robe, garment, dress. **filum, -i,** n., *thread, fibre, texture.*

268   **sumo, -ere, sumpsi, sumptus,** *take, put on.* **umerus, -i,** m.,
      shoulder. **laxus, -a, -um,** *loose(ly), spacious.* **amictus,**
-us, m., *clothing, outer garment, mantle, cloak.* **eat** = '. . .
hang.'

269   **pallidus, -a, -um,** *pale.* With **pallida** supply **puella. purpu-**
      reus, -a, -um, *purple, red, crimson.* **tango, -ere, tetigi,**
tactus, *touch, smear, color, dye.* **virga, -ae,** f., *branch, streak,*
stripe. --It seems uncertain whether Ovid is recommending the use
of rouge on the face or crimson-striped clothes.

270   **niger, -gra, -grum,** *black, dark, swarthy.* **nigrior** is vocative.
      Pharius, -a, -um, *Pharian, Egyptian.* **confugio, -ere, -fugi,**
flee to, have recourse to, resort to. **piscis, -is,** m., *fish.* The
'Egyptian fish' is the crocodile, whose intestines and dung were a
cosmetic ingredient, used to whiten the complexion and remove
freckles.

271   **malus, -a, -um,** *bad, ill-shaped, ugly.* **niveus, -a, -um,**
      snowy, snow-white. **celo, -are, -avi, -atus,** *hide, conceal,*
cover. **aluta, -ae,** f., *soft leather, shoe.*

272   **aridus, -a, -um,** *dry, skinny, lean.* **nec** should come at the
      beginning of the line. **vinclum, -i,** n., *fastening, bond,*
tie, lacing (of a shoe or sandal). **crus, cruris,** n., *leg, shin,*
foot, ankle. **resolvo, -ere, -solvi, -solutus,** *untie, loosen,*
release.

273   **convenio, -ire, -veni, -ventus** (with dat.), *be suitable to,*
      be appropriate to. **scapulae, -arum,** f., *shoulder blades.*
analectris, -idis, f., *shoulder pad.* **altus, -a, -um,** *high, deep.*

angustum circa fascia pectus eat.

Exiguo signet gestu, quodcumque loquetur,   275
cui digiti pingues et scaber unguis erit.

Cui gravis oris odor, numquam ieiuna loquatur
et semper spatio distet ab ore viri.

Si niger aut ingens aut non erit ordine natus
dens tibi, ridendo maxima damna feres.   280

Learn how to laugh and cry fetchingly and how to talk baby talk.
In walking avoid both a sinuously swaying glide and a rustic lope.
Something in between is desired.

Quis credat? Discunt etiam ridere puellae,
quaeritur atque illis hac quoque parte decor!

Sint modici rictus parvaeque utrimque lacunae,
et summos dentes ima labella tegant;

---

274   **angustus, -a, -um,** *narrow, small.* Instead of **angustum,** anoth-
er reading here is **inflatum,** *swollen, swelling, plump.* **cir-
ca** (with acc.), *around.* **fascia, -ae,** f., *band, brassiere.*

275   **exiguus, -a, -um,** *scanty, small, inconspicuous, infrequent.*
signo, -are, -avi, -atus, *mark, emphasize.* **gestus, -us,** m.,
motion, gesture.

276   **cui:** dat. of possession; its antecedent is the subject of
signet. pinguis, -e, *fat, thick.* **scaber, -bra, -brum,**
rough. **unguis, -is,** m., *nail, fingernail.*

277   **cui:** dat. of possession; its antecedent is the subject of
loquatur. gravis, -e, *heavy, strong, unpleasant, offensive.*
odor, -oris, m., *smell, odor.* **numquam,** *never.* **ieiunus, -a, -um,**
(while) hungry.

278   **spatium, -ii,** n., *space, distance, interval.* **disto, -are,**
stand apart, stand away, be distant, be separated.

279   **niger, -gra, -grum,** *black, dingy.* **ingens, -entis,** *huge,
very large.* **ordo, -inis,** m., *regular row, line, order.*
nascor, nasci, natus, *be born, grow.*

280   **dens, dentis,** m., *tooth.* **rideo, -ere, -si, -sus,** *laugh.*
maximus, -a, -um, *greatest.* **damnum, -i,** n., *harm, damage,
loss, penalty.*

281   **Quis credat?** 'Who would believe it?' - a Latin way of saying
'Believe it or not.' **ridere:** 280.

282   **atque:** translate at the beginning of the line. **illis:** dat.
of agent. **hac . . . parte:** 'in this respect.' **decor, -oris,**
m., *elegance, grace, beauty, charm.*

283   **modicus, -a, -um,** *moderate, moderate-sized.* **rictus, -us,** m.,
opening of the mouth. **parvus, -a, -um,** *small.* **utrimque,** *on
both sides, on either side.* **lacuna, -ae,** f., *hollow, dimple.*

284   **dentes:** 280. **imus, -a, -um,** *lowest part of, bottom* or *edge
of.* **labellum, -i,** n., *(little) lip.* **tego, -ere, -xi, -ctus,**
cover, hide, conceal. --That is, the gums should not be exposed.

285   nec sua perpetuo contendant ilia risu,
          sed leve nescio quid femineumque sonet.
       Est, quae perverso distorqueat ora cachinno;
          cum risu quassa est altera, flere putes.
       Illa sonat raucum quiddam atque inamabile: ridet,
290   ut rudit a scabra turpis asella mola.
       Quo non ars penetrat? Discunt lacrimare decenter,
          quoque volunt plorant tempore, quoque modo.
       Quid, cum legitima fraudatur littera voce,
          blaesaque fit iusso lingua coacta sono?

---

285   **perpetuus, -a, -um,** *continual, constant, perpetual.* **con-**
          tendo, -ere, -di, -tus, *stretch, strain, strive, hasten.*
       ilia, -ium, n., *flanks, sides.* **risus, -us,** m., *laughing, laugh,*
       laughter.

286   **nescio quid:** 'I know not what,' i.e., 'something or other,'
          referring here to a kind of laugh and used as subject of **so-**
       net. femineus, -a, -um, *womanly, feminine.* **sono, -are, -avi,**
       -atus, *sound, sound forth, utter a sound.*

287   **Est, quae:** 'There is the girl who,' introducing a relative
          clause of characteristic; hence the subjunctive. **pervers-**
       us, -a, -um, *askew, distorted, disfiguring, hideous.* **distorqueo,**
       -ere, -torsi, -tortus, *twist, distort.* **cachinnus, -i,** m., *loud*
       laugh, coarse laughter, cackle, guffaw.

288   **risu:** 285. **quatio, -ere, --, quassus,** *shake.* **flere:** supply
          eam *(her, she)* as subject.

289   **illa:** 'that one,' 'another.' **sonat:** 286. **raucus, -a, -um,**
          hoarse, harsh, grating, raucous. **quidam, quaedam, quiddam,** *a*
       certain one, a certain thing; here, with **sonat,** *a certain sound,*
       i.e., *some kind of blast.* **inamabilis, -e,** *unlovely.* **rideo, -ere,**
       risi, risus, *laugh.*

290   **rudo, -ere, -ivi, -itus,** *roar, bellow, bray.* Note the parono-
          masia (pun): **ridet** and **rudet.** **scaber, -bra, -brum,** *rough.*
       asella, -ae, f., *(little) she-ass.* **mola, -ae,** f., *millstone.*

291   **quo** (adv.), *whither, where, to what place.* **penetro, -are,**
          -avi, -atus, *penetrate.* **lacrimo, -are, -avi, -atus,** *shed*
       tears, weep, cry. **decenter,** *becomingly, properly, fetchingly.*

292   **quo** modifies **tempore. ploro, -are, -avi, -atus,** *wail, la-*
          ment, weep aloud.

293   **Quid:** 'What?' 'What's to be said?' **legitimus, -a, -um,** *law-*
          ful, right, proper. Modifies **voce** here. **fraudo, -are, -avi,**
       -atus (with abl.), *cheat out of, deprive of.* **littera, -ae,** f.,
       letter. **vox, vocis,** f., *voice, sound.*

294   **blaesus, -a, -um,** *lisping.* **lingua, -ae,** f., *tongue.* **coac-**
          tus, -a, -um, *forced, constrained, unnatural.* **sonus, -i,** m.,
       sound, pronunciation. --A rough line: literally, 'and the tongue,
       constrained with ordered sound, becomes lisping'; quite freely,
       'and girls lisp on purpose.'

In vitio decor est, quaedam male reddere verba: 295
   discunt posse minus, quam potuere, loqui.
Omnibus his, quoniam prosunt, impendite curam.
   Discite femineo corpora ferre gradu:
est et in incessu pars non contempta decoris;
   allicit ignotos ille fugatque viros.   300
Haec movet arte latus, tunicisque fluentibus auras
   accipit, extensos fertque superba pedes;
illa velut coniunx Umbri rubicunda mariti
   ambulat, ingentes varica fertque gradus.
Sed sit,ut in multis,modus hic quoque:rusticus alter
   motus, concesso mollior alter erit.   306

---

295 **decor, -oris,** m., *elegance, grace, charm.* **quidam, quaedam, quoddam,** *certain.* **reddere** = 'to pronounce.'

296 **posse minus, quam potuere, loqui:** 'to be less able to speak than they were able.' **minus** (adv.), *less.* **potuere** = **potuerunt.**

297 **quoniam,** *since, because.* **prosum, prodesse, profui,** *be of use, be advantageous, help.* **impendo, -ere, -di, -sus,** *expend, devote.* **impendite curam:** 'give attention.'

298 **femineus, -a, -um,** *womanly, feminine.* **gradus, -us,** m., *step.*

299 **incessus, -us,** m., *walking, gait.* **contemptus, -a, -um,** *contemptible, (to be) despised, (to be) valued lightly.* **decoris:** 295.

300 **allicio, -ere, allexi, allectus,** *attract.* **ignotus, -a, -um,** *unknown, strange.* **ille** = **incessus.** **fugo, -are, -avi, -atus,** *put to flight, drive away.*

301 **haec:** supply **puella,** as with **illa** (303). **latus, -eris,** n., *side, flank.* **tunica, -ae,** f., *tunic, undergarment, garment, robe.* **fluo, -ere, -xi, -xus,** *flow.*

302 **extensus, -a, -um,** *stretched out, extended.* **extensos** modifies **pedes.** An artificial pacing in the manner of a showroom mannequin or of a chorus girl on parade is indicated. **superbus, -a, -um,** *haughty, proud;* or translate as adverb.

303 **velut,** *just as, like.* **coniunx, -iugis,** m., f., *spouse, wife.* **Umber, -bra, -brum,** *Umbrian* (Umbria was a region of Italy noted for its rusticity; part of the backwoods, as it were). **rubicundus, -a, -um,** *red, ruddy, red-faced.* **maritus, -i,** m., *husband.*

304 **ambulo, -are, -avi, -atus,** *walk, stride.* **ingens, -entis,** *huge, enormous, great.* **varicus, -a, -um,** *with feet spread apart, straddling.* **fert:** 'takes.' **-que** properly should have been attached to **ingentes.** **gradus, -us,** m., *step, pace, stride.*

305 **rusticus, -a, -um,** *rustic, awkward.*

306 **motus, -us,** m., *motion, movement.* **concesso** (neut. abl. of the participle of **concedo,** *allow*): 'than is allowed,' 'than is proper.' **mollior** = 'more affected,' 'more mincing.'

Pars umeri tamen ima tui, pars summa lacerti
   nuda sit, a laeva conspicienda manu.
Hoc vos praecipue, niveae, decet; hoc ubi vidi,
310   oscula ferre umero, qua patet usque, libet.

Girls should know how to sing. Many have found that their voices
make up for their faces. They should be familiar with musical in-
struments as well. Dancing is an invaluable accomplishment. And
though it is a little thing, girls should know how to play various
games, such as dice, chess, and tit-tat-toe (311-366). But much
harder than playing a game skillfully is keeping oneself and one's
temper under control. Their nature prevents girls from engaging in
the more vigorous male sports.

Mille facesse iocos! Turpe est nescire puellam
   ludere: ludendo saepe paratur amor.
Sed minimus labor est sapienter iactibus uti:
370   maius opus mores composuisse suos.
Tum sumus incauti studioque aperimur in ipso,
   nudaque per lusus pectora nostra patent:

---

307 **umerus, -i**, m., *shoulder.* **imus, -a, -um,** *lowest.* **lacertus,
-i,** m., *(upper) arm.*

308 **nudus, -a, -um,** *naked, bare, uncovered.* **laevus, -a, -um,**
left. **conspicio, -ere, -spexi, -spectus,** *look at, gaze upon,
see, observe.* **manu** here = 'side.' --The left side is specified
here probably because in reclining at a Roman dinner, the person
on your couch who could see you best would be ahead of you on your
left, and your left shoulder would be particularly exposed to his
gaze.

309 **praecipue,** *especially, particularly.* **niveus, -a, -um,** *snow-
white, fair-skinned, blonde.* Here vocative.

310 **osculum, -i,** n., *kiss.* **umero:** 307. **qua . . . usque,** *wherev-
er.* **pateo, -ere, -ui,** *lie open, be exposed.* **libet, -ere,
libuit (libitum est),** *it is pleasing, it pleases.*

367 **mille** (indecl. adj.), *a thousand.* **facesso, -ere, facessi,
facessitus,** *do eagerly, perform, engage in, create, invent.*
iocus, -i, m., *joke, pastime, sport, game.* **nescio, -ire, -ivi
(-ii), -itus,** *not know (how), be ignorant.*

368 **ludo, -ere, -si, -sus,** *play, play games, sport.* **paro, -are,
-avi, -atus,** *prepare, get ready, acquire, (arouse).*

369 **minimus, -a, -um,** *smallest, least, slightest.* **labor, -oris,**
m., *labor, task, trouble.* **sapienter,** *sensibly, wisely, clev-
erly.* **iactus, -us,** m., *throw.* **utor, uti, usus** (with abl.), *use.*

370 **compono, -ere, -posui, -positus,** *put together, arrange, set
in order, bring under control.* **suos:** 'one's.'

371 **incautus, -a, -um,** *incautious, off one's guard.* **studium,
-ii,** n., *zeal, eagerness, preoccupation.* **aperio, -ire, ape-
rui, apertus,** *unveil, disclose, reveal; (pass.) reveal one's true
nature.*

372 **nudus, -a, -um,** *naked, bare, exposed.* **lusus, -us,** m., *play,
sport, game.* **pateo, -ere, -ui,** *lie open, be exposed.*

ira subit, deforme malum, lucrique cupido
    iurgiaque et rixae sollicitusque dolor;
crimina dicuntur, resonat clamoribus aether,   375
    invocat iratos et sibi quisque deos.
Nulla fides tabulae! Quae non per vota petuntur!
    Et lacrimis vidi saepe madere genas.
Iuppiter a vobis tam turpia crimina pellat,
    in quibus est ulli cura placere viro.   380
Hos ignava iocos tribuit natura puellis;
    materia ludunt uberiore viri.
Sunt illis celeresque pilae iaculumque trochique
    armaque et in gyros ire coactus equus.

---

373   **ira, -ae,** f., *anger, rage*. **subeo, -ire, -ii, -itus,** *come up, follow, spring up, steal in.* **deformis, -e,** *unsightly, ugly, disgusting, disgraceful.* **malum, -i,** n., *an evil.* **lucrum, -i,** n., *gain.* **cupido, -inis,** f., *desire, passion, lust, greed.*

374   **iurgium, -ii,** n., *quarrel, dispute, violent argument.* **rixa, -ae,** f., *quarrel, brawl, dispute.* **sollicitus, -a, -um,** *anxious, troubled, distressing.* **dolor, -oris,** m., *distress, grief, anguish, vexation.*

375   **resono, -are, -avi, -atus,** *resound, reëcho.* **clamor, -oris,** m., *shout, cry.* **aether, -eris,** m., *air, heaven.*

376   **invoco, -are, -avi, -atus,** *call upon, invoke.* **iratus, -a, -um,** *enraged, angry.* **et:** translate at beginning of line.

377   **fides, -ei,** f., *trust, faith.* **tabula, -ae,** f., *board, game board, gaming table.* **nulla fides tabulae:** '(there is) no faith to a gaming table,' i.e., 'you can't trust the gaming tables.' **votum, -i,** n., *vow, wish.* **quae non per vota petuntur:** 'what (gains) are not sought by means of vows (to the gods)!'

378   **madeo, -ere, -ui,** *be wet, flow.* **gena, -ae,** f., *cheek.*

379   **Iuppiter, Iovis,** m., *Jupiter, Jove,* chief of the gods. **pello, -ere, pepuli, pulsus,** *drive away, avert, turn away.*

380   **ullus, -a, -um** (dat. **ulli**), *any.*

381   **ignavus, -a, -um,** *inactive, lazy, sluggish, (weaker).* **iocus, -i,** m., *joke, pastime, sport, game.* **tribuo, -ere, tribui, tributus,** *assign, allot, give, grant.* **natura, -ae,** f., *nature, innate quality, natural disposition.*

382   **materia, -ae,** f., *stuff, matter, material.* **ludo, -ere, -si, -sus,** *play, play games, sport.* **uber, uberis,** *rich, abundant, plentiful.*

383   **illis:** dat. of possession. **celer, celeris, celere,** *quick, swift, lively.* **pila, -ae,** f., *ball.* **iaculum, -i,** n., *dart, javelin.* **trochus, -i,** m., *hoop.*

384   **gyrus, -i,** m., *circle, circular course, ring.* **cogo, -ere, coegi, coactus,** *collect, force, compel.* --Referred to here is probably the *ludus Troiae,* a kind of sham battle on horseback or elaborate cavalry drill.

Get about; there is no use having a pretty face if no one ever sees it. Have your hook always dangling; a fish (poor?) will bite when you least expect it (385-432). But beware of men who are too smooth.

Sed vitate viros cultum formamque professos,
    quique suas ponunt in statione comas.
435 Quae vobis dicunt, dixerunt mille puellis;
    errat et in nulla sede moratur amor.

*   *   *   *   *   *   *

Nec coma vos fallat liquido nitidissima nardo
    nec brevis in rugas lingula pressa suas,
445 nec toga decipiat filo tenuissima, nec si
    anulus in digitis alter et alter erit.
Forsitan ex horum numero cultissimus ille
    fur sit et uratur vestis amore tuae.
'Redde meum!' clamant spoliatae saepe puellae,

---

433 **vito, -are, -avi, -atus,** *shun, avoid.* **cultus, -us,** m., *culture, cultivation, elegance, polish, refinement.* **profiteor, -eri, -fessus,** *profess, display, make a show of.*

434 **statio, -onis,** f., *post, (proper) place, position.*

435 **mille** (indecl. adj.), *a thousand.*

436 **erro, -are, -avi, -atus,** *wander, stray about, rove.* **sedes, -is,** f., *seat, abode, fixed place.* **moror, -ari, -atus,** *delay, tarry, remain, linger.*

443 **liquidus, -a, -um,** *liquid, flowing, clear.* **nitidus, -a, -um,** *shining, sleek.* **nardum, -i,** n., *nard* (a fragrant oil); *hair oil, brilliantine (?).*

444 **brevis, -e,** *short, little.* **ruga, -ae,** f., *crease, fold, wrinkle.* **lingula, -ae,** f., *little tongue; tongue of a belt, tongue of a shoe, shoe strap.* **premo, -ere, pressi, pressus,** *press.* --The meaning of this line is not quite clear. It evidently refers to a fastidious way of dressing, perhaps with the tongue of the belt adjusted so as to cause the toga to fall in certain precise creases; or with the end of the shoe strap tucked carefully out of sight.

445 **toga, -ae,** f., *toga* (the loose, rather formal outer garment of a Roman male). **decipio, -ere, -cepi, -ceptus,** *ensnare, beguile, deceive, mislead.* **filum, -i,** n., *thread, texture.*

446 **anulus, -i,** m., *ring.* **alter et alter:** *one and another.*

447 **forsitan,** *perhaps.* **numerus, -i,** m., *number.* **cultus, -a, -um,** *cultivated, adorned, polished, elegant;* (superl.) *most elegant,* etc.; *best dressed.*

448 **fur, furis,** m., f., *thief, rogue, knave.* **uro, -ere, ussi, ustus,** *burn, consume.* **vestis, -is,** f., *clothing, clothes.*

449 **spolio, -are, -avi, -atus,** *rob of clothing, rob, plunder.*

'Redde meum!' toto voce boante foro.   450

Don't answer a letter too soon ('mora semper amantes incitat'), but don't delay too long. By your answers make him hope and fear at the same time, but gradually encourage his hopes. If you are afraid of someone else's reading your letters, always let 'he' be 'she' in them (467-498). These things repel men: an angry woman (try looking at yourself in a mirror!), a haughty woman, a gloomy woman.

Si licet a parvis animum ad maiora referre
     plenaque curvato pandere vela sinu,   500
pertinet ad faciem rabidos compescere mores:
     candida pax homines, trux decet ira feras.
Ora tument ira, nigrescunt sanguine venae,
     lumina Gorgoneo saevius igne micant.
'I procul hinc,' dixit 'non es mihi, tibia, tanti,'   505
     ut vidit vultus Pallas in amne suos.

---

450   **totus, -a, -um,** *the whole, all the, the entire.* **boo, -are,** *cry aloud, cry, roar, ring, resound.* **forum, -i,** n., *forum, market place, public square, downtown district.*

499   **parvus, -a, -um,** *little, small;* (neut. plur.) *small things, small matters.*

500   **plenus, -a, -um,** *full, filled, swelling.* **curvatus, -a, -um,** *curved, rounded.* **pando, -ere, pandi, passus & pansus,** *spread out, extend, unfurl.* **velum, -i,** n., *sail.*

501   **pertineo, -ere, -ui,** (with **ad**) *pertain to, relate to, concern, be the concern of.* **rabidus, -a, -um,** *savage, fierce, passionate, angry.* **compesco, -ere, -pescui,** *hold in check, repress, restrain.*

502   **candidus, -a, -um,** *white, bright, fair, beautiful.* **pax, pacis,** f., *peace.* **homo, -inis,** m., f., *human being, man.* **trux, trucis,** *wild, harsh, savage, fierce.* **ira, -ae,** f., *anger, wrath, rage, passion.* **fera, -ae,** f., *wild animal, wild beast.*

503   **tumeo, -ere,** *swell, become swollen.* **ira:** 502. **nigresco, -ere, nigrui,** *become black, grow dark.* **sanguis, -inis,** m., *blood.* **vena, -ae,** f., *vein.*

504   **lumen, -inis,** n., *light, eye.* **Gorgoneus, -a, -um,** *Gorgonian, of the Gorgon* (referring to the Gorgon Medusa, whose glance changed all who looked at her into stone). **saevius** (compar. adv.), *more fiercely, more savagely.* **mico, -are, -avi, -atus,** *flash, gleam, shine.*

505   Ovid speaks of the time Athene picked up the first flute and tried playing on it. She was enjoying her music until she happened to glimpse the distortions of her tootling face reflected in some water. Being a woman, she was horrified and flung the flute away. **procul,** *far, far away.* **hinc,** *hence, from here.* **tibia, -ae,** f., *flute.* **tantus, -a, -um,** *so great, so much.* **tanti** is genitive of value: 'worth so much,' 'worth all that.'

506   **vultus, -us,** m. (sing. and plur.), *countenance, features, face.* **Pallas, -adis & -ados,** f., *Pallas, Athene, Minerva,* goddess of wisdom, the arts, etc. **amnis, -is,** m., *river.*

Vos quoque si media speculum spectetis in ira,
    cognoscat faciem vix satis ulla suam.
Nec minus in vultu damnosa superbia vestro:
510   comibus est oculis alliciendus amor.
Odimus immodicos (experto credite!) fastus:
    saepe tacens odii semina vultus habet.
Spectantem specta, ridenti mollia ride;
    innuet: acceptas tu quoque redde notas.
515 Sic ubi prolusit, rudibus puer ille relictis
    spicula de pharetra promit acuta sua.
Odimus et maestas: Tecmessam diligat Aiax!

---

507 **speculum, -i,** n., *mirror, looking glass.* **ira:** 502.

508 **cognosco, -ere, -gnovi, -gnitus,** *learn, recognize.* **vix,**
    hardly, scarcely. **satis,** *sufficient, sufficiently.* Perhaps
should be omitted in translation here. **ullus, -a, -um,** *any, any-
one.*

509 **minus** (adv.), *less.* Modifies **damnosa. vultu:** 506. **damnosus,**
    -a, -um, *injurious, hurtful, damaging.* **superbia, -ae,** f.,
haughtiness, pride, arrogance. **vester, -tra, -trum,** *your* (plur.).

510 **comis, -e,** *courteous, kind, friendly.* **allicio, -ere, -lexi,**
    -lectus, *attract, entice.*

511 **odi, odisse,** *hate, dislike.* **immodicus, -a, -um,** *excessive,
    immoderate.* **expertus, -i,** m. (from partic. of **experior,** *try,
test*), *one who knows by experience; expert.* **fastus, -us,** m.
(sing. & plur.), *scornful disdain, haughtiness, arrogance, pride.*

512 **tacens, -entis,** *silent.* **odium, -ii,** n., *hatred, ill will,
    dislike.* **semen, -inis,** n., *seed.* **vultus:** 506.

513 **spectantem:** 'one (him, the man) who looks at you'; translate
    ridenti similarly. **rideo, -ere, risi, risus,** *laugh, smile;
smile at* (with dat.). **mollia** (cognate acc.): 'softly,' 'pleas-
antly.'

514 **innuo, -ere, -ui, -utus,** *nod.* The future here indicates a
    supposition rather than a certainty. **acceptus, -a, -um,** *ac-
cepted, received, understood; acceptable, welcome, agreeable.*
nota, -ae, f., *mark, sign, note.*

515 **proludo, -ere, -si, -sus,** *play* or *practice beforehand, warm
    up.* **rudis, -is,** f., *exercise stick, wooden sword, foil.*
puer ille is Cupid.

516 **spiculum, -i,** n., *dart, arrow.* **pharetra, -ae,** f., *quiver.*
    promo, -ere, prompsi, promptus, *bring forth, draw forth, pro-
duce.* **acutus, -a, -um,** *sharp, pointed.*

517 **odi, odisse,** *hate, dislike.* **maestus, -a, -um,** *sad, melan-
    choly, gloomy.* **Tecmessa, -ae,** f.: a princess Ajax captured,
after having killed her father; naturally she may have been mel-
ancholy. **diligo, -ere, dilexi, dilectus,** *love.* **Aiax, -acis,** m.,
Ajax, mighty Greek warrior in the war against Troy.

Nos, hilarem populum, femina laeta capit.

Numquam ego te,Andromache,nec te,Tecmessa,rogarem,

   ut mea de vobis altera amica foret.   520

*   *   *   *   *   *   *

Scilicet Aiaci mulier maestissima dixit   523

   'Lux mea!' quaeque solent verba iuvare viros?

Classify your suitors according to what they are good for. Poets
possess some very good points, and there is a god in them. But
they are poor. A boy new in love will be much more easily fright-
ened off than a veteran (525-576). Love flourishes on difficulties
and repulses. Keep your admirers guessing.

Omnia tradantur (portas reseravimus hosti),

   et sit in infida proditione fides.

Quod datur ex facili, longum male nutrit amorem:

   miscenda est laetis rara repulsa iocis.   580

Ante fores iaceat, 'Crudelis ianua!' dicat,

---

518 **hilaris, -e,** *cheerful, lively, gay, merry.* **populus, -i,** m.,
     people, crowd, throng. **populum** is in apposition with **nos** and
may refer either to the male sex or to the Roman people. **laetus,
-a, -um,** *joyful, cheerful, gay, happy.*

519 **numquam,** *never.* **Andromache, -es,** f.: Hector's noble and he-
     roic wife. As we have already seen (II, 645; III, 109), Ovid
never cared much for her type. Her life was filled with sorrows,
and she had a good deal to weep about. **Tecmessa:** 517.

520 **altera** = 'either one.' **foret** = **esset.**

523 **scilicet** here introduces an incredulous question: 'Is it
     really possible to believe that . . . ?' **Aiaci:** 517. **mu-
lier, -eris,** f., *woman, wife.* **maestissima:** 517.

524 **lux, lucis,** f., *light.* **lux mea:** 'light of my life!' i.e.,
     'darling!' The antecedent of **quae** is **verba.**

577 **trado, -ere, -didi, -ditus,** *hand over, surrender, betray.*
     porta, -ae, f., *gate.* **resero, -are, -avi, -atus,** *unlock,*
open. **hostis, -is,** m., f., *enemy.* By this Ovid means the women.

578 **infidus, -a, -um,** *faithless, treacherous.* **proditio, -onis,**
     f., *betrayal, treachery.* **fides, -ei,** f., *faith, confidence,*
belief. --Ovid is playing with the words **infida** and **fides:** he
wants the women to have faith in his faithless betrayal of the
men.

579 **ex facili,** *easily, readily.* **nutrio, -ire, -ivi (-ii), -itus,**
     nourish, sustain.

580 **misceo, -ere, miscui, mixtus,** *mix, mingle.* **laetus, -a, -um,**
     joyful, cheerful, gay, merry. **rarus, -a, -um,** *rare, occa-*
sional. **repulsa, -ae,** f., *repulse.* **iocus, -i,** m., *joke, pastime,*
sport, game, prank.

581 **foris, -is,** f., *door;* (plur.), *door, doors, entrance.* **crude-
lis, -e,** *hard-hearted, cruel.* **ianua, -ae,** f., *door.*

multaque summisse, multa minanter agat.

Dulcia non ferimus: suco renovemur amaro;

saepe perit ventis obruta cumba suis.

585   Hoc est, uxores quod non patiatur amari:

conveniunt illas, cum voluere, viri;

Adde forem, et duro dicat tibi ianitor ore

'Non potes': exclusum te quoque tanget amor!

Lovers, like horses, do better when they know it is a race. Wives must be faithful to their husbands; for others, deception is sometimes necessary. There are various stratagems, such as notes written and conveyed on a friend's back or written invisibly in new milk (charcoal will make it visible) (589-666). Though he feels that it is a betrayal of his sex, Ovid suggests that men be led to *imagine* that they are held in affection. It should not be hard to do; men are usually conceited.

667   Quo feror insanus? Quid aperto pectore in hostem

mittor et indicio prodor ab ipse meo?

Non avis aucupibus monstrat, qua parte petatur;

---

582   **summisse,** *humbly, submissively.* **minanter,** *threateningly, with threats.*

583   **dulcis, -e,** *sweet, agreeable.* **dulcia:** 'sweet things' = 'unadulterated sweetness,' 'nothing but sweetness.' **sucus, -i,** m., *juice, potion, dose, medicine.* **renovo, -are, -avi, -atus,** *renew, restore, refresh.* **amarus, -a, -um,** *bitter.*

584   **obruo, -ere, -ui, -utus,** *overwhelm, sink.* **cumba, -ae,** f., *boat, skiff.* **suis:** 'its own' = 'favorable.'

585   **uxor, -oris,** f., *wife.* **uxores** is subject of **amari.** **patior, pati, passus,** *endure, allow, permit.*

586   **convenio, -ire, -veni, -ventus,** *come together (with), go to, come to, meet, visit, (see).* **voluere = voluerunt. viri =** *husbands.*

587   **addo, -ere, addidi, additus,** *add.* **foris, -is,** f., *door.* **tibi =** any husband. **ianitor, -oris,** m., *doorkeeper.*

588   **potes:** supply **inire,** *come in.* **excludo, -ere, -si, -sus,** *shut out, lock out.* **tango, -ere, tetigi, tactus,** *touch, affect, take hold of.*

667   **quo,** *whither, where.* **feror =** 'am I rushing.' **insanus, -a, -um,** *mad, insane, foolish.* Perhaps better as adverb here. **apertus, -a, -um,** *open, unprotected, exposed.* **hostis, -is,** m., f., *enemy.*

668   **mitto, mittere, misi, missus,** *send, hurl, throw.* **mittor:** 'do I throw myself,' 'do I charge.' **indicium, -ii,** n., *information, testimony, evidence.* **prodo, -ere, -didi, -ditus,** *betray.* **ab** governs **indicio.**

669   **avis, -is,** f., *bird.* **auceps, aucipis,** m., f., *bird catcher, fowler.* **monstro, -are, -avi, -atus,** *show, point out.*

non docet infestos currere cerva canes.   670
Viderit utilitas! Ego coepta fideliter edam;
Lemniasin gladios in mea fata dabo.
Efficite (et facile est), ut nos credamus amari:
prona venit cupidis in sua vota fides.
Spectet amabilius iuvenem et suspiret ab imo   675
femina, tam sero cur veniatque roget;
accedant lacrimae, dolor et de paelice fictus,
et laniet digitis illius ora suis:
iamdudum persuasus erit; miserebitur ultro
et dicet 'Cura carpitur ista mei!'   680

---

670   infestus, -a, -um, *hostile, dangerous.* curro, -ere, cucurri,
       cursus, *run.* cerva, -ae, f., *hind, deer.* canis, -is, m.,
f., *dog.*

671   utilitas, -atis, f., *utility, profit, advantage, expediency.*
       viderit utilitas: 'let my own advantage look out for itself!'
coeptum, -i, n., *undertaking.* fideliter, *faithfully.* edo, -ere,
edidi, editus, *set forth, publish, relate, give account of.*

672   Lemnias, -adis (dat. plur. -asin), f., *Lemnian woman.* The
       women of the island of Lemnos once murdered all their menfolk
in one night; hence they are typical of Woman in her more aggres-
sive mood. gladius, -ii, m., *sword.* fatum, -i, n., *fate, ruin,*
destruction.

673   efficio, -ere, effeci, effectus, *bring (it) about.* facilis,
       -e, *easy.*

674   pronus, -a, -um, *inclined, prone, ready; readily.* cupidus,
       -a, -um, *desirous, eager.* votum, -i, n., *vow, wish, desire.*
cupidis in sua vota: 'for those who are eager for the fulfillment
of their own desires.' fides, -ei, f., *trust, faith, belief.*

675   amabiliter, *lovingly.* suspiro, -are, -avi, -atus, *sigh.*
       imum, -i, n., *bottom, depth, lowest part.* ab imo = 'from the
depths of her being.'

676   The conventional order would be: rogetque cur tam sero veni-
       at. sero (adv.), *late.* cur, *why.*

677   accedo, -ere, accessi, accessus, *approach, be added.* dolor,
       -oris, m., *pain, distress, grief, vexation.* et connects the
subjects lacrimae and dolor. paelex, -icis, f., *rival* (female).
fictus, -a, -um, *feigned, fictitious, false.*

678   lanio, -are, -avi, -atus, *tear, scratch.*

679   iamdudum, *long since, without delay, instantly, immediately.*
       persuadeo, -ere, -si, -sus, *convince, persuade.* misereor,
-eri, -itus, *feel pity, be filled with compassion.* ultro, *of*
one's own accord, spontaneously.

680   cura: abl. carpo, -ere, -psi, -ptus, *pick, wear away, con-*
       sume. iste, ista, istud, *that of yours, that; he, she, it.*
Here nom. mei: objective gen. with cura.

Praecipue si cultus erit speculoque placebit,
    posse suo tangi credet amore deas.

Feel no real jealousy because of a rival. The sad story of
Cephalus and Procris reveals the folly of that.

Sed te, quaecumque est, moderate iniuria turbet,
    nec sis, audita paelice, mentis inops,
685   nec cito credideris. Quantum cito credere laedat,
    exemplum vobis non leve Procris erit.
Est prope purpureos colles florentis Hymetti
    fons sacer et viridi caespite mollis humus.
Silva nemus non alta facit; tegit arbutus herbam;
690   ros maris et lauri nigraque myrtus olent;
    nec densum foliis buxum fragilesque myricae

---

681 **praecipue,** *especially, particularly.* **cultus, -a, -um,** *culti-*
    vated, elegant, polished, well dressed, well groomed. **spe-**
    culum, -i, n., *looking glass, mirror.*

682 **suo:** probably 'for him' rather than 'his.' **tango, -ere, te-**
    tigi, tactus, *touch, move, affect, impress.* **dea, -ae,** f.,
    goddess.

683 **moderate,** *(only) moderately.* **iniuria, -ae,** f., *wrong, in-*
    jury. **turbo, -are, -avi, -atus,** *disturb, agitate, upset.*

684 **nec sis . . . mentis inops:** 'and don't lose your head.' **au-**
    dio, -ire, -ivi (-ii), -itus, *hear, hear of.* **paelex, -icis,**
    f., *rival.* **inops, inopis** (with gen.), *destitute of, without.*

685 **cito** (adv.), *(too) quickly, (too) soon, at once.* **credideris:**
    subjunctive for imperative. **quantum,** *how much.* **quantum . .**
    laedat: 'how much harm it does.'

686 **exemplum, -i,** n., *example, warning.* **Procris, -is** & **-idis,** f.:
    a princess of Athens and wife of Cephalus.

687 **prope** (with acc.), *near.* **purpureus, -a, -um,** *purple.* **col-**
    lis, m., *hill.* **floreo, -ere, -ui,** *blossom, flower.* **Hymet-**
    tus, -i, m.: a mountain near Athens, famed for its honey.

688 **fons, fontis,** m., *spring, fountain.* **sacer, -cra, -crum,** *sa-*
    cred. **viridis, -e,** *green.* **caespes, -itis,** m., *turf, sod.*
    humus, -i, f., *earth, ground.*

689 **silva, -ae,** f., *woods, forest, trees.* **nemus, -oris,** n.,
    grove. **tego, -ere, texi, tectus,** *cover, hide, conceal.* **ar-**
    butus, -i, f., *wild strawberry tree* (a native of Southern Europe).
    herba, -ae, f., *grass.*

690 **ros maris, roris maris,** m., (lit., *dew of the sea*) *rosemary.*
    laurus, -i, f., *laurel.* **niger, -gra, -grum,** *black, dark.*
    myrtus, -i & **-us,** f., *myrtle.* **oleo, -ere, -ui,** *be fragrant, smell.*

691 **densus, -a, -um,** *thick, dense.* **folium, -ii,** n., *leaf.* **bu-**
    xum, -i, n., *boxwood, box.* **fragilis, -e,** *fragile, frail.*
    myrica, -ae, f., *tamarisk.*

nec tenues cytisi cultaque pinus abest.
Lenibus impulsae zephyris auraque salubri
tot generum frondes herbaque summa tremit.
Grata quies Cephalo; famulis canibusque relictis 695
lassus in hac iuvenis saepe resedit humo,
'Quae'que 'meos releves aestus,' cantare solebat
'accipienda sinu, mobilis aura, veni!'
Coniugis ad timidas aliquis male sedulus aures
auditos memori rettulit ore sonos. 700
Procris ut accepit nomen, quasi paelicis, Aurae,
excidit et subito muta dolore fuit;

---

692 **cytisus, -i,** m., f., *(a kind of) clover.* **cultus, -a, -um,**
cultivated, elegant. **pinus, -us** & **-i,** f., *pine.* **absum, ab-
esse, afui,** *be absent, be missing.* **abest** agrees in number with its
nearest subject.

693 **lenis, -e,** *soft, smooth, mild, gentle.* **impello, -ere, im-
puli, impulsus,** *strike, set in motion, impel.* **zephyrus, -i,**
m., *west wind, zephyr.* **aura:** abl. **salubris, -e,** *health-giving,
healthful, salubrious.*

694 **tot** (indecl. adj.), *so many.* **genus, -eris,** n., *race, sort,
kind.* **frons, frondis,** f., *leafy branch, foliage, leaf.* **fron-
des** is one of the subjects of **tremit.** **herba, -ae,** f., *grass.*
tremo, -ere, -ui, *shake, quiver, tremble.*

695 **gratus, -a, -um,** *pleasing, agreeable.* **quies, -etis,** f.,
rest, quiet. **Cephalus, -i,** m.: husband of Procris. **famu-
lus, -i,** m., *servant, attendant.* **canis, -is,** m., f., *dog.*

696 **lassus, -a, -um,** *weary, tired, exhausted.* **resideo, -ere, re-
sedi,** *remain sitting, rest, linger, tarry.* **humus, -i,** f.,
earth, ground.

697 **quae** introduces a relative clause of purpose (note verb in
2nd person); its antecedent is in next line. **relevo, -are,
-avi, -atus,** *relieve, alleviate, lessen.* **aestus, -us,** m., *heat,
ardor;* in translating here, it must be given a double sense of
physical heat and of passion: *burning.* **canto, -are, -avi, -atus,**
sing, recite.

698 **mobilis, -e,** *nimble, quick, swift.* **aura:** voc. **veni:** imper.

699 **coniunx, coniugis,** m., f., *spouse, wife.* **timidus, -a, -um,**
fearful, timid. **sedulus, -a, -um,** *diligent, officious, med-
dling.* **auris, -is,** f., *ear.*

700 **audio, -ire, -ivi (-ii), -itus,** *hear, overhear.* **memor, me-
moris,** *mindful, remembering, retentive.* **sonus, -i,** m.,
sound, word.

701 **Procris, -is** & **-idis,** f.: wife of Cephalus. **quasi,** *as if, as
though.* **paelex, -icis,** f., *rival.* **Aurae:** to bring out the
reason for Procris' mistake, we might translate (as the context
suggests) by the similar words **aura** and **Laura,** or *breeze* and *Risë.*

702 **excido, -ere, excidi,** *fall down, faint, swoon.* **subitus, -a,
-um,** *sudden.* **mutus, -a, -um,** *dumb, mute, silent.* **dolor,**

palluit, ut serae lectis de vite racemis
   pallescunt frondes, quas nova laesit hiems,
705   quaeque suos curvant matura cydonia ramos,
   cornaque adhuc nostris non satis apta cibis.
Ut rediit animus, tenues a pectore vestes
   rumpit et indignas sauciat ungue genas;
nec mora, per medias passis furibunda capillis
710   evolat, ut thyrso concita Baccha, vias.
Ut prope perventum, comites in valle relinquit,
   ipsa nemus tacito clam pede fortis init.
Quid tibi mentis erat, cum sic male sana lateres,

-oris, m., *pain, distress, grief, anguish.*

703 **palleo, -ere, -ui,** *turn pale.* **serus, -a, -um,** *late.* **vitis,**
   -is, f., *vine, grapevine.* **racemus, -i,** m., *cluster of*
grapes.

704 **pallesco, -ere, pallui,** *turn pale, wither, fade.* **frons,**
   frondis, f., *foliage, leaf.* **hiems, hiemis,** f., *winter.*

705 The antecedent of **quae** is **cydonia,** which is another subject
   of **pallescunt. curvo, -are, -avi, -atus,** *bend, curve.* **matu-**
rus, -a, -um, *ripe, mature.* **cydonia, -orum,** n., *quinces.* **ramus,**
-i, m., *branch.*

706 **cornum, -i,** n., *cornel berry.* **adhuc,** *still, yet.* **satis,** *suf-*
   ficient, sufficiently, enough. **cibus, -i,** m., *food.*

707 **redeo, -ire, -ii, -itus,** *come back, return.* **vestis, -is,** f.,
   clothes, garment.

708 **rumpo, -ere, rupi, ruptus,** *break, tear.* **indignus, -a, -um,**
   unworthy, undeserving, innocent. **saucio, -are, -avi, -atus,**
wound. **unguis, -is,** m., *(finger)nail.* **gena, -ae,** f., *cheek.*

709 **nec mora:** 'and (there is) no delay,' 'without delay.' The
   object of **per** is **vias. passus, -a, -um,** *loose, dishevelled,*
flying. **furibundus, -a, -um,** *raging, mad(ly), furious(ly).*

710 **evolo, -are, -avi, -atus,** *fly away, rush forth.* **thyrsus, -i,**
   m., *thyrsus* (a staff tipped with a pine cone and entwined
with vines, carried by Bacchus and the Bacchantes). **concieo,**
-ere, concivi, concitus, *rouse, excite, stir up.* **Baccha, -ae,** f.,
a Bacchante (female follower of Bacchus, given to mad revels).

711 **prope** (adv.), *near.* **pervenio, -ire, -veni, -ventus,** *come*
   through, come, arrive. **perventum (est):** impersonal passive,
but translate as personal active: 'she came.' **comes, -itis,** m.,
f., *companion, comrade.* **vallis, -is,** f., *valley.*

712 **nemus, -oris,** n., *grove.* **tacitus, -a, -um,** *silent, noise-*
   less. **clam,** *secretly.* **fortis, -e,** *brave, bravely.* **ineo,**
-ire, -ivi (-ii), -itus, *go into, enter.*

713 **Quid tibi mentis erat** = 'What were your thoughts?' **sanus,**
   -a, -um, *healthy, in one's right mind, rational, sane.* **male**
sana: 'badly sane' = 'insane,' 'out of your mind,' 'frantic.'
lateo, -ere, -ui, *lurk, lie hid.*

Procri? Quis adtoniti pectoris ardor erat?

Iam iam venturam, quaecumque erat Aura, putabas   715
   scilicet atque oculis probra videnda tuis.

Nunc venisse piget (neque enim deprendere velles),
   nunc iuvat: incertus pectora versat amor.

Credere quae iubeant, locus est et nomen et index
   et quia mens semper, quod timet, esse putat.   720

Vidit ut oppressa vestigia corporis herba,
   pulsantur trepidi corde micante sinus;

iamque dies medius tenues contraxerat umbras,
   inque pari spatio vesper et ortus erant:

ecce, redit Cephalus silvis, Cyllenia proles,   725

---

714   **Procris, -is & -idis** (voc. **Procri**), f.: wife of Cephalus.
   adtonitus, -a, -um, *stunned, stupefied, astonished.* **ardor,**
-**oris,** m., *fire, burning, ardor, eagerness, impatience.*

715   **iam iam:** 'any moment now.' **venturam = (illam) venturam
   (esse).** **Aura:** see note on 701.

716   **scilicet,** *of course, no doubt, undoubtedly, naturally.* **pro-
   brum, -i,** n., *shameful act.* **videnda:** supply **esse;** indirect
statement after **putabas.**

717   **piget, -ere, piguit & pigitum est,** *it displeases, grieves,
   repents, makes ashamed.* **venisse piget:** 'you regret having
come.' **neque enim:** *for . . . not.* **deprendo, -ere, -di, -sus,**
catch, detect, discover. An object must be supplied.

718   **iuvat:** here used impersonally, parallel to **piget** (717);
   translate 'you are glad (you came).' **incertus, -a, -um,** *un-
certain, wavering, fluctuating.* **pectora:** plur. for sing.: 'your
heart.' **verso, -are, -avi, -atus,** *turn, twist, agitate, disturb.*

719   **Credere quae iubeant . . . est:** 'To bid (i.e., cause) her to
   believe (in her husband's infidelity), there are . . .' **in-
dex, indicis,** m., f., *informer, witness.*

720   **quia** here = 'the fact that.' **esse:** *to exist, to be true.*

721   **opprimo, -ere, oppressi, oppressus,** *press down.* **oppressa** is
   abl. modifying **herba. vestigium, -ii,** n., *footstep, trace,
mark, sign.* **herba, -ae,** f., *grass.*

722   **pulso, -are, -avi, -atus,** *strike, beat.* **trepidus, -a, -um,**
   agitated, anxious, alarmed. **cor, cordis,** n., *heart.* **mico,
-are, -avi, -atus,** *quiver, beat, pulsate.* **sinus:** plural for sin-
gular: *bosom, breast.*

723   **contraho, -ere, -xi, -ctus,** *draw together, contract, shorten,
   lessen.* **umbra, -ae,** f., *shade, shadow.*

724   **par, paris,** *equal.* **spatium, -ii,** n., *space, distance, inter-
   val.* **vesper, -eris & -eri,** m., *evening.* **ortus, -us,** m.,
rising, sunrise, morning.

725   **ecce,** *lo! see! behold!* **redeo, -ire, -ii, -itus,** *come back,
   return.* **Cephalus, -i,** m.: husband of Procris and son of Mer-
cury. **silva, -ae,** f., *wood, forest.* **Cyllenius, -a, -um,** *Cylleni-*

oraque fontana fervida pulsat aqua.

Anxia,Procri,lates;solitas iacet ille per herbas,
　　et 'Zephyri molles auraque,' dixit 'ades!'

Ut patuit miserae iucundus nominis error,
730　　et mens et rediit verus in ora color.

Surgit et oppositas agitato corpore frondes
　　movit, in amplexus uxor itura viri.

Ille, feram vidisse ratus, iuvenaliter artus
　　corripit; in dextra tela fuere manu.

735　Quid facis, infelix? Non est fera; supprime tela!

Me miserum! Iaculo fixa puella tuo est.

---

ian, *of Mercury* (who was born on Mt. Cyllene in Arcadia). **proles,
-is,** f., *offspring, child, descendant, son.*

726　**fontanus, -a, -um,** *from the spring (fountain), spring-.* **fer-
　　vidus, -a, -um,** *glowing, hot.* Modifies **ora** here. **pulso,-are,
-avi, -atus,** *beat, strike, splash.*

727　**anxius, -a, -um,** *fearful, anxious, worried, on pins and nee-
　　dles.* **Procri:** 714. **lateo, -ere, -ui,** *lurk, lie hid.* **soli-
tus, -a, -um,** *accustomed, usual.* **herba, -ae,** f., *grass, herb,
plant.*

728　**zephyrus, -i,** m., *west wind, zephyr.* **ades:** imperative of
　　adsum.

729　**pateo, -ere, -ui,** *lie open, be clear, be evident.* **miserae:**
　　'to the unhappy girl.' **iucundus, -a, -um,** *delightful, agree-
able, pleasing, pleasant.* **error, -oris,** m., *error, mistake.*

730　**rediit:** 725. **verus, -a, -um,** *true, real, genuine, proper.*

731　**surgo, -ere, surrexi, surrectus,** *rise, get up, jump up.* **op-
　　positus, -a, -um,** *opposed, opposing, in the way.* **agito,
-are, -avi, -atus,** *move, impel, agitate, excite.* **frons, frondis,**
f., *leafy branch, foliage, leaf.*

732　**amplexus, -us,** m., *embrace.* **uxor, -oris,** f., *wife.* **itura:**
　　future participle of **eo.**

733　**fera, -ae,** f., *wild animal.* **reor, reri, ratus,** *believe,
　　think, suppose, imagine.* **iuvenaliter,** *in a youthful manner;*
i.e., *with the impulsiveness of youth.* **artus, -us,** m., *joint,
limb.*

734　**corripio, -ere, -ripui, -reptus,** *seize, snatch up.* **artus
　　corripit:** 'snatches up his limbs' = 'jumps up,' 'leaps up.'
dexter, -tra, -trum, *right.* **telum, -i,** n., *dart, spear, javelin,
weapon.* **fuere = fuerunt.**

735　**infelix, -icis,** *unfortunate, unlucky, unhappy, ill-fated.*
　　fera: 733. **supprimo, -ere, -pressi, -pressus,** *hold back,
check, stop.* **tela:** 734.

736　**Me miserum:** acc. of exclamation. **iaculum, -i,** n., *dart,
　　javelin, spear.* **figo, -ere, -xi, -xus,** *fix, transfix,
pierce.*

'Ei mihi!' conclamat. 'Fixisti pectus amicum!
Hic locus a Cephalo vulnera semper habet.
Ante diem morior, sed nulla paelice laesa;
  hoc faciet positae te mihi, terra, levem.   740
Nomine suspectas iam spiritus exit in auras.
Labor, io! Cara lumina conde manu!'
Ille sinu dominae morientia corpora maesto
  sustinet et lacrimis vulnera saeva lavat.
Exit et, incauto paulatim pectore lapsus,   745
  excipitur miseri spiritus ore viri.

But back to the subject! In attending dinner parties, make a point of being late. Your entrance will be more effective for several reasons. Mind your table manners. When dining out, don't eat before you leave home and don't eat quite as much as you are able. Moderation should likewise prevail in drink.

Sed repetamus opus! Mihi nudis rebus eundum est,

---

737 **Ei mihi:** *'Ah me!'* **conclamo, -are, -avi, -atus,** *cry out, exclaim.* **fixisti:** 736. **amicus, -a, -um,** *friendly, loving, dear, of a friend.*

738 **Cephalus, -i,** m.: husband of Procris. **vulnera semper habet:** Procris is thinking not only of the spear wound, but also of the wounds of love and jealousy in the past.

739 **morior, mori, mortuus,** *die.* **paelex, -icis,** f., *rival.*

740 **positae:** 'when I am buried.' **mihi . . . levem:** 'light on me' or 'rest lightly on me.' **terra, -ae,** f., *earth, ground.* Here vocative.

741 **nomine:** abl. of cause with **suspectas. suspectus, -a, -um,** *suspected.* **spiritus, -us,** m., *breath, spirit, soul.* **exeo, -ire, -ii, -itus,** *go out, go forth, depart.*

742 **labor, labi, lapsus,** *slip, sink, pass away.* **io,** *oh! ah!* **carus, -a, -um,** *dear.* Here abl. **lumen, -inis,** n., *light, eye.* **condo, -ere, -didi, -ditus,** *put together, found, shut, close.*

743 **morientia:** 739. **maestus, -a, -um,** *sad, sorrowful.*

744 **sustineo, -ere, -tinui, -tentus,** *hold up, support.* **saevus, -a, -um,** *savage, cruel.* **lavo, -are, lavi, lautus (lotus, lavatus),** *wash, bathe.*

745 **exit:** 741; subject is **spiritus. incautus, -a, -um,** *incautious, heedless, rash.* **paulatim,** *little by little, gradually.* **lapsus:** 742.

746 **excipio, -ere, excepi, exceptus,** *catch, take, receive.* **spiritus:** 741. --It was the custom for the breath of a dying person to be caught in the mouth of the nearest relative.

747 **repeto, -ere, -ivi (-ii), -itus,** *seek again, go back to, return to.* **nudus, -a, -um,** *naked, bare, unadorned.* **res, rei,** f., *thing, fact.* **Mihi nudis rebus eundum est** = 'I must proceed without further embellishments'; i.e., no more stories.

ut tangat portus fessa carina suos.
Sollicite expectas, dum te in convivia ducam,
750   et quaeris monitus hac quoque parte meos.
Sera veni, positaque decens incede lucerna:
grata mora venies; maxima lena mora est.
Etsi turpis eris, formosa videbere potis,
et latebras vitiis nox dabit ipsa tuis.
755 Carpe cibos digitis: est quiddam gestus edendi;
ora nec immunda tota perungue manu.
Neve domi praesume dapes, sed desine citra

---

748 **tango, -ere, tetigi, tactus,** *touch, reach, arrive at.* **por-
tus, -us,** m., *harbor, port.* Here plur. for sing. **fessus, -a,
-um,** *tired, weary.* **carina, -ae,** f., *keel, vessel, boat, ship.*

749 **sollicite,** *anxiously.* **expecto, -are, -avi, -atus,** *wait.*
convivium, -ii, n., *banquet, dinner party.* **duco, -ere, duxi,
ductus,** *lead, conduct.*

750 **monitus, -us,** m., *warning, admonition, counsel, advice.* **hac
. . . parte:** 'in this respect.'

751 **serus, -a, -um,** *late.* **veni:** imperat. **decens, -entis,** *becom-
ing, comely, pretty, charming.* **incedo, -ere, incessi, inces-
sus,** *advance, come in, arrive, appear.* **decens incede** perhaps =
'make a graceful entrance.' **lucerna, -ae,** f., *lamp.*

752 **gratus, -a, -um,** *pleasing, agreeable.* **grata . . . venies:**
'your arrival will be pleasing.' **maximus, -a, -um,** *greatest,
very great.* **lena, -ae,** f., *stimulus of love.* --It does seem the
height of superfluity to *advise* women to be late.

753 **etsi,** *although, even if.* **videbere = videberis.** **poti, -orum,**
(from participle of **poto,** *drink*), m., *those who have drunk,
those who have imbibed, the intoxicated.*

754 **latebra, -ae,** f., *hiding place, concealment.*

755 The Romans regularly ate with their fingers. The advice here
is probably to use *only* the fingers, daintily, rather than
scooping the food in with the whole hand. **carpo, -ere, -psi,
-ptus,** *pick, pluck, eat.* **cibus, -i,** m., *food.* **quidam, quaedam,
quiddam,** *a certain one, a certain thing, someone, something.* **est
quiddam:** 'is something' or 'has a certain importance.' **gestus,
-us,** m., *posture, attitude, motion, gesture.* **edo, edere & esse,
edi, esus,** *eat.*

756 **nec:** place at beginning of line. **immundus, -a, -um,** *unclean,
dirty.* Modifies **manu** here. **totus, -a, -um,** *whole, entire,
all.* Modifies **ora** here. **perunguo, -ere, -unxi, -unctus,** *besmear.*

757 **neve,** *or not, nor; and not, and that not.* **domus, -us & -i,**
f., *house, home.* **praesumo, -ere, -m(p)si, -m(p)tus,** *take be-
forehand or in advance.* **daps** or **dapis, dapis,** f. (sing. & plur.),
feast, banquet, meal, food. --The implication is that you would
have no appetite for your host's dinner if you ate before going
out; this is a good example of safety first, but hardly of polite-

quam cupis: es paulo, quam potes esse, minus;
Priamides Helenen avide si spectet edentem,
    oderit et dicat 'Stulta rapina mea est.'   760
Aptius est deceatque magis potare puellas;
    cum Veneris puero non male, Bacche, facis.
Hoc quoque, qua patiens caput est, animusque pedesque
    constant; nec, quae sunt singula, bina vide!
Turpe iacens mulier multo madefacta Lyaeo.   765

The end has been reached. Girls as well as boys are now in
Ovid's debt.

Lusus habet finem: cygnis descendere tempus,
    duxerunt collo qui iuga nostra suo.   810

---

ness. **citra,** *on this side, on the nearer side.* **citra quam:**
'sooner than.'

758 **cupio, -ere, -ivi (-ii), -itus,** *desire, wish.* **es:** 2nd pers.
    sing. imperative of **edo,** *eat* (755). **paulo . . . minus:** 'a
little less.' **esse:** present infinitive of **edo** (755).

759 **Priamides, -ae,** m., *son of Priam* (king of Troy); i.e., *Paris.*
    Helene, -es (acc. **-en**), f., *Helen* (who eloped with Paris).
avide, *eagerly, greedily.* **edentem:** 755.

760 **odi, odisse,** *hate, dislike, be displeased, be vexed.* **stul-**
    tus, -a, -um, *foolish, silly.* **rapina, -ae,** f., *robbery,*
carrying off, elopement; prize, prey. Refers here either to Helen
herself or to Paris' running off with her.

761 **magis** (adv.), *more, rather.* **poto, -are, -avi, potatus & po-**
    tus, *drink.*

762 **Bacchus, -i,** m., *Bacchus* (god of wine); *wine.* **facis:** 'you
    do' = 'you get along.'

763 **Hoc quoque:** the verb is lacking: '(But do) this too'; i.e.,
    drink. **qua:** 'only to the extent that.' **patiens, -entis,** *en-*
during, permitting, firm, steady, (clear). **caput, -itis,** n.,
head.

764 **consto, -are, -stiti, -status,** *stand together, agree, stand*
    firm, be steady. **singuli, -ae, -a,** *single.* **bini, -ae, -a,**
two at a time, double.

765 **turpe:** neuter nominative after **est** understood: 'a repulsive
    object.' **mulier, -eris,** f., *woman, wife.* **madefacio, -ere,**
-feci, -factus, *moisten, soak, drench, intoxicate.* **Lyaeus, -i,**
m., *Lyaeus* ('the relaxer'), *Bacchus, wine.*

809 **lusus, -us,** m., *play, sport, game, fun.* **finis, -is,** m., *end.*
    cygnus, -i, m., *swan.* Swans sometimes drew Venus' chariot,
and apparently Ovid's, at least when he was writing about love.
descendo, -ere, -di, -sus, *come down (from), descend (from).* **tem-**
pus: supply est.

810 **duco, -ere, duxi, ductus,** *lead, draw.* **collum, -i,** n., *neck.*
    iugum, -i, n., *yoke, chariot.* Plural for singular.

811   Ut quondam iuvenes, ita nunc, mea turba, puellae
         inscribant spoliis 'NASO MAGISTER ERAT.'

---

811   **ut . . . ita**, *as . . . so*.   **quondam**, *once, formerly*.   **turba**,
      -ae, f., *crowd, throng, mob, gang*. In apposition here with
puellae.

812   **inscribo, -ere, -psi, -ptus**, *write on, inscribe on*.   **spolium**,
      -ii, n., *spoil, booty*.   **Naso, -onis**, m.: family name (cogno-
men) of Publius Ovidius Naso.   **magister, -tri**, m., *master, teach-
er, instructor*.   --Cf. II, 744.

P. OVIDI NASONIS

REMEDIA   AMORIS

Cupid is perturbed on reading the title of this book, but Ovid
reassures him. He affirms his continued loyalty, pointing out that
he has always been in love and, as a matter of fact, still is. His
purpose in writing this new work is simply to cut down the number
of suicides caused by unrequited love. Convinced, golden Love,
with a wave of his jewelled wings, directs Ovid to proceed.

Legerat huius Amor titulum nomenque libelli:

  'Bella mihi, video, bella parantur' ait.

'Parce tuum vatem sceleris damnare, Cupido,

  tradita qui totiens, te duce, signa tuli.

Non ego Tydides, a quo tua saucia mater   5

  in liquidum rediit aethera Martis equis.

Saepe tepent alii iuvenes, ego semper amavi,

  et si, quid faciam nunc quoque, quaeris, amo.

Those who do not have the time or the inclination to read all of
the *Remedia Amoris* included herein may find it advisable and more
interesting to skip to line 291. --G.H.T.

1   **titulus, -i**, m., *title.* **libellus, -i**, m., *(little) book.*

2   **bellum, -i**, n., *war.* **paro, -are, -avi, -atus,** *get ready,
prepare.* **aio,** *say, assert.*

3   **parco, -ere, peperci** & **parsi,** *spare; cease, refrain from*
(with Latin infinitive translated by English gerund). **vates,
-is**, m., f., *prophet, poet.* **scelus, -eris**, n., *crime, wickedness.*
damno, -are, -avi, -atus (with gen. of the charge or crime), *condemn, censure.* **Cupido, -inis**, m., *Cupid,* god of love.

4   **trado, -ere, tradidi, traditus,** *hand over, commit, entrust.*
qui: antecedent is **vatem,** but note that its verb is 1st person. **totiens,** *so often, so many times.* **dux, ducis**, m., f., *leader, commander.* **signum, -i**, n., *sign, military standard, banner.*

5   **ego:** supply **sum. Tydides, -ae**, m., *son of Tydeus,* i.e., *Diomedes* (who wounded Venus, mother of Cupid, during the Trojan
War). **a quo:** with **saucia. saucius, -a, -um,** *wounded.*

6   **liquidus, -a, -um,** *liquid, clear, bright, limpid, pure.* **redeo, -ire, -ii, -itus,** *go back, return.* **aether, -eris** (acc.
-era), m., *upper air, ether, heaven.* **Mars, Martis**, m.: god of war
and admirer of Venus; she borrowed his chariot after her escape
from Diomedes.

7   **tepeo, -ere,** *be lukewarm, be without ardor, be indifferent* in
love. **alius, -a, -ud,** *another, other.*

Quin etiam docui qua posses arte parari,
10　　et quod nunc ratio est, impetus ante fuit.
Nec te, blande puer, nec nostras prodimus artes,
　　nec nova praeteritum Musa retexit opus.
Siquis amat quod amare iuvat, feliciter ardet;
　　gaudeat et vento naviget ille suo.
15　At siquis male fert indignae regna puellae,
　　ne pereat, nostrae sentiat artis opem.
Cur aliquis laqueo collum nodatus amator
　　a trabe sublimi triste pependit onus?
Cur aliquis rigido fodit sua pectora ferro?
20　　Invidiam caedis, pacis amator, habes.

9　　**quin etiam**, *nay even, moreover, what's more.* **paro, -are,
-avi, -atus,** *prepare, procure, acquire, get.* --Ovid is
referring to his *Ars Amatoria.*

10　　**quod:** 'what,' 'that which.' **ratio, -onis,** f., *reason, sci-
ence, system.* **impetus, -us,** m., *attack, impulse.*

11　　**blandus, -a, -um,** *pleasant, alluring, charming.* **prodo, -ere,
-didi, -ditus,** *bring forth, betray, abandon.*

12　　**praeteritus, -a, -um,** *past, previous.* **Musa, -ae,** f., *a Muse*
(one of the nine patron goddesses of poetry and other arts
and sciences). **retexo, -ere, -xui,** *unweave, unravel.*

13　　**quod:** 'an object which,' 'one whom.' **amare iuvat:** lit., 'it
delights to love,' i.e., 'he takes pleasure in loving.' **fe-
liciter,** *fortunately, happily.* **ardeo, -ere, arsi, arsus,** *be on
fire, be aglow, burn (with love), be in love.*

14　　**gaudeo, -ere, gavisus sum,** *rejoice, be glad.* **vento . . . suo
= 'with favoring wind' or perhaps 'on his own course.' **navi-
go, -are, -avi, -atus,** *sail.*

15　　**indignus, -a, -um,** *unworthy, intolerable.* **regnum, -i,** n.,
rule, despotism, tyranny.

16　　**sentio, -ire, -si, -sus,** *feel, perceive, experience.*

17　　**cur,** *why.* **laqueus, -i,** m., *noose.* **collum, -i,** n., *neck.*
nodo, -are, -avi, -atus, *knot.* **laqueo collum** (acc. of spec-
ification) **nodatus:** 'knotted as to his neck with a noose,' i.e.,
'with a noose knotted around his neck.' **amator, -oris,** m., *lover.*

18　　**trabs, trabis,** f., *beam, timber.* **sublimis, -e,** *high, lofty.*
tristis, -e, *sad, gloomy.* **pendeo, -ere, pependi,** *hang, be
suspended.* This verb is intransitive and **onus** is nominative,
in apposition with **amator. onus, -eris,** n., *burden, load.*

19　　**cur:** 17. **rigidus, -a, -um,** *stiff, hard, inflexible.* **fodio,
-ere, fodi, fossus,** *dig, pierce, wound, stab.* **ferrum, -i,**
n., *iron, sword.*

20　　**invidia, -ae,** f., *envy, odium, reproach, blame.* **caedes, -is,**
f., *slaughter, murder.* **pax, pacis,** f., *peace.* **amator:** 17.
pacis amator is Cupid.

Qui, nisi desierit, misero periturus amore est,
    desinat; et nulli funeris auctor eris.
Et puer es, nec te quicquam nisi ludere oportet:
    lude! Decent annos mollia regna tuos.
Nam poteras uti nudis ad bella sagittis,   25
    sed tua mortifero sanguine tela carent.
Vitricus et gladiis et acuta dimicet hasta,
    et victor multa caede cruentus eat;
tu cole maternas, tuto quibus utimur, artes,
    et quarum vitio nulla fit orba parens.'   30
*   *   *   *   *   *   *

Haec ego; movit Amor gemmatas aureus alas
    et mihi 'Propositum perfice' dixit 'opus.'   40

Ovid's advice is intended impartially for both men and women who
want to fall out of love. Many famous people might have used his
counsel with profit. With an invocation to Apollo, who appropri-
ately is god of both poetry and healing, the discussion begins.

---

22   **nulli**: dat. **funus, -eris**, n., *funeral, death.* **auctor,**
    -oris, m., f., *author, cause, occasion.*

23   **quisquam, quicquam,** *anyone, anything.* **ludo, -ere, -si, -sus,**
    play, frisk, frolic. **oportet, -ere, -uit,** *it is necessary,*
it is proper; (one) must or *ought.* **nec te quicquam . . . oportet:**
'and you ought not to do anything.'

24   **lude:** 23. **regnum, -i**, n., *rule, dominion, kingdom.*

25   This couplet is easy enough to translate, but the meaning is
    not quite clear. It is doubtful if we have what Ovid actually
wrote. **nam** (conj.), *for.* **utor, uti, usus** (with abl.), *use, em-*
ploy. **nudus, -a, -um,** *naked, bared.* **bellum, -i**, n., *war.* **sagit-**
ta, -ae, f., *arrow.*

26   **mortifer, -era, -erum,** *death-bringing, deadly.* **sanguis,**
    -inis, m., *blood.* **telum, -i**, n., *dart, spear, arrow, weapon.*
careo, -ere, -ui, -itus (with abl.), *be without, be free from.*

27   **vitricus, -i**, m., *stepfather.* Cupid's stepfather would be
    Mars. **gladius, -ii**, m., *sword.* **acutus, -a, -um,** *sharp.* **di-**
mico, -are, -avi, -atus, *fight.* **hasta, -ae**, f., *spear.*

28   **victor, -oris**, m., *victor; victorious.* **caedes, -is**, f.,
    slaughter, killing. **cruentus, -a, -um,** *covered with blood,*
bloody, blood-stained.

29   **maternus, -a, -um,** *of one's mother, mother's.* **tuto**, *safely,*
    without danger. **utimur:** 25.

30   **orbus, -a, -um,** *bereaved, childless.* **parens, -entis**, m.,
    f., *parent, father, mother.*

39   **ego:** supply **dixi. gemmatus, -a, -um,** *jewelled.* **aureus, -a,**
    -um, *golden.* **ala, -ae**, f., *wing.*

40   **propono, -ere, -posui, -positus,** *propose, intend.* **perficio,**
    -ere, -feci, -fectus, *carry out, finish, complete.*

Ad mea, decepti iuvenes, praecepta venite,
　　quos suus ex omni parte fefellit amor.
Discite sanari, per quem didicistis amare;
　　una manus vobis vulnus opemque feret.
45　Terra salutares herbas eademque nocentes
　　nutrit, et urticae proxima saepe rosa est.
Vulnus in Herculeo quae quondam fecerat hoste,
　　vulneris auxilium Pelias hasta tulit.
Sed quaecumque viris, vobis quoque dicta, puellae,
50　credite. Diversis partibus arma damus,
e quibus ad vestros siquid non pertinet usus,
　　attamen exemplo multa docere potest.
Utile propositum est saevas extinguere flammas

41　**decipio, -ere, -cepi, -ceptus,** *ensnare, beguile, deceive.*
praeceptum, -i, n., *precept, instruction, advice.*

42　**suus** = 'your own.' **ex omni parte:** in every respect.'

43　**sano, -are, -avi, -atus,** *heal, cure.*

45　**terra, -ae,** f., *earth, ground, soil.* **salutaris, -e,** *health-*
ful, wholesome, beneficial. **herba, -ae,** f., *grass, plant,*
herb. **idem, eadem, idem,** *the same; likewise, also.* **nocens,**
-entis, *bad, harmful, injurious, poisonous.*

46　**nutrio, -ire, -ivi (-ii), -itus,** *nourish, foster, sustain.*
urtica, -ae, f., *stinging nettle.* **proximus, -a, -um,** *near-*
est, next. **rosa, -ae,** f., *rose.*

47　Telephus, king of Mysia and son of Hercules, was wounded at
　　Troy by the spear of Achilles and was later healed by its
rust. **in Herculeo . . . hoste:** 'in the enemy, the son of Hercu-
les,' i.e., Telephus. **Herculeus, -a, -um,** *Herculean.* **quae:** the
antecedent is **hasta. quondam,** *once, formerly.* **hostis, -is,** m.,
f., *enemy, foe.*

48　**vulneris:** translate the gen. 'for.' **auxilium, -ii,** n., *aid,*
remedy. **Pelias, -adis,** f. adj., *which came from Pelion* (a
mountain in Thessaly whence came the shaft of Achilles' spear).
hasta, -ae, f., *spear.*

49　**quaecumque viris, vobis quoque dicta, puellae, credite:** 'be-
　　lieve that whatever is said to the men is said to you also,
girls.'

50　**diversus, -a, -um,** *opposite, different, opposing.*

51　**e quibus . . . siquid:** 'if any of which (or these). **vester,**
-tra, -trum, *your* (plur.). **pertineo, -ere, -ui,** *relate, con-*
cern, pertain, apply, suit, be suitable. **usus, -us,** m., *use,*
benefit, profit, advantage, need.

52　**attamen,** *nevertheless, yet.* **exemplum, -i,** n., *example.*

53　**utilis, -e,** *useful, profitable.* **propositum,. -i,** n., *plan,*
intention, purpose, aim. **saevus, -a, -um,** *savage, fierce,*

nec servum vitii pectus habere sui:
vixisset Phyllis, si me foret usa magistro,   55
  et per quod noviens, saepius isset iter;
nec moriens Dido summa vidisset ab arce
  Dardanias vento vela dedisse rates.

*   *   *   *   *   *   *

Redde Parim nobis: Helenen Menelaus habebit,   65
  nec manibus Danais Pergama victa cadent;
impia si nostros legisset Scylla libellos,
  haesisset capiti purpura, Nise, tuo.
Me duce, damnosas, homines, compescite curas,

---

cruel. **extinguo, -ere, -nxi, -nctus,** *quench, extinguish.* **flamma, -ae,** f., *flame, fire of love, passion.*

54   **servus, -i,** m., *slave, servant.*

55   **vivo, -ere, vixi, victus,** *live.* **Phyllis, -idis** & **-idos,** f.:
Thracian princess who, deserted by her lover Demophoön, went down to the shore nine times to look for his return, then hanged herself. **foret** = **esset. utor, uti, usus** (with abl.), *use, employ.* **magister, -tri,** m., *master, teacher, instructor.*

56   Rearrange: **et saepius isset (per) iter per quod noviens (ivit). noviens,** *nine times.* **iter, itineris,** n., *way, journey, path, road,*

57   **morior, mori, mortuus,** *die.* **Dido, -us** & **-onis,** f.: queen of Carthage, deserted by her lover, the Trojan Aeneas. **arx, arcis,** f., *citadel, fortress, stronghold, highest point.*

58   **Dardanius, -a, -um,** *Dardanian, Trojan.* **velum, -i,** n., *sail.* **ratis, -is,** f., *raft, boat, vessel, ship.*

65   **Paris, -idis** (acc. **-im),** m.: Trojan prince who carried off Helen; this led to the Trojan War. **Helene, -es** (acc. **-en),** f., *Helen,* most beautiful of women. **Menelaus, -i,** m.: Helen's husband.

66   **Danaus, -a, -um,** *Greek.* **Pergama, -orum,** n., *the citadel of Troy, Troy.* **cado, -ere, cecidi, casus,** *fall.*

67   **impius, -a, -um,** *impious, wicked, undutiful, unfilial.* **Scylla, -ae,** f.: daughter of Nisus; for love of Minos, king of Crete, she cut off her father's lock of purple hair on which his life depended. **libellus, -i,** m., *(little) book.*

68   **haereo, -ere, haesi, haesus,** *stick, cling, remain fastened.* **caput, -itis,** n., *head.* **purpura, -ae,** f., *purple, purple lock.* **Nisus, -i,** m.: king of Megara. --For another historical example, Ovid could cite the case of Edward VIII, who might have kept his throne if he had read the *Remedia Amoris.*

69   **dux, ducis,** m., f., *leader, guide, counsellor.* **damnosus, -a, -um,** *hurtful, injurious, destructive.* **homo, -inis,** m., f., *human being, man.* **compesco, -ere, -pescui,** *hold in check, repress, restrain, subdue.*

70   rectaque cum sociis, me duce, navis eat.

Naso legendus erat tum, cum didicistis amare;
          idem nunc vobis Naso legendus erit.

Publicus assertor dominis suppressa levabo
          pectora: vindictae quisque favete suae.

75   Te precor incipiens, adsit tua laurea nobis,
          carminis et medicae, Phoebe, repertor opis.

Tu pariter vati, pariter succurre medenti:
          utraque tutelae subdita cura tuae est.

First of all, if you feel an unfortunate attack of love coming
on, draw back before it is too late.

          Dum licet, et modici tangunt praecordia motus,

---

70   **rectus, -a, -um,** *straight.* **socius, -ii,** m., *fellow, partner,*
       comrade, companion, ally. **duce:** 69. **navis, -is,** f., *ship.*
--Ovid is back to the figure of a ship as the vehicle of his
instructions.

71   **Naso, -onis,** m., *Naso,* cognomen (family name) of Publius
       Ovidius Naso; *Ovid.*

72   **idem, eadem, idem,** *the same; likewise, also.* **Naso:** 71.

73   **publicus, -a, -um,** *public.* **assertor, -oris,** m., *restorer of*
       liberty, deliverer. Here in apposition with the subject 'I'.
dominis: dat. of agent. Since Ovid is here talking about the slav-
ery of love, there is in this word (which might be from either **do-**
minus, *master,* or **domina**) a nice play on the two ideas of 'master'
(or 'mistress') and 'sweetheart.' **supprimo, -ere, -pressi, -pres-**
sus,*detain, restrain, suppress, oppress.* **levo, -are, -avi, -atus,**
lift up, relieve, release, free.

74   **vindicta, -ae,** f., *rod of liberation* (by whose touch slaves
       were freed). **faveo, -ere, favi, fautus** (with dat.), *be well*
disposed toward, favor.

75   **precor, -ari, -atus,** *pray, invoke, call upon, beseech.* **inci-**
       pio, -ere, -cepi, -ceptus, *begin.* **laurea, -ae,** f., *laurel*
crown, laurel branch (symbolic of Apollo, poets, etc.).

76   **carmen, -inis,** n., *song, poem, poetry.* **medicus, -a, -um,**
       healing, medical. **Phoebus, -i,** m., *Phoebus, Apollo,* god of
light, healing, music, poetry, etc. **repertor, -oris,** m., *dis-*
coverer, inventor.

77   **pariter,** *equally.* **vates, -is,** m., f., *prophet, poet.* **suc-**
       curro, -ere, -curri, -cursus (with dat.), *run to the aid of,*
help, aid, assist. **medens, -entis,** m., *healer, physician.*

78   **uterque, utraque, utrumque,** *each, either, both.* **tutela, -ae,**
       f., *charge, care, protection.* **subdo, -ere, -didi, -ditus**
(with dat.), *place under, subject.* **utraque . . . cura** refers to
the pursuits of poetry and medicine.

79   **modicus, -a, -um,** *(only) moderate.* **tango, -ere, tetigi, tac-**
       tus, *touch, move, affect.* **praecordia, -orum,** n., *breast,*
heart. **motus, -us,** m., *motion, emotion, impulse, passion.*

si piget, in primo limine siste pedem.   80
Opprime, dum nova sunt, subiti mala semina morbi,
    et tuus incipiens ire resistat equus.
Nam mora dat vires: teneras mora percoquit uvas
    et validas segetes, quod fuit herba, facit.
Quae praebet latas arbor spatiantibus umbras,   85
    quo posita est primum tempore, virga fuit;
tum poterat manibus summa tellure revelli,
    nunc stat in immensum viribus acta suis.
Quale sit id, quod amas, celeri circumspice mente
    et tua laesuro subtrahe colla iugo.   90
Principiis obsta: sero medicina paratur,

---

80   **piget, -ere, piguit & pigitum est,** *it is irksome, it is dis-*
       pleasing. **limen, -inis,** n., *threshold.* **sisto, -ere, stiti,**
status, *place, check, stop, halt.*

81   **opprimo, -ere, -pressi, -pressus,** *overwhelm, crush.* **subitus,**
       -a, -um, *sudden, unexpected.* **malus, -a, -um,** *bad, evil, de-*
structive, hurtful. **semen, -inis,** n., *seed.* **morbus, -i,** m.,
disease, malady.

82   **incipio, -ere, -cepi, -ceptus,** *begin.* **resisto, -ere, -stiti,**
stand still, halt, stop, resist.

83   **nam** (conj.), *for.* **percoquo, -ere, -coxi, -coctus,** *cook*
thoroughly, ripen. **uva, -ae,** f., *grape.*

84   **validus, -a, -um,** *strong, vigorous.* **seges, -etis,** f., *field*
of grain, crop. **herba, -ae,** f., *grass.*

85   **quae:** its antecedent is **arbor,** which is subject of **fuit.**
       praebeo, -ere, -ui, -itus, *offer, furnish, supply.* **latus,**
-a, -um, *broad, wide.* **arbor, -oris,** f., *tree.* **spatior, -ari,**
-atus, *walk about, stroll.* The participle here is used as a sub-
stantive: 'those who stroll' = 'strollers.' **umbra, -ae,** f.,
shade, shadow.

86   **quo . . . tempore:** 'at what time' = 'when.' **primum** (adv.),
first. **virga, -ae,** f., *twig, sprout.*

87   **tellus, -uris,** f., *earth, ground.* **revello, -ere, -velli,**
-vulsus & -volsus, *pull from, pull out.*

88   **sto, -are, steti, status,** *stand.* **immensum, -i,** n., *bound-*
less extent, immense size.

89   **qualis, -e,** *of what sort.* **celer, -eris, -e,** *swift, quick.*
       circumspicio, -ere, -spexi, -spectus, *look about, take heed,*
ponder, consider.

90   **laedo, -ere, laesi, laesus,** *hurt, wound, trouble, vex.* **sub-**
       traho, -ere, -traxi, -tractus, *withdraw, remove.* **collum, -i,**
n., *neck.* **iugum, -i,** n., *yoke, collar.*

91   **principium, -ii,** n., *beginning.* **obsto, -are, -stiti, -sta-**
       tus (with dat.), *withstand, oppose, resist.* **sero,** *late, too*
late. **medicina, -ae,** f., *medicine.* **paro, -are, -avi, -atus,**
prepare, get ready, provide.

cum mala per longas convaluere moras.

Sed propera, nec te venturas differ in horas:

qui non est hodie, cras minus aptus erit.

95   Verba dat omnis amor reperitque alimenta morando;

optima vindictae proxima quaeque dies.

Flumina pauca vides de magnis fontibus orta;

plurima collectis multiplicantur aquis. . . .

But if you let your love get a start on you, there is not much
to be done at first. The doctor's advice can be more readily
heeded after the first attack has subsided.

Si tamen auxilii perierunt tempora primi,

et vetus in capto pectore sedit amor,

maius opus superest; sed non, quia serior aegro

110   advocor, ille mihi destituendus erit.

     *   *   *   *   *   *   *

115   Qui modo nascentes properabam pellere morbos,

---

92   **malum, -i,** n., *an evil;* (plur.) *disease.* **convalesco, -ere, -valui,** *grow strong, gain strength.* **convaluere = convaluerunt.**

93   **propero, -are, -avi, -atus,** *hasten, hurry.* **differo, differre, distuli, dilatus,** *defer, put off, delay.* **hora, -ae,** f., *hour.* **nec te venturas differ in horas:** 'and do not put it off until a future hour.'

94   **hodie,** *today.* **cras,** *tomorrow.* **minus** (adv.), *less.*

95   **verba dat =** 'deceives.' Cf. *Ars Amatoria* II, 166. **reperio, -ire, repperi, repertus,** *find, procure, obtain.* **alimentum, -i,** n., *nourishment, food.* **moror, -ari, -atus,** *delay, linger.*

96   **optimus, -a, -um,** *best.* **vindicta, -ae,** f., *rod of liberation* (cf. 74); *liberation.* **proximus, -a, -um,** *nearest, next, successive, approaching.*

97   **flumen, -inis,** n., *river.* **paucus, -a, -um,** *few.* **fons, fontis,** m., *spring, fountain.* **orior, -iri, ortus,** *rise, originate.*

98   **plurimus, -a, -um,** *most, very much, very many.* **colligo, -ere, -legi, -lectus,** *gather, collect.* **multiplico, -are, -avi, -atus,** *multiply, increase, augment.*

107   **auxilium, -ii,** n., *aid, remedy.* **auxilii . . . primi:** !

108   **vetus, -eris,** *old, of long standing.*

109   **supersum, -esse, -fui,** *be left, remain.* **serus, -a, -um,** *late.* **aeger, -gri,** m., *sick person, patient.*

110   **advoco, -are, -avi, -atus** (with dat.), *call to, summon to.* **destituo, -ere, -ui, -utus,** *forsake, abandon, desert.*

115   **qui =** 'I who.' **nascens, -entis,** *being born, arising, (just) beginning, nascent.* **propero, -are, -avi, -atus,** *hasten, hurry.* **pello, -ere, pepuli, pulsus,** *drive, drive away.* **morbus, -i,** m., *disease, malady.*

admoveo tardam nunc tibi lentus opem.
Aut nova, si possis, sedare incendia temptes,
    aut ubi per vires procubuere suas.
Cum furor in cursu est, currenti cede furori;
    difficiles aditus impetus omnis habet.   120
Stultus, ab obliquo qui cum descendere possit,
    pugnat in adversas ire natator aquas.
Impatiens animus, nec adhuc tractabilis arte,
    respuit atque odio verba monentis habet.
Adgrediar melius tum, cum sua vulnera tangi   125
    iam sinet et veris vocibus aptus erit.
Quis matrem, nisi mentis inops, in funere nati

---

116 **admoveo, -ere, -movi, -motus,** *bring to, apply.* **tardus, -a,**
     -um, *slow, tardy, delayed.* **lentus, -a, -um,** *slow, without*
haste.

117 **nova:** 'while new.' **sedo, -are, -avi, -atus,** *calm, quench,*
     stop, check. **incendium, -ii,** n., *fire; flame.* **tempto, -are,**
-avi, -atus, *try.* The subjunctive here is best translated as an
imperative.

118 **procumbo, -ere, -cubui, -cubitus,** *fall forward, sink, become*
     exhausted.

119 **furor, -oris,** m., *frenzy, madness, fury.* **cursus, -us,** m., *run-*
     ning, course, (full) speed, (full) career. **curro, -ere, cu-**
curri, cursus, *run, speed.* **cedo, -ere, cessi, cessus,** *go, yield.*

120 **difficilis, -e,** *difficult, hard (to resist or manage), trou-*
     blesome. **aditus, -us,** m., *approach, beginning, onset, on-*
slaught. **impetus, -us,** m., *attack, impulse, ardor, passion.*

121 Rearrange: **Stultus (est) natator qui, cum ab obliquo descen-**
     dere possit, pugnat ire in adversas aquas. stultus, -a, -um,
foolish, silly. **ab obliquo,** *sideways, obliquely.* **descendo, -ere,**
-di, -sus, *descend, go down (stream).*

122 **pugno, -are, -avi, -atus,** *fight, struggle.* **in adversas . . .**
     aquas: 'against the current.' **natator, -oris,** m., *swimmer.*

123 **impatiens, -entis,** *impatient.* **adhuc,** *yet, still.* **tractabi-**
     lis, -e, *manageable.*

124 **respuo, -ere, -ui,** *spit back, reject, repel, refuse.* **odium,**
     -ii, n., *hatred, dislike.* **odio . . .** **habet:** 'regards with
dislike,' 'hates.' **moneo, -ere, -ui, -itus,** *remind, admonish, ad-*
vise, warn. The participle = 'one who . . .'

125 **adgredior, -di, adgressus,** *approach, begin.* **melius** (adv.),
     better, more successfully. **tango, -ere, tetigi, tactus,**
touch, handle.

126 **sino, -ere, sivi, situs,** *let, allow, permit.* **verus, -a, -um,**
     true, genuine, frank.

127 **mater, matris,** f., *mother.* **inops, inopis** (with gen.), *desti-*
     tute of, without. **funus, -eris,** n., *funeral, death.* **natus,**
-i, m., *son.*

flere vetet? Non hoc illa monenda loco est;
cum dederit lacrimas animumque impleverit aegrum,
130   ille dolor verbis emoderandus erit.
Temporis ars medicina fere est:data tempore prosunt,
et data non apto tempore vina nocent.
Quin etiam accendas vitia inritesque vetando,
temporibus si non adgrediare suis.

When you are in a condition to take advice, above all shun idle-
ness. Love flourishes on idleness. Law, politics, or the army will
help to occupy your mind.

135   Ergo ubi visus eris nostrae medicabilis arti,
fac monitis fugias otia prima meis.
Haec, ut ames, faciunt; haec, ut fecere, tuentur;
haec sunt iucundi causa cibusque mali.
Otia si tollas, periere Cupidinis arcus,

---

128   **veto, -are, -ui, -itus,** *forbid.* **monenda est:** 124.

129   **dederit:** here *give = shed.* **impleo, -ere, -evi, -etus,** *fill,*
     satisfy, satiate. **aeger, -gra, -grum,** *sick, suffering.*

130   **dolor, -oris,** m., *pain, ache, distress, grief.* **emoderor,**
     -ari, *moderate, soothe.*

131   **temporis:** 'of the right moment,' 'of seizing the psychologi-
     cal moment.' **medicina, -ae,** f., *medicine.* **fere,** *almost.*
data modifies **vina,** subject of both **prosunt** and **nocent. prosum,**
prodesse, profui, *be useful, do good, benefit, help.*

132   **vinum, -i,** n., *wine.* **noceo, -ere, nocui, nocitus,** *do harm.*

133   **quin etiam,** *nay even, furthermore, besides, what's more.* **ac-**
cendo, -ere, -ndi, -nsus, *kindle, inflame, arouse, excite.*
inrito, -are, -avi, -atus, *excite, stimulate, irritate, stir up.*
veto, -are, -ui, -itus, *forbid, prohibit.*

134   **temporibus . . . suis:** 'at the proper time.' **adgredior, -di,**
     adgressus, *approach, attack, begin.* **adgrediare = adgrediaris.**

135   **ergo,** *accordingly, therefore.* **medicabilis, -e,** *curable.*

136   **monitum, -i,** n., *advice, counsel.* **otium, -ii,** n., *leisure,*
     inactivity, idleness. **prima:** either 'first of all' or 'the
beginnings of.'

137   **haec:** i.e., **otia. tueor, -eri, tuitus,** *watch, preserve,*
     keep. **haec, ut fecere, tuentur:** 'this (idleness), when it
has caused (you to fall in love), keeps (you in love).'

138   **iucundus, -a, -um,** *pleasant, agreeable, delightful.* **cibus,**
     -i, m., *food, nourishment.* **malum, -i,** n., *evil, mischief,*
misfortune.

139   **otia:** 136. **tollo, -ere, sustuli, sublatus,** *raise, take away,*
     remove, do away with. **periere = perierunt. Cupido, -inis,**
m., *Cupid, god of love.* **arcus, -us,** m., *bow.*

contemptaeque iacent et sine luce faces. 140
Quam platanus vino gaudet, quam populus unda,
  et quam limosa canna palustris humo,
tam Venus otia amat; qui finem quaeris amoris
  (cedit amor rebus), res age: tutus eris.
Languor et immodici sub nullo vindice somni 145
  aleaque et multo tempora quassa mero
eripiunt omnes animo sine vulnere nervos;
  adfluit incautis insidiosus Amor.
Desidiam puer ille sequi solet, odit agentes:
  da vacuae menti, quo teneatur, opus. 150
Sunt fora, sunt leges, sunt, quos tuearis, amici:

---

140 **contemno, -ere, -tempsi, -temptus,** *despise, disdain.* **lux,
    lucis,** f., *light.* **fax, facis,** f., *torch* (one of the attri-
butes of Cupid).

141 **platanus, -i,** f., *plane tree* (on whose roots wine was some-
    times poured in return for the shade it afforded parties).
vinum, -i, n., *wine.* **gaudeo, -ere, gavisus sum,** *rejoice in, take
pleasure in, be pleased with.* **populus, -i,** f., *poplar tree.*

142 **limosus, -a, -um,** *muddy, miry, marshy.* **canna, -ae,** f., *reed.*
    paluster, -tris, -tre, *of the marsh* or *swamp.* **humus, -i,** f.,
earth, ground, soil.

143 **otia:** 136. **qui:** 'you who.' **finis, -is,** m., *end, limit.*

144 **cedo, -ere, cessi, cessus,** *go, yield to.* **res, rei,** f.,
    thing, affair, deed, business matter, business. **tutus, -a,
-um,** *safe, out of danger.*

145 **languor, -oris,** m., *languor, sluggishness, inactivity, lazi-
    ness.* **immodicus, -a, -um,** *excessive, immoderate.* **vindex,
-icis,** m., f., *defender, liberator, punisher.* **sub nullo vindice:**
'with no one to hinder.' **somnus, -i,** m., *sleep, slumber.*

146 **alea, -ae,** f., *game of dice, dicing, gambling with dice.*
    quassus, -a, -um, *shaken, throbbing.* **merum, -i,** n., *unmixed
wine.*

147 **eripio, -ere, eripui, ereptus,** *snatch away, take away.* **ner-
vus, -i,** m., *sinew, nerve, vigor, energy, strength.*

148 **adfluo, -ere, -xi, -xus** (with dat.), *flow to, (glide into,
    worm one's way into).* **incauti, -orum,** m., *the incautious,
the heedless.* **insidiosus, -a, -um,** *cunning, artful, deceitful.*

149 **desidia, -ae,** f., *idleness, inactivity.* **sequor, sequi, secu-
    tus,** *follow, attend.* **odi, odisse,** *hate, dislike.* **agentes:**
'the busy.'

150 **vacuus, -a, -um,** *empty, vacant, unoccupied, idle.* **quo:** the
    antecedent is **opus.**

151 **forum, -i,** n., *market place, forum* (center of public life),
    law court. **lex, legis,** f., *law.* **tueor, -eri, tuitus,** *look
at, defend, protect.* **amicus, -i,** m., *friend.*

152   vade per urbanae splendida castra togae;
        vel tu sanguinei iuvenalia munera Martis
            suscipe: deliciae iam tibi terga dabunt.

Life in the country and hunting are also good distractions. At
night you will be so tired that sleep, not thoughts about the
girl, will overwhelm you. Fishing and travel are worth trying,
too.

        Rura quoque oblectant animos studiumque colendi;
170   quaelibet huic curae cedere cura potest.
        Colla iube domitos oneri supponere tauros,
            sauciet ut duram vomer aduncus humum;
        obrue versata Cerealia semina terra,
            quae tibi cum multo faenore reddat ager.
175   Adspice curvatos pomorum pondere ramos,

---

152   **vado, -ere,** *go.* **urbanus, -a, -um,** *belonging to the city,
    city-, civic, civil.* **splendidus, -a, -um,** *bright, shining,
brilliant, distinguished.* **castra, -orum,** n., *camp.* **toga, -ae,**
f., *toga* (the rather formal outer garment of a Roman civilian, in
contrast with military garb). --This line perhaps refers to a
political career. Candidates wore shining white togas (**candidatus**
= 'one clothed in white').

153   **vel,** *or.* **tu:** omit with imperative. **sanguineus, -a, -um,**
    bloody, bloodthirsty. **iuvenalis, -e,** *youthful.* **Mars, Mar-
tis,** m.: god of war.

154   **suscipio, -ere, -cepi, -ceptus,** *undertake.* **deliciae, -arum,**
    f., *delight, pleasure, voluptuousness, frolics, (amorous
thoughts); darling, sweetheart.* **tergum, -i,** n., *back.* **tibi terga
dabunt:** 'will take to flight from you.'

169   **rus, ruris,** n., *the country, fields, farm.* **oblecto, -are,
    -avi, -atus,** *delight, please, divert.* **studium, -ii,** n.,
zeal, fondness, study, pursuit.

170   **quilibet, quaelibet, quodlibet,** *any . . . whatsoever.* **cedo,
    -ere, cessi, cessus,** *go, yield to, be second to.*

171   **collum, -i,** n., *neck.* **domo, -are, -ui, -itus,** *tame, subdue.*
    onus, oneris, n., *load, burden.* **suppono, -ere, -posui,
-positus** (with acc. & dat.), *place . . . under.* **taurus, -i,** m.,
bull, ox.

172   **saucio, -are, -avi, -atus,** *wound, dig into, tear up.* **vomer,
    -eris,** m., *plowshare.* **aduncus, -a, -um,** *hooked, curved.* **hu-
mus, -i,** f., *earth, ground, soil.*

173   **obruo, -ere, -ui, -utus,** *overwhelm, bury, sow.* **verso, -are,
    -avi, -atus,** *turn, overturn.* **Cerealis, -e,** *of Ceres* (goddess
of agriculture). **semen, -inis,** n., *seed.* **terra, -ae,** f., *land,
soil, ground, earth.*

174   **faenus, faenoris,** n., *interest.* **reddat:** note subjunctive;
    relative clause of purpose. **ager, agri,** m., *field, land.*

175   **adspicio, -ere, -spexi, -spectus,** *look at, behold, see,
    watch.* **curvo, -are, -avi, -atus,** *bend, curve.* **pomum, -i,**
n., *fruit, apple.* **ramus, -i,** m., *branch.*

ut sua, quod peperit, vix ferat arbor onus;
adspice labentes iucundo murmure rivos;
    adspice tondentes fertile gramen oves.
Ecce, petunt rupes praeruptaque saxa capellae;
    iam referent haedis ubera plena suis.   180
Pastor inaequali modulatur harundine carmen,
    nec desunt comites, sedula turba, canes.
Parte sonant alia silvae mugitibus altae,
    et queritur vitulum mater abesse suum.
Quid, cum suppositos fugiunt examina fumos,   185
    ut relevent dempti vimina curva favi?

---

176   **sua** modifies **arbor** and refers to **onus**.   **pario, -ere, peperi,
      paritus** & **partus,** *bring forth, bear, produce.*   **vix,** *scarcely,
hardly, with difficulty.*   **arbor, -oris,** f., *tree.*   **onus:** 171.

177   **adspice:** 175.   **labor, labi, lapsus,** *glide, slip, flow.*   **iu-
      cundus, -a, -um,** *pleasant, pleasing, delightful.*   **murmur,
murmuris,** n., *murmur.*   **rivus, -i,** m., *small stream, brook.*

178   **adspice:** 175.   **tondeo, -ere, totondi, tonsus,** *shear, crop,
      graze upon.*   **fertilis, -e,** *fertile.*   **gramen, -inis,** n.,
grass, pasture.*   **ovis, -is,** f., *sheep.*

179   **ecce,** *lo! behold! see!*   **rupes, -is,** f., *rock, cliff.*   **prae-
      ruptus, -a, -um,** *steep, abrupt, rugged.*   **saxum, -i,** n., *rock.*
capella, -ae, f., *she-goat.*

180   **haedus, -i,** m., *young goat, kid.*   **uber, -eris,** n., *udder.*
      plenus, -a, -um, *full.*

181   **pastor, -oris,** m., *shepherd.*   **inaequalis, -e,** *uneven, une-
      qual.*   **modulor, -ari, -atus,** *measure rhythmically, play.*   **ha-
rundo, -inis,** f., *reed, reed pipe* (made of several reeds of dif-
ferent lengths).   **carmen, -inis,** n., *song, poem, poetry.*

182   **desum, -esse, -fui,** *be absent, be missing.*   **comes, -itis,** m.,
      f., *companion, comrade.*   **sedulus, -a, -um,** *busy, industrious.*
turba, -ae,** f., *crowd, throng, band.*   **canis, -is,** m., f., *dog.*

183   **sono, -are, -ui, -itus,** *sound, resound.*   **alius, -a, -ud,** *an-
      other, other.*   **silva, -ae,** f., *wood, forest.*   **mugitus, -us,**
m., *lowing, bellowing, moo.*   **altus, -a, -um,** *high, deep.*

184   **queror, -i, questus,** *complain, lament.*   **vitulus, -i,** m.,
      calf.*   **mater, -tris,** f., *mother.*   **absum, abesse, afui,** *be
absent, be missing.*

185   **Quid, cum** = 'What about the time when.'   **suppono, -ere, sup-
      posui, suppositus,** *put under, place beneath.*   **examen, -inis,**
n., *swarm of bees.*   **fumus, -i,** m., *smoke.*

186   **relevo, -are, -avi, -atus,** *lighten, relieve.*   **demo, -ere,
      dempsi, demptus,** *take away, remove.*   **vimen, -inis,** n., *pli-
ant twig, osier, wickerwork, wickerwork beehive.*   **curvus, -a, -um,**
curved.*   **favus, -i,** m., *honeycomb.*   **favi** is subject of **relevent.**

Poma dat autumnus; formosa est messibus aestas;
    ver praebet flores; igne levatur hiems.
Temporibus certis maturam rusticus uvam
190   deligit, et nudo sub pede musta fluunt;
temporibus certis desectas alligat herbas,
    et tonsam raro pectine verrit humum.
Ipse potes riguis plantam deponere in hortis,
    ipse potes rivos ducere lenis aquae.
195 Venerit insitio: fac ramum ramus adoptet,
    stetque peregrinis arbor operta comis.
Cum semel haec animum coepit mulcere voluptas,
    debilibus pinnis inritus exit Amor.

---

187 **pomum, -i,** n., *fruit* of a tree; *apple,* etc. **autumnus, -i,** m., *autumn, fall.* **messis, -is,** f., *harvest.* **aestas, -atis,** f., *summer.*

188 **ver, veris,** n., *spring.* **praebeo, -ere, -ui, -itus,** *offer, furnish, supply.* **flos, -oris,** m., *flower, blossom.* **levo, -are, -avi, -atus,** *lighten, relieve, ease, alleviate.* **hiems, -emis,** f., *winter.*

189 **certus, -a, -um,** *fixed, definite, certain.* **maturus, -a, -um,** *ripe, mature.* **rusticus, -i,** m., *countryman, rustic, peasant.* **uva, -ae,** f., *grape.*

190 **deligo, -ere, -legi, -lectus,** *select, gather, pick.* **nudus, -a, -um,** *naked, bare.* **mustum, -i,** n., *new wine, must.* **fluo, -ere, -xi, -xus,** *flow.* --An unsavory but time-honored method of pressing out the juice from the grapes.

191 **certis:** 189. **deseco, -are, -cui, -ctus,** *cut, mow.* **alligo, -are, -avi, -atus,** *bind.* **herba, -ae,** f., *grass, crop.*

192 **tondeo, -ere, totondi, tonsus,** *shear, crop, mow.* **rarus, -a, -um,** *far apart, wide-toothed, rare, few.* **pecten, -inis,** m., *comb, rake.* **verro, -ere, verri, versus,** *scrape, sweep.* **humus, -i,** f., *earth, ground, soil.*

193 **riguus, -a, -um,** *well-watered.* **planta, -ae,** f., *sprout, sprig, shoot, young plant, slip; sole.* **depono, -ere, -posui, -positus,** *set down, set out, plant.* **hortus, -i,** m., *garden.*

194 **rivus, -i,** m., *small stream, channel, canal, ditch.* **duco, -ere, duxi, ductus,** *lead, guide, direct, draw, construct.* **lenis, -e,** *smooth, gentle, calm.*

195 **insitio, -onis,** f., *grafting, season for grafting.* **ramus, -i,** m., *branch.* **adopto, -are, -avi, -atus,** *adopt.*

196 **sto, -are, steti, status,** *stand.* **peregrinus, -a, -um,** *strange, alien, not one's own.* **arbor, -oris,** f., *tree.* **operio, -ire, operui, opertus,** *cover.*

197 **semel,** *once.* **(coepio, -ere,) coepi, coeptus,** *begin, commence.* **mulceo, -ere, -si, -sus,** *soothe, delight.* **voluptas, -atis,** f., *enjoyment, pleasure, delight.*

198 **debilis, -e,** *lame, feeble, weak.* **inritus, -a, -um,** *useless,*

Vel tu venandi studium cole: saepe recessit
  turpiter a Phoebi victa sorore Venus.   200
Nunc leporem pronum catulo sectare sagaci,
  nunc tua frondosis retia tende iugis,
aut pavidos terre varia formidine cervos,
  aut cadat adversa cuspide fossus aper.
Nocte fatigatum somnus, non cura puellae,   205
  excipit et pingui membra quiete levat.
Lenius est studium, studium tamen, alite capta
  aut lino aut calamis praemia parva sequi,

---

ineffectual, devoid of results, having no effect.   **exeo,**
-ire, -ii, -itus, *go out, go away, depart.*

199 **vel,** *or.* **venor, -ari, -atus,** *hunt.* **studium, -ii,** n., *zeal,*
  fondness, study, interest, pursuit. **recedo, -ere, recessi,**
recessus, *give ground, retire, withdraw.*

200 **turpiter,** *basely, shamefully, humiliatingly.* **Phoebus, -i,**
  m., *Phoebus, Apollo* (brother of Diana, goddess of chastity
and the chase). **soror, -oris,** f., *sister.*

201 **lepus, -oris,** m., *hare.* **pronus, -a, -um,** *leaning forward,*
  swiftly flying. **catulus, -i,** m., *young dog, puppy.* **sector,**
-ari, -atus, *follow after, chase, pursue.* **sectare** is imperative.
sagax, -acis, *keen-scented, sagacious, shrewd.*

202 **frondosus, -a, -um,** *leafy.* **rete, -is,** n., *net.* **tendo, -ere,**
  tetendi, tentus & tensus, *stretch.* **iugum, -i,** n., *yoke,*
mountain ridge.

203 **pavidus, -a, -um,** *trembling, fearful, timid.* **terreo, -ere,**
  -ui, -itus, *frighten, terrify.* **varius, -a, -um,** *different,*
changing, various; varicolored, of various colors. **formido,**
-inis, f., *fear, terror, fright; a 'fright-line'* (a cord hung with
feathers of different colors to frighten and drive game into
nets). **cervus, -i,** m., *stag, deer.*

204 **cado, -ere, cecidi, casus,** *fall, perish.* **adversus, -a, -um,**
  turned toward, opposite, opposing, hostile. **cuspis, -idis,**
f., *point, point of a spear, spear.* **fodio, -ere, fodi, fossus,**
dig, pierce, wound. **aper, apri,** m., *wild boar.*

205 **fatigo, -are, -avi, -atus,** *weary, tire, fatigue.* With **fatiga-**
  tum supply **te.** **somnus, -i,** m., *sleep, slumber.*

206 **excipio, -ere, -cepi, -ceptus,** *take, receive, capture.* **pin-**
  guis, -e, *fat, calm, undisturbed.* **membrum, -i,** n., *limb.*
quies, -etis, f., *rest, quiet, repose.* **levo, -are, -avi, -atus,**
lighten, relieve, ease, refresh.

207 **lenis, -e,** *gentle, mild, calm.* **studium, -ii,** n., *zeal, in-*
  terest, pursuit. **ales, -itis,** m., f., *bird.*

208 **linum, -i,** n., *thread, net.* **calamus, -i,** m., *reed, limed*
  twig (for catching birds). **praemium, -ii,** n., *reward, prize,*
booty. **parvus, -a, -um,** *little, small.* **sequor, sequi, secutus,**
follow, pursue, seek.

      vel, quae piscis edax avido male devoret ore,
210   abdere sub parvis aera recurva cibis.
      Aut his aut aliis, donec dediscis amare,
      ipse tibi furtim decipiendus eris.
      Tu tantum, quamvis firmis retinebere vinclis,
      i procul et longas carpere perge vias.
215   Flebis, et occurret desertae nomen amicae,
      stabit et in media pes tibi saepe via;
      sed quanto minus ire voles, magis ire memento:
      perfer et invitos currere coge pedes.
      Nec pluvias opta, nec te peregrina morentur
220   sabbata nec damnis Allia nota suis;

---

209   quae: its antecedent is aera; note that its verb is in the
      subjunctive. piscis, -is, m., fish. edax, -acis, gluttonous, greedy. avidus, -a, -um, eager, hungry, greedy. devoro,
-are, -avi, -atus, swallow, gulp down, devour.

210   abdo, -ere, abdidi, abditus, hide, conceal. parvis: 208.
      aes, aeris, n., copper, bronze; fishhook. recurvus, -a, -um,
bent back, curved. cibus, -i, m., food. --The infinitive abdere,
like sequi (208), goes back to lenius est studium (207).

211   With his and aliis understand studiis. donec, as long as,
      while, until. dedisco, -ere,-didici, unlearn, forget, learn
not.

212   furtim, by stealth, secretly. decipio, -ere, decepi, deceptus, beguile, deceive.

213   tantum (adv.), only. quamvis, although. firmus, -a, -um,
      firm, strong, powerful. retineo, -ere, -ui, -tentus, keep
back, hold fast, restrain. retinebere = retineberis. vinclum,-i,
n., bond, fetter, tie, chain.

214   i: imperative of eo. procul, far away. carpo, -ere, -psi,
      -ptus, pick; (with viam) take a trip, make a journey. pergo,
-ere, perrexi, perrectus, continue, proceed.

215   occurro, -ere, occurri, occursus, present itself, occur, re-
      cur to one's thoughts. desertus, -a, -um, deserted, for-
saken, abandoned.

216   sto, -are, steti, status, stand, tarry, linger, halt. et:
      translate at beginning of line.

217   quanto minus: 'by how much less' = 'the less.' magis, (the)
      more. memento is imperative of memini, -isse, remember.

218   perfero, -ferre, -tuli, -latus, carry through, see it
      through, endure to the end. invitus, -a, -um, unwilling,
reluctant. curro, -ere, cucurri, cursus, run, hasten. cogo,
-ere, coegi, coactus, collect, force, compel.

219   pluvia, -ae, f., rain, shower. opto, -are, -avi, -atus, wish
      for, hope for. peregrinus, -a, -um, strange, foreign. mo-
ror, -ari, -atus, delay, retard, detain.

220   sabbata, -orum, n., the Sabbath, the day of rest of the Jews.

nec quot transieris, sed quot tibi, quaere, supersint

   milia, nec, maneas ut prope, finge moras.

Tempora nec numera nec crebro respice Romam,

   sed fuge: tutus adhuc Parthus ab hoste fuga est.

Like medicine, this advice may be bitter, but it will be good
for you. You can become used to anything. Don't return to the city
too soon.

Dura aliquis praecepta vocet mea: dura fatemur   225

   esse, sed ut valeas, multa dolenda feres.

Saepe bibi sucos, quamvis invitus, amaros

   aeger, et oranti mensa negata mihi.

There were a great many Jews in Rome. **damnum**, **-i**, n., *in-
jury, misfortune, disaster.* **Allia**, **-ae**, f., *the Allia,* a little
river north of Rome where the Romans were disastrously defeated by
the Gauls July 18, 390 or 387 B.C. Anniversaries of this battle
were considered days of bad luck, equivalent to Friday the thir-
teenth. Obviously Ovid considers that a person using this date or
the Sabbath or rain as an excuse for not starting his journey is
simply weakening in his resolve to make the break with the girl.
notus, **-a**, **-um**, *known, well-known, famous.*

221 Rearrange as follows: **nec quaere quot milia transieris, sed
     quot tibi supersint.** **transeo**, **-ire**, **-ivi** (**-ii**), **-itus**, *pass
over, traverse, travel.* **supersum**, **-esse**, **-fui**, *be left, remain.*

222 **mille** (plur., **milia**, **-ium**), *a thousand; a thousand paces, a
     mile.* **maneo**, **-ere**, **mansi**, **mansus**, *stay, remain.* **prope**,
near. **fingo**, **-ere**, **finxi**, **fictus**, *imagine, contrive, invent.*

223 **tempora:** 'the time,' 'the days,' 'the hours.' **nec:** translate
     at the first of the line. **numero**, **-are**, **-avi**, **-atus**, *count.*
crebro, *repeatedly, frequently.* **respicio**, **-ere**, **respexi**, **respec-
tus**, *look back at.* **Roma**, **-ae**, f., *Rome.*

224 **tutus**, **-a**, **-um**, *safe.* **adhuc**, *still, yet.* **Parthus**, **-i**, m.,
     the Parthian. The Parthians were Rome's most stubborn enemy.
Their favorite method of fighting was to discharge their arrows in
a vicious shower at their opponents as they (the Parthians) turned
their horses to retreat. This annoying procedure is one of the
earliest examples of hit-and-run tactics. **hostis**, **-is**, m., f.,
enemy, foe. **fuga**, **-ae**, f., *flight, running away.*

225 **praeceptum**, **-i**, n., *precept, advice, instruction, direction.*
     voco, **-are**, **-avi**, **-atus**, *call.* **fateor**, **-eri**, **fassus**, *con-
fess, admit.*

226 **valeo**, **-ere**, **-ui**, **-itus**, *be strong, be healthy.* **doleo**, **-ere**,
     -ui, **-itus**, *suffer, lament.* **dolenda:** 'things to be lamented,'
'disagreeable things.'

227 **sucus**, **-i**, m., *juice, dose, medicine.* **quamvis**, *although.*
     invitus, **-a**, **-um**, *unwilling, against one's will, reluctant.*
amarus, **-a**, **-um**, *bitter.*

228 **aeger**, **-gra**, **-grum**, *ill, sick.* **oro**, **-are**, **-avi**, **-atus**, *beg,
     plead.* **mensa**, **-ae**, f., *table, meal, food.* **nego**, **-are**, **-avi**,
-atus, *say no, deny, refuse.* With **negata** supply **est.**

       Ut corpus redimas, ferrum patieris et ignes
230   arida nec sitiens ora levabis aqua:
       ut valeas animo, quicquam tolerare negabis?
          At pretium pars haec corpore maius habet.
       Sed tamen est artis tristissima ianua nostrae,
          et labor est unus tempora prima pati.
235   Adspicis ut prensos urant iuga prima iuvencos
          et nova velocem cingula laedat equum?
       Forsitan a Laribus patriis exire pigebit,
          sed tamen exibis; deinde redire voles,
       nec te Lar patrius, sed amor revocabit amicae,
240   praetendens culpae splendida verba tuae.

---

229   **redimo, -ere, -emi, -emptus,** *buy back, redeem, release, free
    from disease.* **ferrum, -i,** n., *iron, knife.* **patior, pati,**
passus, *undergo, endure, suffer, allow.*

230   **aridus, -a, -um,** *dry, parched.* **nec:** to be translated at
    first of line. **sitio, -ire, -ivi (-ii),** *thirst, be thirsty.*
levo, -are, -avi, -atus, *raise, relieve, ease, refresh.*

231   **valeas:** 226. **quisquam, quicquam,** *anyone, anything.* **tolero,
    -are, -avi, -atus,** *bear, endure.* **negabis:** 228.

232   **pretium, -ii,** n., *worth, value, price.* --I.e., peace of mind
    is even more precious than health of body.

233   This couplet means that the initial stages are the worst.
    tristis, -e, *sad, harsh, disagreeable, bitter.* **ianua, -ae,**
f., *door, entrance, gateway, approach, (first stage).*

234   **labor, -oris,** m., *labor, toil, hardship, trouble.* **tempora =**
    'days of separation.' **pati:** 229.

235   **adspicio, -ere, adspexi, adspectus,** *behold, see.* **ut,** *how.*
    prendo, -ere, -di, -sus, *seize, catch.* **uro, -ere, ussi, us-**
tus, *burn, rub sore, chafe.* **iugum, -i,** n., *yoke, ridge.* **iuven-**
cus, -i, m., *young bullock, young ox.*

236   **velox, -ocis,** *swift, fleet, speedy.* **cingula, -ae,** f., *belt,
    girth.*

237   **forsitan,** *perhaps.* **Lares, -um & -ium,** m., *household gods;
    home.* **patrius, -a, -um,** *father's, paternal, ancestral.* **ex-**
eo, -ire, -ii, -itus, *go out, go away, depart.* **piget, -ere, pi-**
guit & pigitum est, *it annoys, it troubles, it disgusts, it makes
sorry.* **(te) pigebit:** 'you will be reluctant.'

238   **exibis:** 237. **deinde,** *then, next.* **redeo, -ire, -ii, -itus,**
    go back, come back, return.

239   **Lar, Laris,** m., *household god, home.* **patrius:** 237. **revoco,
    -are, -avi, -atus,** *call back, recall.*

240   **praetendo, -ere, -di, -tus** (with acc. & dat.), *spread . . .
    in front of, use . . . to hide.* **culpa, -ae,** f., *fault,
blame, failure.* **splendidus, -a, -um,** *bright, splendid, showy,
fine, specious.*

Cum semel exieris, centum solacia curae
et rus et comites et via longa dabit.
Nec satis esse putes discedere: lentus abesto,
dum perdat vires sitque sine igne cinis.
Quod nisi firmata properaris mente reverti, 245
inferet arma tibi saeva rebellis Amor;
quidquid et afueris, avidus sitiensque redibis,
et spatium damno cesserit omne tuo.

Magic won't do you any good (249-290). The simplest cure for love is the use of some will power. But for those who are not so strong-willed, Ovid suggests a little psychotherapy: make a list of your darling's faults, and then go over the list repeatedly.

Si te causa potens domina retinebit in Urbe, 291
accipe, consilium quod sit in Urbe meum.

---

241 **semel,** *once.* **exieris:** 237. **centum** (indecl. adj.), *a hundred.* **solacium, -ii,** n., *comfort, consolation, solace, compensation.*

242 **rus, ruris,** n., *country, fields.* **comes, -itis,** m., f., *companion, comrade.*

243 **satis,** *enough, sufficient.* **putes:** subjunctive for imperative. **discedo, -ere, -cessi, -cessus,** *go away, depart, leave.* **lentus, -a, -um,** *slow, lingering, for a long time.* **absum, abesse, afui,** *be away, be absent.* **abesto:** future imperative.

244 **perdo, -ere, -didi, -ditus,** *waste, destroy, lose.* **cinis, -eris,** m., *ashes, embers.*

245 **quod** (with **nisi**), *but.* The negative in **nisi** is best taken with **firmata:** 'if you hasten to return with your mind not strengthened.' **firmo, -are, -avi, -atus,** *strengthen, fortify.* **propero, -are, -avi, -atus,** *hasten, hurry.* **properaris = properaveris.** **revertor, -ti, reversus,** *come back, return.*

246 **infero, -ferre, -tuli, illatus,** *bring against;* (with **arma**) *make an attack on.* **arma, -orum,** n., *arms, weapons.* **saevus, -a, -um,** *savage, fierce, cruel.* **rebellis, -is,** *insurgent, rebellious.*

247 **quidquid et afueris:** 'and however long you have been away.' **afueris:** 243. **avidus, -a, -um,** *eager, hungry, greedy.* **sitiens, -entis,** *thirsting, thirsty, athirst.* **redeo, -ire, -ii, -itus,** *go back, come back, return.*

248 **spatium, -ii,** n., *space, space of time, interval, period.* **damnum, -i,** n., *harm, injury, loss.* **cedo, -ere, cessi, cessus,** *go; eventuate, happen, result, turn out, work.* **damno cesserit . . . tuo:** 'will have worked to your disadvantage,' 'will have resulted in your loss.'

291 **potens, -entis,** *strong, powerful.* **domina:** in apposition with **Urbe,** 'mistress of the world'; or as adj., 'the Queen City.' **retineo, -ere, -ui, -tentus,** *detain, keep, hold.* **urbs, urbis,** f., *city;* especially, the city of Rome.

292 **consilium, -ii,** n., *plan, advice, counsel.* **Urbe:** 291.

Optimus ille fuit vindex, laedentia pectus
     vincula qui rupit dedoluitque semel;
295   sicui tantum animi est, illum mirabor et ipse
     et dicam 'Monitis non eget iste meis.'
Tu mihi, qui, quod amas, aegre dediscis amare
     nec potes et velles posse, docendus eris.
Saepe refer tecum sceleratae facta puellae
300   et pone ante oculos omnia damna tuos.
'Illud et illud habet, nec ea contenta rapina est;
     sub titulum nostros misit avara Lares.
Sic mihi iuravit, sic me iurata fefellit,
     ante suas quotiens passa iacere fores!

---

293 **optimus, -a, -um,** *best.* **vindex, -icis,** m., f., *deliverer, liberator;* here = 'liberator of himself.'

294 **vinculum, -i,** n., *bond, fetter, chain.* **qui:** antecedent is **ille. rumpo, -ere, rupi, ruptus,** *break, burst, sever.* **dedoleo, -ere, -ui,** *leave off grieving, cease to grieve.* **semel,** *once, once for all.*

295 **sicui** (dat. of poss.) **tantum animi** (part. gen.) **est:** 'if anyone has that much will power.' **tantum, -i,** n., *so much.* **miror, -ari, -atus,** *wonder at, admire.*

296 **monitum, -i,** n., *admonition, advice, counsel, instruction.* **egeo, -ere, -ui** (with abl.), *need, lack.* **iste, ista, istud,** *that (one), that of yours, this (one); he, she, it.*

297 **mihi:** dat. of agent with **docendus eris. quod amas:** object of **amare. aegre,** *with difficulty, reluctantly.* **dedisco, -ere, dedidici,** *unlearn, learn how not to.*

298 **velles** (imperf. subjunctive of **volo**): 'would like.'

299 **refer tecum:** 'repeat to yourself,' 'recall to your mind,' 'go over with yourself.' **sceleratus, -a, -um,** *bad, wicked, naughty.* **factum, -i,** n., *deed, act, action.*

300 **damnum, -i,** n., *hurt, loss, injury.*

301 **illud et illud:** 'this and that of mine.' **is, ea, id,** *this, that; he, she, it.* **ea** here is abl., modifying **rapina. contentus, -a, -um,** *content, satisfied.* **rapina, -ae,** f., *robbery, plundering, pillage, plunder, booty.*

302 **titulus, -i,** m., *inscription, placard, notice of sale.* **sub titulum** = 'under the auctioneer's hammer.' **mitto, -ere, misi, missus,** *cause to go, send.* **avarus, -a, -um,** *greedy, covetous.* **Lares, -um,** m., *household gods, home.*--Ovid means that the girl's greedy extravagance has forced the man to sell his home.

303 **iuro, -are, -avi, -atus** (also deponent), *swear.* **fallo, -ere, fefelli, falsus,** *deceive, trick, cheat.*

304 **quotiens,** *how often, how many times, as often as.* **patior, pati, passus,** *endure, allow, permit.* **iacere:** supply **me** as subject. **foris, -is,** f., *door, gate.*

Diligit ipsa alios, a me fastidit amari;   305
   institor (heu!) noctes, quas mihi non dat, habet!'
Haec tibi per totos inacescant omnia sensus,
   haec refer, hinc odii semina quaere tui.
Atque utinam possis etiam facundus in illis
   esse! Dole tantum: sponte disertus eris.   310
Haeserat in quadam nuper mea cura puella:
   conveniens animo non erat illa meo;
curabar propriis aeger Podalirius herbis
   et, fateor, medicus turpiter aeger eram.
Profuit adsidue vitiis insistere amicae,   315
   idque mihi factum saepe salubre fuit.

---

305 **diligo, -ere, -lexi, -lectus,** *choose out, esteem, love.*
    alius, -a, -ud, *another, other.* **fastidio, -ire, -ivi (-ii),**
  -itus, *disdain, despise, scorn.*

306 **institor, -oris,** m., *agent, peddler, traveling salesman.*
    heu, *alas! oh unhappy day!* **noctes:** 'nights' = 'dates.'

307 **totus, -a, -um,** *all, the whole, entire.* **inacesco, -ere, ina-**
    cui, *turn sour, ferment.* **sensus, -us,** m., *feeling, sense.*

308 **refer:** see note on 299. **hinc,** *hence, from here, from this*
    source. **odium, -ii,** n., *hatred, ill will, dislike.* **semen,**
  -inis, n., *seed, origin.*

309 **utinam,** *would that! if only! I wish that.* **facundus, -a, -um,**
    eloquent. **illis** refers to the same things as **haec** above.

310 **doleo, -ere, -ui, -itus,** *feel pain, suffer, grieve.* **tantum**
    (adv.), *only.* **sponte,** *of one's own accord, spontaneously.*
  disertus, -a, -um, *fluent.*

311 **haereo, -ere, haesi, haesus,** *stick, become fixed, attach one-*
    self. **quidam, quaedam, quoddam,** *a certain, some.* **nuper,**
  recently, not long ago. **cura** (nom.): 'fancy.' **puella:** abl. with
  in quadam.

312 **conveniens, -entis,** *harmonious, appropriate to, fit, suit-*
    able.

313 **curo, -are, -avi, -atus,** *care for, cure, heal.* **proprius, -a,**
    -um, *one's (my) own.* **aeger, -gra, -grum,** *ill, sick.* **Podali-**
  rius, -ii, m.: a celebrated Greek physician in the Trojan War.
  Here in apposition with the subject 'I'; Ovid visualizes himself
  as a sick physician, cured by his own medicine. **herba, -ae,** f.,
  herb, plant, grass.

314 **fateor, -eri, fassus,** *confess, admit.* **medicus, -i,** m., *phy-*
    sician, doctor. **turpiter,** *shamefully.* **aeger:** 313.

315 **prosum, prodesse, profui,** *be useful, be of use, do good,*
    help. **adsidue,** *continually, constantly.* **insisto, -ere,**
  institi (with dat.), *press upon, dwell upon, consider at length.*

316 **factum, -i,** n., *deed, act.* Could also be construed as parti-
    ciple of **facio** here. **salubris, -e,** *health-giving, wholesome,*
  beneficial.

'Quam mala' dicebam 'nostrae sunt crura puellae!'
nec tamen, ut vere confiteamur, erant.
'Bracchia quam non sunt nostrae formosa puellae!'
320   et tamen, ut vere confiteamur, erant.
'Quam brevis est'; nec erat. 'Quam multum poscit amantem!'
haec odio venit maxima causa meo.

Since good qualities are often closely akin to bad ones, by
using the worse terms for things you may make the young lady seem
less attractive than she is. Coax her to do the things she does
least well. Try to catch her before she has primped herself.

Et mala sunt vicina bonis; errore sub illo
pro vitio virtus crimina saepe tulit.
325   Qua potes, in peius dotes deflecte puellae
iudiciumque brevi limite falle tuum.
Turgida, si plena est, si fusca est, nigra vocetur;
in gracili macies crimen habere potest;

---

317   **malus, -a, -um,** *bad, bad-looking, ugly, ill-shaped.* **crus,
cruris,** n., *leg.*

318   **vere,** *truly, aright; (the truth).* **confiteor, -eri, -fessus,**
acknowledge, confess, admit.

319   **bracchium, -ii,** n., *arm.*

320   **vere:** 318. **confiteamur:** 318.

321   **brevis, -e,** *short, little, small.* **posco, -ere, poposci** (with
two accusatives), *ask . . . for, beg from, demand from.*
amans, -antis, m., *lover.*

322   **odium, -ii,** n., *hatred, ill will, dislike, aversion.* **venit =**
'became.' **maximus, -a, -um,** *greatest, most important, chief.*

323   **malum, -i,** n., *bad thing, evil, bad quality.* **vicinus, -a,
-um,** *neighboring, near, similar, akin.* **bonum, -i,** n., *good
thing, good quality.* **error, -oris,** m., *error, mistake.*

324   **pro** (with abl.), *before, for, instead of, in place of, as
though.* **virtus, -utis,** f., *manliness, courage; worth, excel-
lence, merit, virtue.*

325   **in peius** (neut. comp. of **malus**): 'to the worse.' **dos, dotis,**
f., *dowry, gift, endowment, good quality.* **deflecto, -ere,
-xi, -xus,** *turn aside, turn.*

326   **iudicium, -ii,** n., *judgment, opinion, discernment.* **brevis,
-e,** *short, narrow, little, sma'!.* **limes, -itis,** m., *path,
boundary, distinction, difference.* By this word Ovid refers to the
narrow dividing line which separates many good qualities from the
corresponding bad qualities. Examples follow in succeeding lines.

327   **turgidus, -a, -um,** *swollen, inflated, (fat, flabby).* **plenus,
-a, -um,** *full, plump, well rounded, well filled out.* **fus-
cus, -a, -um,** *dark, swarthy, brunette.* **niger, -gra, -grum,** *black.*
voco, -are, -avi, -atus, *call.*

328   **gracilis, -e,** *slight, slender, slim.* With **gracili** supply **pu-**

et poterit dici petulans, quae rustica non est,
  et poterit dici rustica, siqua proba est.   330
Quin etiam, quacumque caret tua femina dote,
  hanc moveat, blandis usque precare sonis:
exige uti cantet, siqua est sine voce puella;
  fac saltet, nescit siqua movere manum.
Barbara sermone est? Fac tecum multa loquatur.   335
  Non didicit chordas tangere? Posce lyram!
Durius incedit? Fac inambulet.   *   *
     *   *   *   *   *   *   *

Si male dentata est, narra, quod rideat, illi.
  Mollibus est oculis? Quod fleat illa, refer.   340
Proderit et subito, cum se non finxerit ulli,

---

ella. macies, -ei, f., *thinness, skinniness, emaciation.*
crimen habere: 'have a reproach = 'be the criticism.'

329 petulans, -antis, *forward, impudent, bold, (unladylike).*
  rusticus, -a, -um, *rustic, simple, provincial, prudish.*

330 rustica: 329. probus, -a, -um, *good, virtuous, well-behaved.*

331 quin etiam, *nay even, furthermore, besides, what's more.* ca-
    reo, -ere, -ui, -itus (with abl.), *be without, lack, not*
have. dote: 325.

332 moveat = 'display.' The subjunctive depends on precare, with
  ut omitted. blandus, -a, -um, *flattering, coaxing.* usque,
continuously, constantly. precor, -ari, -atus, *entreat, pray,
beg, beseech.* precare is imperative. sonus, -i, m., *sound, word.*

333 exigo, -ere, -egi, -actus, *drive out; demand.* canto, -are,
  -avi, -atus, *sing.*

334 salto, -are, -avi, -atus, *dance* (including graceful gesticu-
    lation with the arms). nescio, -ire, -ivi (-ii), -itus, *not*
know (how).

335 barbarus, -a, -um, *barbarous, uncultivated, rude, crude.*
  sermo, -onis, m., *talk, conversation, speech.*

336 chorda, -ae, f., *catgut, string* of a musical instrument.
    tango, -ere, tetigi, tactus, *touch, strike, pluck, handle.*
posco, -ere, poposci, *ask for (urgently), demand, request.* lyra,
-ae, f., *lyre.*

337 durius (comp. adv.), *rather or too stiffly or awkwardly.*
    incedo, -ere, incessi, incessus, *step along, proceed, walk.*
inambulo, -are, *walk up and down, pace to and fro, promenade.*

339 dentatus, -a, -um, *toothed.* narro, -are, -avi, -atus, *tell,
  relate.* rideo, -ere, -si, -sus, *laugh at.* illi: dative.

340 mollibus: 'weak' perhaps = 'watery.'

341 prosum, prodesse, profui, *be useful, be of use, do good,
  help.* subito, *suddenly, unexpectedly.* fingo, -ere, finxi,
fictus, *mould, fashion, shape, adorn, dress, get ready.* ullus,
-a, -um (dat. ulli), *any, anyone, anybody.*

ad dominam celeres mane tulisse gradus.

Auferimur cultu: gemmis auroque teguntur

omnia; pars minima est ipsa puella sui.

345   Saepe ubi sit,quod ames,inter tam multa requiras:

decipit hac oculos aegide dives Amor.

Improvisus ades: deprendes tutus inermem;

infelix vitiis excidet illa suis.

Non tamen huic nimium praecepto credere tutum est:

350   fallit enim multos forma sine arte decens.

Tum quoque, compositis cum collinit ora venenis,

ad dominae vultus (nec pudor obstet!) eas.

Pyxidas invenies et rerum mille colores,

---

342 **celer, -eris, -e,** *swift, quick.* **mane,** *in the morning, early in the morning.* **gradus, -us,** m., *step, pace.*

343 **aufero, auferre, abstuli, ablatus,** *carry away, mislead, dupe, deceive.* **cultus, -us,** m., *cultivation, dress, attire, ornament, decoration.* **gemma, -ae,** f., *jewel, gem.* **aurum, -i,** n., *gold.* **tego, -ere, texi, tectus,** *cover, hide, conceal.*

344 **minimus, -a, -um,** *smallest, least.*

345 **quod:** antecedent is subject of **sit.** **inter** (with acc.), *between, among, amid.* **requiro, -ere, -sivi (-sii), -situs,** *seek, inquire, ask.*

346 **decipio, -ere, decepi, deceptus,** *deceive, beguile.* **aegis, -idis,** f., *shield, defense.* **dives, -itis,** *rich.* --The idea is that girls with money can use jewelry, apparel, and cosmetics as a kind of shield to cover their lack of good looks.

347 **improvisus, -a, -um,** *unforeseen, unexpected(ly).* **ades:** imperative of **adsum.** **deprendo, -ere, -di, -sus,** *catch, surprise.* **tutus, -a, -um,** *safe, without danger.* **inermis, -e,** *unarmed.*

348 **infelix, -icis,** *unfortunate, unhappy, unlucky.* **excido, -ere, excidi,** *fall down, fall, be lost, fail, lose out.*

349 **nimium** (adv.), *too much.* **praeceptum, -i,** n., *precept, advice, instruction.* **tutum:** 347.

350 **enim** (postpositive conj.), *for.* **decens, -entis,** *becoming, comely, handsomely shaped, well formed, handsome, personable, noble.* --At last, a handsome tribute to the female sex, or part of it!

351 **compono, -ere, -posui, -positus,** *put together, mix.* **collino, -ere, -levi, -litus,** *besmear, cover over.* **venenum, -i,** n., *drug, poison, color, paint.*

352 **vultus, -us,** m. (sing. & plur.), *countenance, face.* **pudor, -oris,** m., *shame, sense of shame, feeling of decency, modesty, good manners (?).* **obsto, -are, -stiti, -status,** *stand in the way, hinder.* **eas:** subjunctive for imperative.

353 **pyxis, -idis,** f., *box, cosmetic jar.* **invenio, -ire, inveni, inventus,** *come upon, find, discover.* **res, rei,** f., *thing,*

et fluere in tepidos oesypa lapsa sinus.

Illa tuas redolent, Phineu, medicamina mensas: 355

non semel hinc stomacho nausea facta meo est.

Ovid says he has been criticized lately for his writings; but so were Homer and Vergil. Envy always attacks the highest ('Summa petit livor'). Ovid is to elegiac poetry what Vergil is to epic. But back to the subject. Use your moments with the girl to place her in the most unfavorable light possible (357-440). You can lessen your love by having two girls simultaneously.

Hortor et, ut pariter binas habeatis amicas

(fortior est, plures siquis habere potest);

secta bipertito cum mens discurrit utroque,

alterius vires subtrahit alter amor.

Grandia per multos tenuantur flumina rivos,   445

cassaque, seducto stipite, flamma perit.

Non satis una tenet ceratas ancora puppes,

---

object. **mille** (indecl. adj.), *a thousand.*

354 **fluo, -ere, -xi, -xus,** *flow, run down, drip.* The infinitive is in indirect discourse after **invenies. tepidus, -a, -um,** *warm.* **oesypum, -i,** n., *oesypum,* a *cosmetic* made from the sweat and dirt of unwashed wool; it had a strong, rank odor. **labor, labi, lapsus,** *slip, glide, (melt).*

355 **redoleo, -ere, -ui,** *smell of, smell like.* **Phineus, -ei** & **-eos** (voc. **-eu**), m.: a Thracian king, the food on whose table was dirtied by the Harpies (filthy birds with women's heads). **medicamen, -inis,** n., *drug, paint, cosmetic.* **mensa, -ae,** f., *table.*

356 **semel,** *once, just once.* **hinc,** *hence, from this.* **stomachus, -i,** m., *stomach.* **nausea, -ae,** f., *seasickness, nausea.*

441 **hortor, -ari, -atus,** *urge.* **pariter,** *equally, at the same time.* **bini, -ae, -a,** *two at a time, two at the same time.* --This is good advice - if you can afford it.

442 **fortis, -e,** *strong, brave.*

443 **seco, -are, -avi, -tus,** *cut, divide, separate.* **bipertito** (adv.), *in(to) two parts.* **discurro, -ere, -curri** & **-cucurri, -cursus,** *run different ways, run back and forth.* **utroque** (adv.), *in both directions, both ways, each way.*

444 **subtraho, -ere, -xi, -ctus,** *take away from, lessen.*

445 **grandis, -e,** *great, large.* **tenuo, -are, -avi, -atus,** *lessen, diminish, reduce.* **flumen, -inis,** n., *river.* **rivus, -i,** m., *small stream, channel, canal.*

446 **cassus, -a, -um,** *vain, useless, futile.* **seduco, -ere, -xi, -ctus,** *draw aside, set aside, divide.* **stipes, -itis,** m., *log.* **flamma, -ae,** f., *flame.*

447 **satis** (adv.), *sufficiently, adequately, satisfactorily.* **ceratus, -a, -um,** *smeared with wax, waxed.* **ancora, -ae,** f., *anchor.* **puppis, -is,** f., *stern, ship.*

nec satis est liquidis unicus hamus aquis.

Qui sibi iam pridem solacia bina paravit,

450   iam pridem summa victor in arce fuit.

Every love may be supplanted by a new one. History (i.e., my-
thology) is full of such cases. Do you wonder where you may find
another sweetheart? Go, cries Ovid, read my *Ars Amatoria*. You will
soon have a shipload of girls (451-488). Even though you are on
fire with love, appear to the girl colder than ice. By pretending
that what isn't so is so, you will soon make it really so.

Quod siquid praecepta valent mea, siquid Apollo

490   utile mortales perdocet ore meo,

quamvis infelix media torreberis Aetna,

frigidior glacie fac videare tuae;

et sanum simula, ne, siquid forte dolebis,

sentiat, et ride, cum tibi flendus eris.

---

448 **satis** (indecl. adj.), *enough, sufficient, adequate.* **liqui-
dus, -a, -um,** *flowing, liquid, clear.* **unicus, -a, -um,** *one
and no more, one only, single.* **hamus, -i,** m., *hook.*

449 **iam pridem,** *long ago.* **solacium, -ii,** n., *comfort, consola-
tion, solace.* **bini, -ae, -a,** *two at a time, two at the same
time.* **paro, -are, -avi, -atus,** *prepare, acquire, obtain, get.*

450 **iam pridem:** 449. **victor, -oris,** m., *conqueror, victor.* **arx,
arcis,** f., *stronghold, citadel.* --In ancient cities, no vic-
tory was final until the citadel (usually the highest point) was
captured.

489 **quod** (before **si**), *but.* **praeceptum, -i,** n., *precept, instruc-
tion, teaching, counsel.* **valeo, -ere, -ui, -itus,** *be strong,
be worth.* **Apollo, -inis,** m.: god of light, poetry, prophecy and
oracles, etc.

490 **utilis, -e,** *useful, beneficial, profitable.* **mortales, -ium,**
m., f., *men, mortals, mankind.* **perdoceo, -ere, -cui, -ctus,**
teach thoroughly, teach.

491 **quamvis,** *although.* **infelix, -icis,** *unhappy, unfortunate, un-
lucky.* **torreo, -ere, torrui, tostus,** *burn.* **Aetna, -ae,** f.:
the famous volcano of Sicily; used here symbolically of the fires
of love.

492 **frigidus, -a, -um,** *cold, cool.* **glacies, -ei,** f., *ice.* **vide-
are = videaris. tuae:** supply **amicae** or **puellae.**

493 **sanus, -a, -um,** *sound, sound of heart, whole, well, cured.*
With **sanum** supply **te esse. simulo, -are, -avi, -atus,** *pre-
tend.* **forte,** *by chance, perchance.* **doleo, -ere, -ui, -itus,**
suffer, feel pain, grieve.

494 **sentio, -ire, -si, -sus,** *feel, perceive, notice, observe.*
rideo, -ere, -si, -sus, *laugh.* **tibi flendus eris:** 'you will
have to be wept for by yourself,' i.e., 'you will feel more like
weeping for yourself.'

Non ego te iubeo medias abrumpere curas: 495
  non sunt imperii tam fera iussa mei.
Quod non est, simula, positosque imitare furores:
  sic facies vere, quod meditatus eris.
Saepe ego, ne biberem, volui dormire videri:
  dum videor, somno lumina victa dedi.   500
Deceptum risi, qui se simulabat amare,
  in laqueos auceps decideratque suos.
Intrat amor mentes usu, dediscitur usu:
  qui poterit sanum fingere, sanus erit.

If she breaks dates with you, don't let her realize that you
mind in the least. Soon she will begin to worry when she sees you
apparently growing cold. But you must deceive yourself, too, and
not let yourself know that you are trying to fall out of love, or
you will balk (505-522). If you are too weak to break away, try
the opposite tactics: see the girl morning, noon, and night, until
you are so tired of her that you never want to see her again.

---

495 **medias . . . curas:** 'your love midway *or* at its height.'
     abrumpo, -ere, -rupi, -ruptus, *break off.*

496 **imperium, -ii,** n., *command, authority, sovereignty, rule.*
     ferus, -a, -um, *wild, savage, cruel.* **iussum, -i,** n., *order,*
command.

497 **simula:** 493. **imitor, -ari, -atus,** *imitate, portray.* **furor,**
     -oris, m., *frenzy, fury, madness, passion.* --'Pretend that
what is not (the case is) and imitate a passion that has been laid
aside (i.e., that is over and done with).'

498 **facies:** 'you will bring about.' **vere,** *truly, really.* **medi-**
     tor, -ari, -atus, *consider, intend, practice.*

499 **dormio, -ire, -ivi (-ii), -itus,** *sleep.* --So it might be
     inferred that Ovid was not a heavy drinker.

500 **somnus, -i,** m., *sleep, slumber.* **lumen, -inis,** n., *light,*
     eye.

501 **decipio, -ere, decepi, deceptus,** *ensnare, deceive, fool.*
     deceptum modifies **virum** understood, the antecedent of **qui.**
rideo, -ere, risi, risus, *laugh at.* **simulo, -are, -avi, -atus,**
pretend.

502 The pretended lover is compared to a bird snarer who falls
     into his own trap. **laqueus, -i,** m., *noose, snare, trap.*
auceps, -cupis, m., f., *birdcatcher, fowler.* **decido, -ere, deci-**
di, *fall.* **-que** should be translated at the beginning of the line.

503 **intro, -are, -avi, -atus,** *enter.* **usus, -us,** m., *use, experi-*
     ence, habit, custom. **dedisco, -ere, dedidici,** *unlearn, for-*
get.

504 **sanus, -a, -um,** *sound, sound of heart, whole, well, cured.*
     fingo, -ere, finxi, fictus, *imagine, feign, pretend.*

Et quisquam praecepta potest mea dura vocare?
En, etiam partes conciliantis ago.
525 Nam quoniam variant animi, variabimus artes;
mille mali species, mille salutis erunt.
Corpora vix ferro quaedam sanantur acuto;
auxilium multis sucus et herba fuit.
Mollior es neque abire potes vinctusque teneris,
530 et tua saevus Amor sub pede colla premit:
desine luctari. Referant tua carbasa venti,
quaque vocant fluctus, hac tibi remus eat.
Explenda est sitis ista tibi, qua perditus ardes;
cedimus: e medio iam licet amne bibas.

---

523 **quisquam, quicquam,** *anyone, anything.* **praeceptum, -i,** n., *precept, advice, instruction, direction.* **voco, -are, -avi, -atus,** *call.*

524 **en,** *lo! behold! see!* **concilio, -are, -avi, -atus,** *bring together, unite, make friendly, reconcile.* The participle is here used as a substantive: 'of one who . . .'

525 **nam** (conj.), *for.* **quoniam,** *since, inasmuch as.* **vario, -are, -avi, -atus,** *change, alter, vary.*

526 **mille** (indecl. adj.), *a thousand.* **malum, -i,** n., *evil, pest, mischief, disease.* **species, -ei,** f., *shape, form, appearance.* **salus, -utis,** f., *safety, health, cure.*

527 **vix,** *with difficulty, scarcely, hardly.* **ferrum, -i,** n., *iron, knife.* **quidam, quaedam, quoddam,** *certain, some.* **sano, -are, -avi, -atus,** *heal, cure, restore to health.* **acutus, -a, -um,** *sharp.*

528 **auxilium, -ii,** n., *help, aid, relief, remedy.* **sucus, -i,** m., *juice, potion, dose, medicine.* **herba, -ae,** f., *plant, herb.*

529 **abeo, -ire, -ivi (-ii), -itus,** *go away, depart, leave off.* **vincio, -ire, vinxi, vinctus,** *bind, fetter, tie.*

530 **saevus, -a, -um,** *savage, fierce, cruel.* **collum, -i,** n. (sing. & plur.), *neck.* **premo, -ere, pressi, pressus,** *press, press down, crush.*

531 **luctor, -ari, -atus,** *wrestle, struggle.* **carbasa, -orum,** n., *sails.*

532 **voco, -are, -avi, -atus,** *call.* **fluctus, -us,** m., *wave.* **hac** (adv.), *here, this way.* **remus, -i,** m., *oar.*

533 **expleo, -ere, -evi, -etus,** *fill, satisfy.* **sitis, -is,** f., *thirst.* **iste, ista, istud,** *that . . of yours, that.* **perditus, -a, -um,** *destroyed, hopeless, desperate.* Better translated as adverb here. **ardeo, -ere, arsi, arsus,** *be on fire, burn.*

534 **cedo, -ere, cessi, cessus,** *retreat, yield, allow, permit.* **amnis, -is,** m., *stream, river.*

Sed bibe plus etiam, quam quod praecordia poscunt; 535
  gutture fac pleno sumpta redundet aqua.

Perfruere usque tua, nullo prohibente, puella:
  illa tibi noctes auferat, illa dies.

Taedia quaere mali: faciunt et taedia finem;
  iam quoque, cum credes posse carere, mane, 540

dum bene te cumules et copia tollat amorem,
  et fastidita non iuvet esse domo.

Your cure will be more difficult if you are concerned about someone else's getting your girl. You can forget all about love if you start worrying about your other troubles: debts, a strict father, crops, business investments. 'Et quis non causas mille doloris habet?' (543-578). Beware of solitude; while you are alone, the face of your beloved will be ever present in your imagination. Always have with you some close friend. The cause of Phyllis' death was the lack of a companion.

Quisquis amas, loca sola nocent: loca sola caveto!

  Quo fugis? In populo tutior esse potes. 580

Non tibi secretis (augent secreta furores)

---

535 **praecordia, -orum,** n., *heart.* **posco, -ere, poposci,** *demand.*

536 **guttur, -uris,** n., *gullet, throat.* **plenus, -a, -um,** *full.* **sumo, -ere, sumpsi, sumptus,** *take, take up, drink, swallow.* **redundo, -are, -avi, -atus,** *run over, overflow.*

537 **perfruor, -frui, -fructus** (with abl.), *enjoy, enjoy the company of.* **usque,** *without interruption, continuously, constantly.* **prohibeo, -ere, -ui, -itus,** *restrain, hinder, prevent.*

538 **noctes:** 'nights,' 'evenings.' **aufero, auferre, abstuli, ablatus,** *take away, consume, occupy.*

539 **taedium, -ii,** n., *weariness, tediousness, loathing, satiety, more than enough.* **malum, -i,** n., *evil, misfortune, pest.* **finis, -is,** m., *limit, end.*

540 **careo, -ere, -ui, -itus,** *be without, lack, do without, stay away.* **maneo, -ere, mansi, mansus,** *stay, remain, continue.*

541 **cumulo, -are, -avi, -atus,** *fill, overload.* **copia, -ae,** f., *abundance, fullness.* **tollo, -ere, sustuli, sublatus,** *raise, take away, remove, kill, destroy.*

542 **fastiditus, -a, -um,** *loathed, scorned, despised.* **domus, -us** & **-i,** f., *house, home.* **domo** is abl. of place where instead of locative, since it is modified by an adjective.

579 **quisquis amas:** 'whoever you are that love.' **noceo, -ere, -ui, -itus,** *hurt, do harm, do mischief.* **caveo, -ere, cavi, cautus,** *beware of, guard against, avoid.* **caveto** is fut. imperat.

580 **quo** (adv.), *whither, where.* **populus, -i,** m., *people, throng, crowd.* **tutus, -a, -um,** *safe, secure.*

581 **secretum, -i,** n., *solitude, secrecy, solitary place.* **augeo, -ere, auxi, auctus,** *increase, strengthen.* **furor, -oris,** m. (sing. & plur.), *frenzy, madness, fury, passion, desire.*

est opus; auxilio turba futura tibi est.

Tristis eris, si solus eris, dominaeque relictae
ante oculos facies stabit, ut ipsa, tuos.

585   Tristior idcirco nox est quam tempora Phoebi:
quae relevet luctus, turba sodalis abest.

Nec fuge colloquium, nec sit tibi ianua clausa,
nec tenebris vultus flebilis abde tuos.

Semper habe Pyladen aliquem, qui curet Orestem:

590   hic quoque amicitiae non levis usus erit.

Quid nisi secretae laeserunt Phyllida silvae?

Certa necis causa est: incomitata fuit.

---

582   **auxilium, -ii,** n., *help, aid, relief.* **auxilio** is dat. of pur-
pose. **turba, -ae,** f., *crowd, throng, mob.* **futura . . . est:**
active (first) periphrastic of **sum.**

583   **tristis, -e,** *sad, gloomy, melancholy, unhappy.*

584   **sto, -are, steti, status,** *stand, remain, linger.* **ut ipsa:**
'as though it were she herself.'

585   **tristior:** 583.   **idcirco,** *on this account, for this reason.*
Phoebus, -i, m., *Phoebus, Apollo* (god of the sun), *sun.*

586   **relevo, -are, -avi, -atus,** *lighten, lessen, console.* **luctus,**
-us, m., *sorrow, grief, affliction.* **turba:** 582. **sodalis,**
-is, m., f., *comrade.* Used by the poets also as an adj., so that
turba sodalis = *group of friends, group of comrades.* **absum, ab-**
esse, afui, *be away, be absent.*

587   **colloquium, -ii,** n., *conversation, 'bull session'* (?).
ianua, -ae, f., *door.* **claudo, -ere, clausi, clausus,** *close,*
shut.

588   **tenebrae, -arum,** f., *darkness.* **vultus, -us,** m. (sing. &
plur.), *countenance, face.* **flebilis, -e,** *tearful, doleful.*
abdo, -ere, abdidi, abditus, *hide, conceal.*

589   The friendship of Orestes and Pylades was a celebrated one,
like that of David and Jonathan. The meaning of the line,
then, is always to have some devoted friend close to you. **Pyla-**
des, -ae & -is (acc. **-en**), m.: the close friend of Orestes. **curo,**
-are, -avi, -atus, *care for, take care of, look after, be solic-*
itous for. **Orestes, -is & -ae,** m.: the son of Agamemnon and Cly-
temnestra.

590   **amicitia, -ae,** f., *friendship.* **usus, -us,** m., *use, employ-*
ment, benefit, profit, advantage.

591   **secretus, -a, -um,** *lonely, solitary.* **Phyllis, -idis** (acc.
-ida), f.: Thracian princess who, deserted by her lover
Demophoön, went down to the shore nine times to watch for his re-
turn, then hanged herself. **silva, -ae,** f., *wood, forest.*

592   **certus, -a, -um,** *established, settled, fixed, certain.* **nex,**
necis, f., *violent death, death.* **incomitatus, -a, -um,**
unaccompanied, unattended, without a companion.

Ibat, ut Edono referens trieterica Baccho
  ire solet fusis barbara turba comis,
et modo,qua poterat,longum spectabat in aequor,   595
  nunc in harenosa lassa iacebat humo.
'Perfide Demophoon!' surdas clamabat ad undas,
  ruptaque singultu verba loquentis erant.
Limes erat tenuis longa subnubilus umbra,
  qua tulit illa suos ad mare saepe pedes.   600
Nona terebatur miserae via: 'Viderit!' inquit
  et spectat zonam pallida facta suam,
adspicit et ramos; dubitat, refugitque quod audet,
  et timet, et digitos ad sua colla refert.

---

593   **Edonus, -a, -um,** *Edonian, Thracian.* The frenzied worship of
      Bacchus flourished in Thrace, and especially on Mt. Edon.
referens (modifies **turba**): 'renewing.' **trieterica, -orum,** n.,
triennial festival of Bacchus. **Bacchus, -i,** m.: the god of wine.

594   **fusus, -a, -um,** *spread out, flowing, dishevelled.* **barbarus,**
     -a, -um, *strange, barbarous, wild.* **turba, -ae,** f., *crowd,*
throng, mob.

595   **aequor, -oris,** n., *surface of the sea, sea.*

596   **harenosus, -a, -um,** *sandy.* **lassus, -a, -um,** *faint, weary,*
     tired, exhausted. **humus, -i,** f., *earth, ground.*

597   **perfidus, -a, -um,** *faithless, false, perfidious, treacherous.*
     Demophoon, -ontis, m.: a son of Theseus, for love of whom
Phyllis killed herself; it seems he did return to her eventually,
but too late. **surdus, -a, -um,** *deaf.*

598   **rumpo, -ere, rupi, ruptus,** *break, interrupt.* **singultus, -us,**
     m., *sobbing.* **verba loquentis:** 'the words of her, speaking' =
'her words, as she spoke.'

599   **limes, -itis,** m., *path, road, boundary.* **subnubilus, -a, -um,**
     somewhat overcast, gloomy, darkened. **umbra, -ae,** f., *shade,*
shadow.

600   **mare, -is,** n., *sea.*

601   **nonus, -a, -um,** *ninth, (for the ninth time).* **tero, -ere,**
     trivi, tritus, *rub, tread, traverse.* **miserae:** supply **puel-**
lae (dat. of agent). **viderit:** 'let him see!' or 'he'll see!';
perhaps 'I'll show him!' **inquam** (3rd pers. sing. **inquit**), *say.*

602   **zona, -ae,** f., *belt, girdle.* **pallidus, -a, -um,** *pale.* **fac-**
     ta: 'becoming' = 'turning.'

603   **adspicio, -ere, adspexi, adspectus,** *look at, see.* **ramus, -i,**
     m., *branch, bough.* **dubito, -are, -avi, -atus,** *doubt, hesi-*
tate. **refugio, -ere, refugi,** *run away from, avoid, shun, shrink*
from. **audeo, -ere, ausus,** *dare, dare to do, attempt, venture.*

604   **collum, -i,** n. (sing. & plur.), *neck.* **refert:** 'brings back'
    = 'keeps putting.'

605   Sithoni, tunc certe vellem non sola fuisses:
          non flesset positis Phyllida silva comis.
       Phyllidis exemplo nimium secreta timete,
          laese vir a domina, laesa puella viro!

But avoid the company of people who are in love; when the house
next door is burning, it is hard to keep your own from catching
fire! Avoid chance encounters with your erstwhile sweetheart.
Don't go for walks where you know she is accustomed to walk. More
than that, you must tell her sisters and her cousins and her aunts
goodbye forever. If you happen to meet them, don't even ask how
the girl is (609-642). Utter no complaints about her. By keeping
quiet you have a better revenge and it is easier to forget. It is
unbecoming to a gentleman to allow hatred to replace love. Just
cease to be interested.

       Tu quoque, qui causam finiti reddis amoris
          deque tua domina multa querenda refers,
645   parce queri; melius sic ulciscere tacendo,
          ut desideriis effluat illa tuis.
       Et malim taceas, quam te desisse loquaris:

---

605   **Sithonis, -idis** (voc. **-i**), f., *Sithonian girl, Thracian girl*
          (i.e., Phyllis). **tunc,** *then, at that time.* **certe,** *certain-*
ly, surely, at least. **vellem . . . fuisses:** a 'vain' wish (con-
trary to what was actually the case), past time: 'I wish you had
been.'

606   **flesset = flevisset. positis,** with **comis, =** '(having been)
          shed.' **Phyllis, -idis** (acc. **-ida**), f.: Thracian princess who
hanged herself for love of Demophoön. **silva, -ae,** f., *wood(s),
forest.* --With great art Ovid passes over the obvious end of his
story. The sad fate of Phyllis is merely indicated by the mourning
of the trees.

607   **Phyllidis:** 606. **exemplum, -i,** n., *example, case, warning,
          lesson.* **nimium,** *too much, too, excessive(ly).* **secretum, -i,**
n., *secret thing; solitude, secrecy, solitary place.*

608   **vir:** vocative. **puella:** vocative.

643   **finio, -ire, -ivi (-ii), -itus,** *end, finish, terminate.*

644   **queror, queri, questus,** *complain, lament.* **multa querenda:**
          'many things to be complained of,' 'many complaints,' 'many
criticisms.'

645   **parco, -ere, peperci,** *spare, cease, stop, refrain from.*
          melius (comp. adv.), *better, more satisfactorily.* **ulciscor,
-sci, ultus,** *avenge oneself, obtain revenge.* **ulciscere** is 2nd per-
son singular, future indicative. **taceo, -ere, tacui, tacitus,** *be
silent, say nothing, keep quiet.*

646   **desiderium, -ii,** n., *longing, regret.* **effluo, -ere, -xi,**
          flow out, pass away, disappear, vanish.

647   **malo, malle, malui,** *wish rather, prefer.* **malim** (pres. subj.):
          'I should prefer (that).' **taceas:** 645. **desisse** (syncopated
form) **= desiisse;** supply **amare.**

qui nimium multis 'Non amo' dicit, amat.
Sed meliore fide paulatim extinguitur ignis,
   quam subito. Lente desine: tutus eris.   650
Flumine perpetuo torrens solet acrior ire;
   sed tamen haec brevis est, illa perennis aqua.
Fallat et in tenues evanidus exeat auras
   perque gradus molles emoriatur amor.
Sed modo dilectam scelus est odisse puellam: 655
   exitus ingeniis convenit iste feris.
Non curare sat est: odio qui finit amorem,
   aut amat aut aegre desinet esse miser.

It is shameful that men and women, lately in love, should become
enemies and even go to court (659-672). If you and the girl happen
to be thrown together after the break, you must summon up all your
resources. Don't try to make yourself attractive to her. Show her
that she is just one out of many.

---

648 **nimium,** *too much, too.* --A profound observation!

649 **melior, -ius,** *better.* **fides, -ei,** f., *faith, confidence,
assurance.* **paulatim,** *little by little, gradually, by de-
grees.* **extinguo, -ere, -nxi, -nctus,** *put out, extinguish.*

650 **subito,** *suddenly, all at once.* **lente,** *slowly.* **desine:**
supply **amare. tutus, -a, -um,** *safe, secure, out of danger.*

651 **flumen, -inis,** n., *river.* **perpetuus, -a, -um,** *continuous,
uninterrupted, constant, (steadily flowing).* **torrens,
-entis,** m., *torrent.* **acer, acris, acre,** *violent, fierce.* Better
translated here as adverb.

652 **brevis, -e,** *short, brief, short-lived, of brief duration.*
perennis, -e, *through the year, unceasing, never failing,
everlasting.*

653 **fallat:** 'let (love) fade away imperceptibly.' **evanidus, -a,
-um,** *vanishing, passing away.* **exeo, -ire, -ii, -itus,** *go
away, depart.*

654 **gradus, -us,** m., *step, stage, degree.* **molles:** 'easy' or
'gradual.' **emorior, -i, emortuus,** *die out, perish, cease.*

655 **modo:** 'recently'; with **dilectam. dilectus, -a, -um,** *loved,
beloved, dear.* **scelus, sceleris,** n., *wicked thing, crime,
wickedness.* **odi, odisse,** *hate.*

656 **exitus, -us,** m., *outcome, result, conclusion, termination,
end.* **ingenium, -ii,** n., *nature, disposition, character, tem-
per, genius.* **convenio, -ire, -veni, -ventus** (with dat.), *be suit-
able to, be appropriate to.* **iste, ista, istud,** *that, that of
yours, such.* **ferus, -a, -um,** *wild, rude, savage, barbarous.*

657 **non** goes with **curare. curo, -are, -avi, -atus,** *care, care
for.* **sat** (indecl.), *enough, sufficient.* **odium, -ii,** n.,
hatred, enmity. **finio, -ire, -ivi (-ii), -itus,** *end, terminate,
finish.*

658 **aegre,** *with difficulty, hardly, scarcely.*

Quod si vos aliquis casus conducet in unum,
    mente memor tota, quae damus arma tene.
675 Nunc opus est armis; hic, o fortissime, pugna!
    Vincenda est telo Penthesilea tuo.
Nunc tibi rivalis, nunc durum limen amanti,
    nunc subeant mediis inrita verba deis.
Nec compone comas, quia sis venturus ad illam,
680   nec toga sit laxo conspicienda sinu.
Nulla sit ut placeas alienae cura puellae;
    iam facito, e multis una sit illa tibi!

Warnings: We are slow to cease loving because we always hope for better luck. Don't believe a girl's words or her tears. Never give her the reasons why you are giving her up or recount to her her failings; if you do, she will argue with you and convince you that you are wrong.

---

673 **quod si**, *but if.* **casus, -us**, m., *event, accident, chance.* **conduco, -ere, -duxi, -ductus**, *bring . . . together.* **in unum**: 'into the same place.'

674 **memor, -oris**, *mindful, remembering, heedful.* **totus, -a, -um**, *whole, all, entire.* **tota** modifies **mente**.

675 **o**, *O, oh!* **fortis, -e**, *strong, brave, fearless.* **pugno, -are, -avi, -atus**, *fight, give battle.*

676 **telum, -i**, n., *weapon, dart, spear.* **Penthesilea, -ae**, f.: a queen of the Amazons who was killed at Troy by Achilles; she here typifies all womankind in the war of the sexes. Cf. *Ars Amatoria* III, 1-2.

677 **tibi**: with **subeant. rivalis, -is**, m., *rival.* **limen, -inis**, n., *threshold* (where excluded lovers often lay). **amans, -antis**, m., *lover.* The dative here follows **durum**.

678 **subeo, -ire, -ii, -itus**, *come up, come into one's mind, occur to.* **medius, -i**, m., *mediator, arbiter.* **mediis . . . deis**: 'with the gods called upon to be mediators.' **inritus, -a, -um**, *vain, useless, without effect.* **inrita verba**: 'your useless words (prayers? remonstrances?)' or possibly 'her worthless oaths.'

679 **compono, -ere, -posui, -positus**, *put in order, arrange, smooth.*

680 **toga, -ae**, f., *toga* (the loose outer garment worn in public by Roman citizens). **laxus, -a, -um**, *loose, unfastened, open.* **conspiciendus, -a, -um**, *worth seeing, noticeable, conspicuous.* -- The Roman men about town wore their togas creased at the waist and open at the breast. Ovid might advise the modern young man to leave his trousers unpressed or his tie crooked.

681 The **ut** clause depends on **cura**, the subject of **sit. alienus, -a, -um**, *belonging to someone else; unfriendly.*

682 **e multis una**: note the similarity to the motto of the United States. Ovid, however, came first.

Desinimus tarde, quia nos speramus amari;   685
   dum sibi quisque placet, credula turba sumus.
At tu nec voces (quid enim fallacius illis?)
   crede nec aeternos pondus habere deos;
neve puellarum lacrimis moveare, caveto:
   ut flerent, oculos erudiere suos.   690
Artibus innumeris mens oppugnatur amantum,
   ut lapis aequoreis undique pulsus aquis.
Nec causas aperi quare divortia malis,
   nec dic quid doleas (clam tamen usque dole),
nec peccata refer, ne diluat: ipse favebis,   695
   ut melior causa causa sit illa tua.

---

685 **tarde,** *slowly, tardily.* **spero, -are, -avi, -atus,** *hope, ex-
    pect; believe.*

686 **credulus, -a, -um,** *credulous, ready to believe, believing.*
    turba, -ae, f., *crowd, throng, mob, gang.*

687 **voces** ('words'): acc.; a subject of **habere. enim** (postposi-
    tive conj.), *for.* **fallax, -acis,** *deceitful, deceptive.*

688 **aeternus, -a, -um,** *eternal, immortal.* **pondus, -eris,** n.,
    weight. --Lovers, in swearing their love, would call upon
the gods.

689 **-ve,** *or, and.* **moveare = movearis. caveo, -ere, cavi, cau-
    tus,** *take care, beware, be on one's guard.* **caveto:** future
imperative.

690 **erudio, -ire, -ivi (-ii), -itus,** *teach.* **erudiere = erudie-
    runt.**

691 **innumerus, -a, -um,** *countless, innumerable.* **oppugno, -are,
    -avi, -atus,** *attack, assail.* **amans, -antis,** m., f., *lover.*

692 **lapis, -idis,** m., *stone, rock.* **aequoreus, -a, -um,** *of the
    sea.* **undique,** *from* or *on all sides.* **pello, -ere, pepuli,
pulsus,** *strike, beat.*

693 **aperio, -ire, aperui, apertus,** *uncover, disclose, make known.*
    quare, *why.* **divortium, -ii,** n., *separation.* **malo, malle,
malui,** *prefer.*

694 **doleo, -ere, -ui, -itus,** *feel pain, grieve (for), be ag-
    grieved.* **clam,** *secretly, privately.* **usque,** *constantly, con-
tinuously.*

695 **peccatum, -i,** n., *fault, error.* **diluo, -ere, -ui, -utus,**
    dissolve, lessen, do away with, explain (something) away.
faveo, -ere, favi, fautus, *be favorable, be well-disposed, favor.*

696 **melior, -ius,** *better.* The first **causa** is ablative, the sec-
    ond is nominative; **illa** ('that . . . of hers') is nominative,
tua is ablative.

Qui silet, est firmus; qui dicit multa puellae
698   probra, satisfieri postulat ille sibi.

It will help to compare your girl with women who are really beautiful. Make comparisons also on the basis of character. Don't reread her old love letters which you have saved. Burn them up. Get rid of her portraits, if you can. Why have your resistance undermined by a dumb likeness?

Confer Amyclaeis medicatum vellus aënis
    murice cum Tyrio: turpius illud erit;
vos quoque formosis vestras conferte puellas:
710   incipiet dominae quemque pudere suae.
Utraque formosae Paridi potuere videri,
    sed sibi collatam vicit utramque Venus.
Nec solam faciem, mores quoque confer et artem;

---

697 **sileo, -ere, -ui,** *be silent, say nothing.* **firmus, -a, -um,** *strong, powerful.*

698 **probrum, -i,** n., *disgraceful act, (case of) improper behavior, reproach, disgrace, insult.* **satisfacio, -ere, -feci, -factus** (pass., **satisfio, -fieri, -factus**) (with dat.), *satisfy.* **satisfieri . . . sibi:** 'it to be satisfied to himself' = 'to be satisfied.' **postulo, -are, -avi, -atus,** *demand, desire, wish, want.* --Starting with **qui dicit,** Ovid means roughly this: A man who specifies what he has against a girl is giving her a chance to explain it away, and indeed wants her to.

707 **confero, -ferre, -tuli, collatus,** *bring together, compare.* **Amyclaeus, -a, -um,** *of Amyclae* (a town in Laconia, Greece, which manufactured an inferior purple dye). **medicatus, -a, -um,** *medicated; colored, dyed.* **vellus, -eris,** n., *wool, fleece.* **aënum, -i,** n., *bronze vat.*

708 **murex, -icis,** m., *purple, purple dye.* **Tyrius, -a, -um,** *Tyrian, of Tyre* (the Phoenician city noted for its fine purple dye). **turpius:** 'uglier' or 'less handsome.'

709 **formosis** (dat. after **conferte**): 'with really beautiful girls.' **vester, -tra, -trum,** *your* (plur.). **conferte:** 707.

710 **incipio, -ere, incepi, inceptus,** *begin.* **pudet, -ere, puditum est,** *it makes ashamed.* **incipiet . . . quemque pudere:** lit., 'it will begin to make each one ashamed of,' i.e., 'each one will begin to be ashamed of.'

711 'Both goddesses could have seemed beautiful to Paris.' **uterque, utraque, utrumque,** *each, both.* **utraque,** though singular, is the subject of a plural verb. It refers to Juno and Minerva, rivals of Venus in the beauty contest when Paris awarded the prize of the golden apple to Venus. **Paris, -idis,** m.: son of Priam, the king of Troy. **potuere = potuerunt.**

712 **sibi** (dat. with **collatam**): 'with herself.' **confero, conferre, contuli, collatus,** *bring together, compare (with).* **utramque:** 711.

713 **confer:** 712. **artem:** *conduct* (a less obvious meaning of **ars**).

tantum iudicio ne tuus obsit amor.

Exiguum est, quod deinde canam; sed profuit illud   715
exiguum multis, in quibus ipse fui.

Scripta cave relegas blandae servata puellae:
constantes animos scripta relecta movent.

Omnia pone feros (pones invitus) in ignes
et dic 'Ardoris sit rogus iste mei!'   720

Thestias absentem succendit stipite natum:
tu timide flammae perfida verba dabis?

Si potes, et ceras remove! Quid imagine muta
carperis? Hoc periit Laodamia modo.

---

714   **tantum** (adv.), *only.* **iudicium**, **-ii**, n., *judgment.* **obsum,
-esse, -fui** (with dat.), *get in the way of, hinder, hurt.*

715   **exiguus, -a, -um**, *small, little, trifling.* **deinde**, *next.*
cano, -ere, cecini, cantus, *sing, sing of, proclaim.* **prosum,
prodesse, profui** (with dat.), *be useful, be of use, benefit, help.*

716   **exiguum:** 715. Since it is neuter here, supply 'thing.'

717   **scriptum, -i**, n., *writing, letter.* **caveo, -ere, cavi, cau-
tus**, *beware.* **cave** with the subjunctive = 'don't.' **relego,
-ere, relegi, relectus**, *read again, reread.* **blandus, -a, -um**,
enticing, alluring, charming. **servo, -are, -avi, -atus**, *save,
keep, preserve.*

718   **constans, -antis**, *firm, steadfast, steady.* **scripta:** 717.
relecta: 717.

719   **ferus, -a, -um**, *wild, savage, fierce.* **invitus, -a, -um**, *un-
willing(ly), reluctant(ly), against one's will.*

720   **ardor, -oris**, m., *flame, fire, ardor, ardent affection, burn-
ing love.* **rogus, -i**, m., *funeral pyre.* **iste, ista, istud,**
that, that of yours; this. --Note the play on the words **ardoris**
and **rogus:** 'the funeral pyre of my burning love.'

721   **Thestias, -adis**, f., *daughter of Thestius,* i.e., *Althaea,* who
brought about the death of her son, Meleager, by thrusting
back into the fire a brand, on the preservation of which his life
depended. **absens, -entis**, *absent.* **succendo, -ere, succendi, suc-
census**, *set on fire, burn.* **stipes, -itis**, m., *log, (brand).*
natus, -i, m., *son.*

722   **timide**, *fearfully, timidly.* **flamma, -ae**, f., *blaze, flame.*
perfidus, -a, -um, *faithless, false, unreliable.*

723   **cera, -ae**, f., *wax, wax figure, portrait bust, portrait.* **re-
moveo, -ere, removi, remotus**, *remove.* **imago, -inis**, f.,
likeness, statue, bust, picture. **mutus, -a, -um**, *dumb, mute,
silent.*

724   **carpo, -ere, -psi, -ptus**, *pluck, weaken, wear away, consume.*
Laodamia, -ae, f.: wife of Protesilaus. After his death, she
lavished her affection on a portrait of him; when this was burned
by her father, she threw herself into the flames and died.

Avoid all places which can bring back fond memories of happy
moments spent with your beloved. An effective (though drastic) way
to put an end to a love affair is to lose your money. Stay away
from theaters, where lovers are constantly enacted. Love poetry is
just as bad. Don't read it - even mine, says Ovid. The worst thing
about breaking off an affair is imagining someone else in your
place; so just suppose she has been left all alone. When you are
able to give a hearty greeting to a rival suitor, then you are
cured. It is just as well to drink no wine (725-810). And so the
end has been reached; Ovid's ship has come into its harbor.

811   Hoc opus exegi: fessae date serta carinae!
      Contigimus portus, quo mihi cursus erat.
      Postmodo reddetis sacro pia vota poetae,
        carmine sanati femina virque meo.

---

811   **exigo, -ere, exegi, exactus,** *drive out, demand, complete,*
      finish. **fessus, -a, -um,** *weary, tired.* **serta, -orum,** n.,
wreaths of flowers, garlands. **carina, -ae,** f., *vessel, boat ,*
ship.

812   **contingo, -ere, contigi, contactus,** *touch, reach, arrive at.*
      portus, -us, m., *harbor, haven, port.* **quo** (adv.), *whither,*
where, to which. **cursus, -us,** m., *course, voyage, journey.*

813   **postmodo,** *afterwards, soon.* **sacer, -cra, -crum,** *dedicated,*
      holy, sacred. **pius, -a, -um,** *dutiful, due, pious.* **votum,**
-i, n., *vow, wish.* **poeta, -ae,** m., *poet.*

814   **carmen, -inis,** n., *song, poem.* **sano, -are, -avi, -atus,**
      heal, cure, restore to health. **femina:** vocative. **vir:**
vocative.